Expressing the Shape and Colour of Personality

*In gratitude to
Dr Glenys Parkinson
for her inspiring personality,
her warm friendship and,
above all, for her dedication to
her work with children*

Expressing the Shape and Colour of Personality

Using Lowenfeld Mosaics in Psychotherapy and Cross-Cultural Research

THÉRÈSE MEI-YAU WOODCOCK

sussex
ACADEMIC
PRESS

BRIGHTON • PORTLAND

2 4 6 8 10 9 7 5 3 1

First published 2006 in Great Britain by
SUSSEX ACADEMIC PRESS
PO Box 2950
Brighton BN2 5SP

and in the United States of America by
SUSSEX ACADEMIC PRESS
920 NE 58th Ave   Suite 300
Portland, Oregon 97213-3786

British Library Cataloguing in Publication Data
A CIP catalogue record for this book is available from the British Library.

Library of Congress Cataloging-in-Publication Data
Woodcock, Thérèse Mei-Yau.
  Expressing the shape and colour of personality : using Lowenfeld mosaics in psychotherapy and cross-cultural research / Thérèse Mei-Yau Woodcock.
      p.   cm.
  Includes bibliographical references and index.
  ISBN 1-84519-090-4 (p/b : alk. paper)
  1. Lowenfeld Mosaics.   I. Title.

Publication of this book has been supported through the generous provisions of the Dr Margaret Lowenfeld Trust.

Typeset and designed by G&G Editorial, Brighton & Eastbourne
Printed and bound by The Alden Press, Oxford
This book is printed on acid-free paper

Contents

Illustrations and tables

The Mosaic illustrations are taken from a collection of hand-coloured originals, assembled over nearly forty years; this accounts for the variation in colour and colouring.

Illustrations

Tables

Foreword

By the turn of the twentieth century concern for the well-being of children in the workplace had become a national issue. Through the combined efforts of social reformers from many walks of life emerged a clear model of adult guidance for a child exposed to early adversities that would prevent the development of morals and behaviours that would allow him or her to take their place in society as responsible adults. Child guidance methods focused on groups of children we would now refer to as high risk for emotional and behavioural disorders such as those who lived without parents, had taken to crime and were illiterate or illegitimate. The management involved better education, moral training, lessons in socialized behaviour and attending to physical needs wherever possible. In the aftermath of the First World War Western Europe began to rebuild its societies and communities and began to take a fresh look at the consequences for the individual of exposure to severe adverse events. A new psychology began to emerge in which there was a greater acceptance than ever before that personal traumatic experiences were causal features of mental distress and psychiatric disorders. Much of this new humanistic psychology was accelerated into clinical practice in adults who were war survivors in the physical sense. In the decade that followed this trauma model was also being applied to vulnerable children and began to influence the theory and practice of the guidance movement.

One of the great pioneers of this new psychology was Margaret Lowenfeld (1890–1973), a paediatrician whose professional and personal interest in how children physically grow and mentally develop began when, recently qualified as a doctor, she was involved in relief work in her ancestral Poland after the First World War and wondered what enabled some children to survive and flourish despite their traumatic experiences. Early in her career she engaged in medical research (in childhood rheumatism and in breast feeding) and retained a strong belief in the need for research and evaluation in whatever field she was engaged. Her outstanding contribution sprang from the recognition that play is an important activity in children's development and that language may for many be an unsatisfactory medium to express their difficult experiences. As a consequence she invented non-verbal techniques that enabled them to convey their thoughts and feelings without resort to words.

Margaret Lowenfeld developed a number of non-verbal techniques of which one, the Lowenfeld Mosaics is the subject of this volume. The Mosaics tool uses differently shaped and coloured tiles to produce a powerful yet user friendly diag-

International Specialized Book Services, Inc.
920 NE 58th Avenue, Suite 300 • Portland, OR 97213-3786 • USA
(503) 287-3093 • FAX (503) 280-8832

ISBS is pleased to send you the accompanying book for review consideration. Please send tearsheets of the published review. ISBS, at the above address, should be shown as the exclusive distributor of this book.

Document ID: 251878

Title: **Expressing the Shape and Colour of Perso**

Author: **Woodcock**

List Price: **67.50**

Publisher: **Sussex Academic Press**

Please detach and return bottom half of card or you may go to www.isbs.com/reviews and complete this form on-line.

- -

Your response is necessary for our records. Thank you.

Title: **Expressing the Shape and Colour of Perso**

Date: **03/15/06**

Publisher: **Sussex Academic Press**

Journal Name: **Child & Family Behavior Therapy / 44332**

This card acknowledges receipt of book on _____

Book Review Editor: _____

❑ Yes, the book will be reviewed. Review date: _____

❑ No, the book will not be reviewed. Reason: _____

_____

❑ We do not review books. Please remove us from your list.

❑ The proper person and address to whom review copies should be sent are_____

_____

_____

nostic and therapeutic instrument; they have also proved useful in comparative studies of children from different cultures. Other Lowenfeld tools include the Lowenfeld World Technique, which uses trays filled with sand and collections of miniature toys, representing all aspects of their daily lives, to enable children to portray their inner worlds, and Lowenfeld Kaleidoblocs, a psychological test. Though most of her work was with emotionally disturbed children, she devised the Lowenfeld Poleidoblocs, now still widely used in primary schools in Britain, to help young children learn about fundamental mathematical principles.

In the late 1920s Dr Lowenfeld established one of the first child guidance clinics in Britain in Notting Hill, London. This she developed into the Institute for Child Psychology, which trained child psychotherapists in her theories and techniques while continuing to be the local child guidance centre (funded eventually by the National Health Service); this gave the students a unique experience of the practicalities of the child guidance field during their training. In the Science Museum, London, a display cabinet in the History of Medicine section is devoted to Lowenfeld's inventions. The Lowenfeld Archives and the Institute of Child Psychology Library are housed in the Centre for Family Research of Cambridge University.*

In this volume, Thérèse Mei-Yau Woodcock, a distinguished child psychotherapist trained by Margaret Lowenfeld, provides a lucid readable and elegant account of the Lowenfeld Mosaic tool and its application in psychotherapy. Thérèse Woodcock shows how the methods and procedures can be of value in assessment and treatment of emotional and behavioural difficulties in children, adolescents and adults. By taking us through case studies and combining this rich clinical data with a clear account of the application of the Mosaic technique, the reader will be introduced to the dynamic world of a classic non-verbal projective method. As well as chapters devoted to working specifically with children and adolescents, there are clear and concise accounts of using the Mosaics as an assessment tool. Finally, Thérèse introduces the application of Mosaics into work with young people with developmental language and learning difficulties, thereby opening up the opportunities, already taken in many places throughout the world, to use these procedures and methods in pre-school and early educational settings. This illustrates the flexibility and adaptability of the Lowenfeld Mosaic technique to a wide variety of social and cultural settings. Thérèse demonstrates this further in her account of the cross-cultural research she personally conducted, using Mosaics in assessing and comparing non-verbal constructs of self-percept in Chinese and American children.

This is a delightful and thoughtful introduction to the work of Margaret Lowenfeld by one of her most able and devoted students, who, throughout her own career, has striven to maintain non-verbal Lowenfeld techniques as part of the "tools of the trade" in child and adolescent mental health practice and research.

---

* The Lowenfeld Archives are now housed in the Wellcome Library for the History and Understanding of Medicine, whilst the Institute of Child Psychology Library remains at the Centre for Family Research, Cambridge University. Author's note.

That there is an international recognition and use of Lowenfeld Mosaics in child mental services, educational establishments and social services world wide is a tribute to both their enduring value and the importance of recognizing that the most biological of processes, play, should be at the centre of how we approach children with emotional and behavioural difficulties.

Ian Goodyer
Cambridge
April 2005

Preface

The inspiration for this book has come from my personal experience of the effectiveness of Lowenfeld's form of Projective Play Therapy through over thirty-five years of practice and nearly thirty years of teaching.

The aim of the work is to impart both my enthusiasm and experience in using the Lowenfeld Mosaics, the lesser known of Lowenfeld's therapeutic techniques, the other being the World Technique, better known in the United States as Sandplay.

Chapter 1 introduces the power of the Mosaics to liberate communication. Chapter 2 gives the history of how Lowenfeld came to design the Mosaics. Chapters 3 and 7 describe the Mosaic language of shape and colour, its development and its ability to portray the client's personality in action. Chapter 4 gives three examples of adult responses. In Chapters 5 and 6 I describe the therapeutic procedure from the moment of introducing the Mosaics to a client to suggesting ways in which the therapist could respond, using the Lowenfeld approach to therapy.

Chapters 8, 9 and 10 provide richly illustrated case studies of Mosaic work with children and adolescents in therapy and assessment. In Chapter 11 I discuss in detail two treatment series of Mosaics, showing the contrasting personalities of two young people.

Chapters 12, 13 and 14 recount my cross-cultural research work, using the Mosaics as the research instrument. There were two pieces of work, involving two separate groups of subjects. The first is with a group of severely deaf persons with complex emotional problems; the second is a study of cultural differences between Chinese children growing up and being educated within three different cultural backgrounds: China, the UK and the United States.

Chapters 15 and 16 attempt to elucidate the theoretical underpinnings of the Lowenfeld approach: her theories of E and Protosystem Thinking. I end with a personal account of my own Mosaic process, beginning with the first Mosaic I made at the Institute of Child Psychology, where I trained under Lowenfeld, and ending with my latest Mosaic made after my book was accepted for publication.

Guidelines on how to use the Lowenfeld Mosaics are given in the appendices. The list of further reading material includes both works that are alluded to in the main text and others that put the present volume in a wider context. All technical terms relating to the Lowenfeld Mosaics have been clarified as far as possible within the text.

Generally, I use "she" to refer to the therapist or Mosaic presenter, and "he" to refer to the client or Mosaic-maker when not discussing a named Mosaic example. Not all Mosaic examples are clinical cases. To conform to common practice, minor details have been changed in the named examples to maximise confidentiality and minimise identification.

Acknowledgements

My first and greatest debt is to my late friend and colleague, Dr Glenys Parkinson, who was the first to give me the courage to contemplate the idea that I might personally contribute towards making the Lowenfeld theories and practices better known. I would have been content to facilitate others, but Glenys wanted me to develop an entire course of professional training. It was fortunate that I was working for Professor Ian Goodyer at the time, at the Developmental Psychiatry Section at the University of Cambridge's Department of Psychiatry, for he looked favourably upon the idea; better still, he gave me a free hand. He was backed by the Dr Margaret Lowenfeld Trust; the whole project was supported personally by the then Chairman of the Trust, Dr Beric Wright. And it was he who finally raised the funds that made the project possible.

All this has truly only been possible because of all the people whose lives have crossed my path, chief of whom are the children and families who have helped me to help them. Throughout the years I have been teaching about Lowenfeld, the students on the Mosaic seminars, workshops and training courses have added further insights on the role of the therapist in using the Lowenfeld Mosaics. Furthermore, they have helped to clarify my understanding of Lowenfeld's theories and practice and increased the sum of my knowledge of the book's subject. Of my colleagues and others who have assisted me in the writing of this book, I would like especially to mention Lee Balfour, Shona Comben, Drs Althea and John de Carteret, Dr Christine Heath, Paul Henderson, Victoria Neumark, Lynn Pan, Sally Roberts, Susie Summers, Malcolm Ward, Rebecca Wolff, and in particular Jasper Woodcock, whose contribution has been inestimable. Any errors, omissions and obfuscations throughout the text are entirely my responsibility.

1 Meet Adam

"He won't talk to me. My son says he feels like killing himself. He keeps saying he doesn't know why." Adam's mother had rung up a community health centre the day before. Now he sat before me in the consulting room, where I had laid out a set of Lowenfeld Mosaics (see Figure 3.1) for him to use.

A big, ungainly but solemn young man of fourteen, he silently worked on his Mosaic. When he had finished he looked up. I held his gaze. "Tell me about what you've just done."

Mosaic 1.1
Adam

"It's a pattern . . . a symmetrical pattern."

"Yes . . . I noticed that you started at the corners of the tray."

"I was trying to balance the colours and shapes symmetrically. To make it more interesting I did it like this, diagonally."

"Yes, you worked in two interweaving movements, inwards from the edge but also criss-crossing the tray. When you got to the middle you stopped."

"Yes, the space in the middle is important."

"Important?"

He pondered for a while, eyes on the Mosaic. He looked up. His voice was quiet but firm and steady. "This" – indicating his Mosaic – "feels like a contracting coffin. I am in the middle" – indicating the space in the middle – "squeezed so hard that I've become invisible."

"Invisible? To whom?"

He did not answer. After a pause I referred back to his Mosaic: "Let's look at this more closely." I showed him how he had made his Mosaic, making the movements with my own hand, crossing and re-crossing the central space, my hand movements contracting towards the centre of the tray. I could feel the tightening, the contracting. Adam was watching me. The feeling in my hands made a powerful impression on me.

"Yes," I said. At the same moment I saw something else. "You took much longer as you approached the middle. What was happening there?"

"I found it difficult to get the right effect."

So there was a "right" effect after all. "Yes?"

"I knew there had to be a space in the middle. It had to be the right shape, that was the problem."

"Let's look at it again. I seem to remember that you took some time to put down the pair of red and yellow diamonds here: the red diamond above the yellow one, placed together as a pair [fourth row in from the left]. And it got progressively more difficult."

"Yes." Judging this to be the right moment I continued, "I think I see something. There seem to be two figures making up the space in the middle."

He looked down at his Mosaic. After a longer pause, he spoke, his voice suffused with emotion, summing up his feelings about his situation by reiterating his earlier statement about his Mosaic feeling "like a contracting coffin. I am in the middle squeezed so hard that I've become invisible." He now saw that the two figures holding the central space were his parents.

His bleak situation, in which he knew no sympathy, understanding nor a way out, was here powerfully conveyed by the notion of a contracting coffin that had rendered him invisible. And what was particularly moving was *his* surprise at the ease with which he was able to talk so openly, the Mosaic having offered him, finally, a medium of expression he could use.

What was Adam's life in reality, so feelingly and succinctly described as living "in a contracting coffin, [being] in the middle, squeezed so hard that I've become invisible"? What had happened between the desperate cry of "I don't know why," his inability to explain himself to his mother and the eloquence which the making of the Mosaic had brought about?

Adam was an only child. The family lived in a three-storey house. Both his parents worked at home, the father on the top floor, the mother on the ground floor. Adam inhabited the middle floor, where he ate, slept, did his schoolwork and where the family occasionally met up. The central portion of his Mosaic, including his difficulty in "formulation", corresponded therefore to the central reality of his life. He was in the middle, between his parents, "in a contracting coffin", being "squeezed so hard that I've become invisible". Adam had not set out to formulate his problem thus. He had set out to make a symmetrical pattern.

From Adam's point of view, his parents both doted on and neglected him, in different and confusing ways, their words never seeming to Adam to match what they did. Often they contradicted each other such that Adam was left in a helpless dilemma, unable to act.

This was reflected in the manner of his Mosaic-making – the criss-crossing motion of his hand across the tray, as well as in the identical nature of the figures corralling the space in the middle of the Mosaic. I was alerted to this latter notion by the first appearance of a pair of red and yellow diamonds placed on the board simultaneously, marking the difference (the colours red and yellow) as well as the similarity (the diamond shape) between the two parents (placed together as a couple, a unit). These figures were created from a continuous motion crossing the central space and placed in opposition to each other but holding the space together, and the space grew smaller and smaller with each move, becoming "a contracting coffin", where he was being "squeezed so hard, he had become invisible". This captured the feeling of something that earlier Adam could only think of in terms of a "symmetrical pattern", of the "space" having to be the "right shape".

But it was only after I had pointed out my observation about the two diamonds placed together simultaneously that the full force of his feelings began to crystallize into words that expressed the reality of his life at home, which was that the home created by his parents had the constricting effect of making him feel he was "invisible" to them. The words thus summarised a dynamic portrait that had been feelingly painted in the colours and shapes of the Lowenfeld Mosaics.

During his primary school years, he was thought to be a slow learner. The parents were convinced this was a character defect, that he was simply lazy. They saw Adam's problem in terms of academic success. Their chief efforts went into finding a school with a high academic reputation, and they commissioned a professional report to assess Adam's academic potential to that end. This report established that he had this potential, but revealed that dyslexia was the cause of his slow progress at school, not laziness. Nevertheless, Adam's parents decided to send him to a well-known, academically high-powered, sports-orientated school which had no facilities for dyslexic pupils. They ignored the dyslexia mentioned in the report, stuck doggedly to their view of him as "lazy" and maintained that sports would cure him of it. He thus received no help, continued to do badly at school and became ever more miserable. The parents continued their belief in his laziness as the sole cause of his academic failure and misery.

He stood out in the school in several ways, but chiefly because he felt he did not belong. Adam was rather large, round in build, with a clumsy gait, and he disliked sport of any kind. He felt denigrated and bullied as a misfit by some of his teachers and his peers, but his parents refused to send him elsewhere, on the grounds that his was "a very good school".

All these contradictions, the multi-faceted nature of Adam's life and experience of himself within his home and school environment, were economically summed up through his Mosaic process as well as his Mosaic. Go through the way he actually made the Mosaic. Those diagonally propelled hand movements, stressing the "cross" formation – "I was trying to balance the colours and shapes symmetrically; to make it more interesting, I did it like this, diagonally" – which repeatedly traverse across the central empty space, here representing Adam. And it was with the recognition that it was the figures of his parents corralling the contracting central space that formed the final piece to the jigsaw of his intense and confused feelings. Instead of growing in strength and stature, and able to develop his skills, Adam suddenly found that he was diminishing into invisibility.

This factual information did not come out in any logical order, nor at a single meeting. The seeming sense of cause and effect presented here was, at the time of telling, a jumble of facts round a singular but intense feeling of despair. Having made the Mosaic, Adam felt empowered to engage with his family, which for him was the chief merit of our first meeting. A coherent, feeling picture of his life was presented in his first Mosaic and gave him the opportunity, with the therapist's support, to convey his feelings directly to his parents, who finally acknowledged the necessity to address Adam's evident unhappiness within the family context.

What has the act of projection using the Lowenfeld Mosaics to do with the release of self-expression and communication?

Communication in situations like Adam's is obviously not about giving straightforward information, like "My family lives in a three-storey house," or even "I feel unloved and unnoticed." The Mosaic-maker at first does not know how he feels and thinks in relation to the specific situation he perceives himself to be in. It is feelings that have to be communicated, and the linearity and logic of verbal language make it impossible to convey the global nature of feelings. The Mosaics, on the other hand, are non-verbal, and through their use feelings begin to emerge, be externalized and communicated. With this distance granted by the Mosaic process and product, the Mosaic-maker can begin to make sense of the pattern formed by the many strands of his life.

For Adam, it was the moment he recognised that it was the figures of his parents who were cradling the contracting space which formed the final piece to the jigsaw of his feelings that brought the desperate cry of "I want to kill myself" to his mother. It was the use of the Lowenfeld Mosaics that finally enabled Adam to articulate what had at first been inexpressible.

2 Telling my story with shapes and colours

Humanity has always found it necessary to include non-verbal forms in its repertoire of expressive communication. Drawing, painting, music and dance are the major forms, but today there is increasing awareness of the importance of our non-verbal vocabularies, our gestures, facial expressions and body language. They add nuance and depth to the meanings invested in our everyday life as well as in our more conscious attempts to communicate with words. No one would dispute the paucity of a personal relationship conducted through words alone. Sooner or later, people want to meet, see, hear, touch and smell each other. Thus a variety of means is needed for satisfactory social intercourse. Margaret Lowenfeld (1890–1973) seems to have understood why human beings have this need for non-verbal communication and where it comes from.

By the late 1920s and 1930s, after years of watching children play (Lowenfeld 1991), Lowenfeld became convinced that from the very beginning we are equipped to be able to make sense of the world around us, to think about our personal experience. This thinking makes use of our senses of touch, smell, taste, hearing, sight, as well as our kinaesthetic sense. Through the dynamic, global and multidimensional picture of our world that is built up by our senses, we formulate images, ideas about what the world within and around us is like. She called this Protosystem Thinking (Lowenfeld 2004b: 94–6).[1]

With the development of her concept of Protosystem Thinking, Lowenfeld began to realise that through our early thoughts and feelings about the world around us, we simultaneously begin to form a picture of ourselves within this world, a picture built up of impressions of responses to us from those we have constant contact with. Our parents' view of us, whether positive or negative, gives us our first glimpse of who we are within this primary social circle. The very culture of our family would define a certain sense of what is a "good" person, what is the "good life". And it is within this formative matrix that our sense of ourselves begins to take shape in our minds. It would define both our idea of ourselves and that of the actions we take. When something is amiss in our lives, that is the time we wish to discover the roots of our predicament. And to do that, we need to return to a

---

1 This concept will be explored in greater detail in Chapter 16.

time when we began to form ideas about the world around us as well as our place in it, to the time of our beginning. Since words are not our first vocabulary, we have to begin by trying to access this world through our primary vocabulary, the multi-dimensional vocabulary of our senses.

How then do we access and express these thoughts, thoughts about the world which surrounds us, about their meaning in relation to ourselves? When does it become imperative that we have access to these thoughts? In ordinary living, if we think about ourselves, or the way we behave at all, we assume that our behaviour has a rational foundation. We tend not to question ourselves, or our motives, until something goes awry with our lives. We then begin to wonder what it was that has brought the present dissonance in our lives. We begin to question both our actions and our motives. We may even begin to doubt ourselves and perhaps for the first time wonder what it is in ourselves that has led us into this unhappy situation. At times of profound grief and loss, we can only howl and weep. Often we are left wordless. It is at such times that we begin to delve deep into ourselves for comfort to take us out of our present predicament and look for new perspectives that will carry us forward.

It is just at this point that the Lowenfeld Mosaics comes into its own, as an instrument for eliciting our non-verbal thoughts and feelings. Ultimately it is also a tool for demonstrating the personality in action. But how did Lowenfeld come to design this personality projective tool – the Lowenfeld Mosaics – and develop her particular approach to psychotherapeutic work? What was the reality in her own life which prompted an idea that creating a pattern or a picture using objects rather than words makes it possible for people to make sense of their personal experiences? Margaret Lowenfeld's own account went like this.

It was in 1919, the year after the end of the First World War, and while the Russo-Polish War was still in progress. Lowenfeld, then a young student, went from England with a typhus mission to Eastern Europe as part of a medical team. At that particular time in British history, the fact that she was allowed by her parents to study medicine was remarkable enough. In Europe so soon after the war, for her to enlist in the peace effort, to be given a position of authority, spoke of a certain commitment to healing. Once there, she was deployed to help to repair some of the ravages of war. This included "the attempt to feed and clothe many thousands of demobilized Polish students", assisting "in sanitary provisions" for prisoners of war, and doing "welfare . . . work for troops on a four hundred mile front" (Lowenfeld 2004c: 1). At the same time, once out of her uniformed role, she, although a "landowning citizen of Poland", became "a powerless and indistinguishable unit [in the] disintegrated [Polish] countryside [that was] decimated by typhoid, dysentery, cholera, tuberculosis and an influenza epidemic, with no medical stores" (p. 1).

Her experiences of the extremes of feeling helpful and being helpless "led [her] later to a direct understanding of certain aspects of the inner life of children" (2004c: 2). At the same time she was faced with two profound questions. The first was that "contrary to all expectations, certain children and young adults deprived of everything that psychiatry [then and even now] considers essential to health and development, nevertheless grew into vigorous and creative people" (p. 2). So, how did this come about? She realised then that we are indeed unique individuals, that our uniqueness lies in our singular view of the world, which is formed through our earliest understanding of ourselves, the world around us and our place in it. And it is this personal view of the world that largely governs our ability to manage our present adversities as well as to find the resources to see potential opportunities for survival beyond them.

She considered the second question was the more urgent. She thought we urgently needed to understand the kind of ideas we have and how we come to formulate them. Writing after the Second World War, she formulated the second question as "What exactly was taking place in individuals who carried out the type of actions which words like Auschwitz and Ravensbrück have since made too familiar to us?" (Lowenfeld 2004c: 2).

Lowenfeld was asking how it is that certain beliefs which, when put in place, knowingly bring about horrific large-scale consequences can come to be thought of as not only acceptable, but good? And this is not simply a matter of historical interest, because these beliefs are endlessly present all round us, for instance, in the myriad debates about freedom and democracy, the factors and reasons which would justify going to war, whether society is a proper concept, or what constitutes a family, a good marriage or a happy relationship. All these are important concepts, important to our view of ourselves and how we conduct our lives. How then are our views arrived at?

Her quest was to find a means for us to access and express these thoughts, to see the process by which they are arrived at, and how these inform our actions. Her discovery of early non-verbal thinking, Protosystem Thinking, became fundamental to her search for a means of communicating these thoughts and feelings, allowing us to glimpse the thoughts and feelings which form the basis of our actions.

Lowenfeld came from a family with connections scattered across Europe. She spoke several European languages, so it is not surprising to learn that her post-World War I work later included a period of "strenuous four-language interpretation" (Lowenfeld 2004c: 2). It was through this work that she came to the conclusion that language was not necessarily a helpful instrument to enhance interpersonal understanding. After her war-work, this became clearer to her on her return to England, when much to her own surprise, Lowenfeld found during her personal analyses that it was impossible to convey in words "the essence of the experiences out of which the queries grew" (p. 2).

She felt the answer could lie within psychiatry, specifically in medical research. Following her relief work in Poland and whilst doing her postgraduate training in clinical research methods in a hospital in Glasgow, Lowenfeld began to glimpse the possibility of a different approach to her enquiries. She describes the dawning of this approach during this training in some detail.

> I began to notice in the faces and bodies of the children I was studying, expressions, postures and gestures that resembled those with which I had become familiar in prison camps and famine areas. Language I had already

discarded as too uncertain a tool; the manipulation of relationships seemed irrelevant to problems whose essence was the absence of relationships. It then occurred to me to wonder if anything could be done with objects instead of persons, and whether it would not be possible to devise a scientific experiment where one could represent to children by means of small objects what one guessed they might be undergoing.

Taking courage therefore, I set out to try acting before children with objects, what I conceived that they might be experiencing, and with immediate result. The children understood at once . . . With this experiment a door came open and I found the children and myself in contact with one another.

(Lowenfeld 2004c: 2)

Her account of Betty, a girl of under three years old, as told to me sometime during my child psychotherapy training, remains fresh in my memory still. Betty had had an obstruction in her bowels. She had an operation to cut out the obstructed sections and the two parts were sewn together again. From the doctors' point of view, it was an entirely successful operation, and they fully expected her to make a quick and complete recovery. Contrary to these expectations, Betty's health began to fail. She became listless and seemed to be physically fading away. Lowenfeld's curiosity was aroused, and as a medical researcher in the department, she began to devise a way to test out her ideas about using objects to act out what she thought Betty might be thinking and feeling about the operation which the doctors had recently performed on her.

Betty was not often awake, but on one occasion when she was, Lowenfeld enacted a series of tableaux in front of Betty, using a length of tube and a jug of water. Betty watched every movement with seeming interest. She first showed Betty the tube with a kink tied up in the middle. Lowenfeld poured some water into the top of this tied-up tube and demonstrated that no water could get through it. In full view of Betty, Lowenfeld then cut away the kinked section, joined the two ends together with bandages, and again poured water down the tube. This time the water came tumbling out at the other end. Betty responded with a wan smile. That seemed to have been the moment when Betty began to recover. Lowenfeld was visibly moved by the memory of that moment, and I can still feel my own excitement as I imagined what Lowenfeld might have felt when she first saw that smile. I believe it was to a case such as Betty's that Lowenfeld was alluding when she found the door which "came open and . . . found the children and myself in contact with one another" (2004c: 2).

From her experience with children like Betty, Lowenfeld began to realise that thinking through images alone, without the use of words, is possible. What then does this non-verbal thinking consist of? Are there many ways of accessing this non-verbal thought? Perhaps this is why we have always needed drawing, painting and dance to express as well as to understand ourselves.

What did Adam mean when he told his mother that he felt like killing himself but did not know why he had this feeling? He had no words to tell her.

Could one of the reasons that his mother felt "he won't talk to me" be that the source of his feeling "to kill myself" was not explicable in words even to himself? What he needed was a means of expressing his feelings. Feeling is complex and is more easily expressed through a medium which is capable of saying many different, often contradictory, things simultaneously, one which more resembles our personal experiences, one which engages all our senses at once. And certainly a medium that engages more than our verbal skills, a medium which is more able to reflect the global nature of our experience.

Margaret Lowenfeld's experience with Betty and children like her led first to the design of the World Technique, now more widely known as Sandplay. The Lowenfeld Mosaics came from another source of personal experience. During her travels to visit her large multilingual family around Europe, she was caught by the colourful patterns in the folk costumes worn by the people in processions at many of their local festivals, especially in districts round western Poland, where her family owned large estates. Lowenfeld found a fascinating commonality as well as distinct local variations: "The basic patterns of form and colour that are shared by peasant communities over wide areas have their own local variations in the individual villages" (Lowenfeld 2004a: 31).

Her curiosity was aroused by this observation, and she began "to wonder whether any way could be found through which such differences could be investigated" (Lowenfeld 2004a: 31). She had two questions in mind:

> Were these basic patterns of form and colour the expression of creative faculties in these communities from days long past, and were they perpetuated now through force of habit or tradition? Or was some characteristic inherent in the people concerned reflected in these creations so that their perpetuation arose out of a relationship between the people and their communal expressions which remains real today?
>
> (Lowenfeld 2004a: 31–2)[2]

This interest in pattern and pattern making evolved into a tool for investigating a personality in action. In her broad-ranging researches, she found that the Lowenfeld Mosaics can also be "an instrument of exploration rather than standardization" (Lowenfeld 2004a: 115). Not only were there distinctive differences in individual responses, but the Lowenfeld Mosaics seemed also to provide "a useful instrument for increasing the understanding both of the potentialities of different children within the limits of a given culture; and of the relation of the development shown by individual children to the general pattern of development of all children" (p. 105). In its final form, the Lowenfeld Mosaics "provides an opportunity to observe the personality in spontaneous action" (Anderson and Hood-Williams undated: 6)

I now see that my own journey to the Lowenfeld Mosaics began with my

---

2 Lowenfeld's discoveries in relation to cultural differences will be discussed in a later chapter.

first landing at Heathrow airport. A Chinese from Hongkong, I was in England to further my education. Some years later, being cut off from the support of an extended family and needing urgently to understand my maternal role in an alien culture, I sought to acquire some knowledge. I did not feel that an academic course alone would answer. It was then suggested that I find out about courses in child psychotherapy. At the time there were three. Lowenfeld's Institute of Child Psychology in London seemed to me then to provide the broadest education about the inner life in British culture of the time.

At my interview at the Institute, I was given a set of Lowenfeld Mosaics, I thought to while away the time whilst I waited to be "properly" assessed. I was totally entranced by and became completely absorbed with playing with the shapes and colours. I can still recall vividly this first Mosaic of mine. It was an utterly satisfying emotional experience. At the centre of the Mosaic was an aeroplane, multicoloured and flying upwards. In the bottom right corner of the Mosaic I had created a small tree.[3] Indeed, I had come to England by plane, but that journey I now understood was also a quest for understanding. In later Mosaics, this tree grew and bore fruit; I became a child psychotherapist and my journey into the human heart and mind continued.

I came to England to further my education. Two professional lifetimes, as a librarian and a teacher, later, I entered my third professional career, which, on reflection, has been my life-transforming work.

---

3 This Mosaic is presented in Chapter 17.

3 The Lowenfeld Mosaic language of shape and colour

We all understand that therapeutic work has two aspects. The first has to do with the personal experiences of the children, young people and adults we see. We try to understand the client's present through assembling a picture of his past. With children, it is usually through reports that have come with the child, by talking to the adult figures who are most closely associated with them, and/or by asking the child to tell us directly. Thus the past forms the background to any therapeutic endeavour. The second aspect is that it is work which is centred on expression, communication and understanding. Thus the means by which these personal experiences are expressed, and in what or whose terms these expressions are understood, become central to the therapeutic enterprise.

Now let us look at the nature of ordinary experience. Try to recall a recent experience you have had, for instance, the start of today. How would you tell it? How would you express the moment of your awakening? Would you naturally use words? Try this out for yourself. Describe in words your experience of that moment of awakening consciousness.

What exactly came into your mind when you were doing this? Did you notice how you went about recalling the experience? How did you select the moment that was the beginning of your experience? If you had no hesitation, what was it that made it decisive? How did you go about describing your experience? Did you encounter any problems at all? Did you have to grope for words, for instance? If not, can you explain why not?

What do you observe about your description? You will surely have perceived that whilst the experience took only one moment of your time, the act of describing it took much longer. Why is this? The difference surely lies in the difference between the nature of personal experience and that of verbal expression. It is because experience is instantaneous, simultaneous, global and multidimensional, whereas verbal expression is linear, sequential and time-bound in nature. Verbal language (since most verbal languages are based on Aristotelian bivalent logic)[4] requires us to prioritize the elements of experience, which is highly complex and

---

4 The language of the Aymara people, in Bolivia and Peru, is based on trivalent logic, where something can be "both perhaps true and perhaps not true" and where it is possible to arrive at conclusions from doubtful or barely plausible premises (Guzman 1985: v).

subtle, and not necessarily dominated by the single priority needed to begin a sentence, any telling of a moment. Moreover, words have general meanings, while an experience, any experience, is singular in nature, that is, uniquely personal in every respect. The same words, however, would not have the same meaning for different persons, nor even to the same person at another time or under different circumstances.

However, verbal language is perhaps not our only vehicle for expressing our thoughts and feelings and reflecting upon ourselves. In this context, we are all aware of the expressiveness of sign language, and we know about the importance of body language. What about infants, how do they express themselves? How do babies make sense of the world around and within them? We now know babies think. What do they think with? And babies do express themselves. How do they do that? We know of course that we all express ourselves most immediately through our actions. Might that be the case for infants as well? But what are the faculties involved when we are in contemplation, when we are reflecting upon the events of our day, our relationships, ourselves? Might there be a way that is not dependent upon verbal articulacy?

Margaret Lowenfeld, faced with the question of finding a non-verbal language that would allow the global, multidimensional, simultaneous nature of personal experience to be expressed and reflected upon, realised that our senses held the key, that we make sense of our experiences through our senses: touch, smell, taste, sight, hearing and the kinaesthetic. Of these, that of touch, to my thinking, is fundamental. Our senses are not only used to understand our sensorial experiences; they are fundamental to our sensorial thinking. They are also what we use to express what we think and feel about those experiences. Therefore all the tools devised by Lowenfeld involve the use of several senses, but most particularly touch. She has left us with three tools: the Poleidoblocs to assist and demonstrate our mathematical thinking, the World Technique (now more popularly known as Sandplay), and the Mosaics.

The Lowenfeld Mosaic material, the Mosaic language, consists of a tray, usually fitted with a piece of white paper, and a box containing 456 coloured tiles that are grouped by shape. There are five different shapes: a square, a rhombus or diamond, an isosceles triangle or a half-square, an equilateral triangle and finally, a scalene triangle (see Figure 3.1). Each shape is available in six colours, red, blue, yellow, black, green and white, and they are clearly displayed and arranged on their sides in the box and usually in this order.

All these shapes are mathematically interrelated. The dimensions of the five shapes are based on the length of the sides of the square: the sides of the rhombus are the same length as that of the square; the isosceles triangle is formed by bisecting the square diagonally; the sides of the equilateral triangle are the same length as the hypotenuse of the isosceles triangle; and bisecting the equilateral triangle gives the size of the scalene triangle. All this in turn determined the size of the tray, the dimensions of which were chosen so that complete edged patterns could be made with certain shapes, and the tray could be entirely covered. The colours and shapes, together with their interrelationships are shown in Figure 3.2.

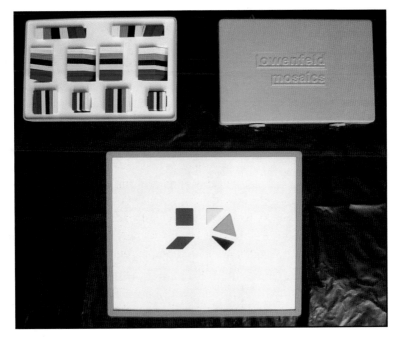

Figure 3.1
Box and tray

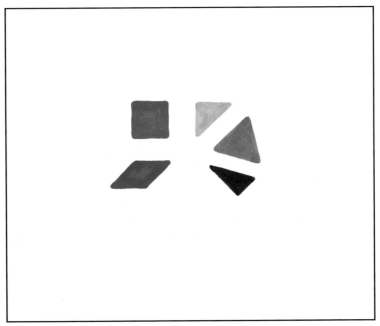

Figure 3.2
The five Mosaic shapes, showing their interrelationships and displaying all the colours, except for white

This simple material forms the vocabulary of the Mosaic communication. As can be seen, the vocabulary as such is quite limited. However, this very limitation is one of its strengths.

Let us first look at the special features of this vocabulary (see Figures 3.1 and 3.2).

- The dimensions of the tray are obvious.
- The colours are clearly displayed.
- The location of the shapes is quickly learnt, and can be seen and distinguished at a glance.
- Their differences and their relationships, both among the shapes and in relation to the tray, can be perceived and certainly visually demonstrated virtually without verbal explanation.
- For children, especially younger children, if not for adults also, there is the added attraction of the bright colours and the opportunity to play.
- It requires the minimum of skill to use.
- The limitations are clearly defined, both by the size of the tray space offered as well as by the numbers of colours and shapes available.

These limitations are an important element of the Lowenfeld Mosaics as a projective tool in reflecting the personality actively engaged with the world around it. They reproduce "life as lived" by all of us, which is in a state of dynamic transition, always circumscribed by our own singular natures and circumstances, within a particular culture and historical time, and, most crucially, by our view of ourselves. Given these characteristics, the combined Mosaic process and product is always unique to the person making a Mosaic, at the moment of its making.

This self-portraiture thus demonstrates more closely how we approach real-life situations. None of us behave in a vacuum. We are all required to respond to life's "givens", and it is how we respond which distinguishes us from one another. In Mosaic terms, the Mosaics and the tray are the givens. And in my experience, no two Mosaics are ever alike, not even those made by the same person at different times. Even so, throughout an individual Mosaic series, the individual style of approach is always evident.[5] Of cultural interest, it is noteworthy that the Japanese prefer soft shades to primary colours, and so, of the two Lowenfeld techniques, they tend to use only the World Technique or Sandplay.

One of the inherent characteristics of Mosaic-making is that it allows the emergence of thoughts and feelings through the simultaneous use of two of our strongest senses, touch and sight. Richard Gregory, who is distinguished for his work on perception, has written regarding the importance of touch to our ability to make sense of what we see that "effective seeing depends on interactive experience of objects . . . We would be blind if brought up in a . . . world of sight without touch" (Gregory 1997: 13). The use of Mosaics thus enables us to recreate the meaning of our personal experience in reverse, so to speak, through seeing and touching the Mosaic pieces.

Sight and touch are two of our three main sensory modalities, the third being voice/hearing. Each tile has both a colour (sight) and a shape (primarily touch), and depending on the effect one wishes to create, one needs to choose just the right colour-shape combination to express what one wishes to "say". The presence of these two dimensions is also clear to both the observer and Mosaic-maker alike.

---

5 See Chapter 11 for a description of two contrasting styles of approach to a similar problem.

The Lowenfeld Mosaics' vocabulary thus has two distinctive features: the use of our senses to make direct contact with our experience, and the uniqueness of meaning that can be invested in the shapes and colours of their Mosaic by the user. There is no meaning specific to each of the colour-shapes, except that invested by the individuals using them. Unlike words, there is no dictionary, no common understanding for meanings attributed to these colour-shapes. Other people will accept, for instance, one's preference for red rather than blue. They can clearly understand that this liking for the red in the box may not have the same source as their own liking. Likewise, people can also easily see that another's preference for the red need not evoke the same kind of feeling or image in them.

Recognising this difference, having the knowledge that other people's liking for a particular colour or shape is unlikely to conjure up the same feelings and thoughts in you, makes it possible for us to believe that the meaning of our individual Mosaic response can emerge, and that our communication can be understood in its personal context.

Many practitioners who have used the Mosaics understand that "the process of acquiring experience in its use resembles that of acquiring a new language" (Lowenfeld 2004a: 152). In practice, Mosaics can be used to communicate thoughts, feelings and experiences, which is essentially about something dynamic and simultaneously multidimensional and global. We ourselves may not be able to fully understand what is being expressed, but it is a statement we can return to and explore time and time again. In the next chapter, I will tell you about Claire, whose Mosaic simultaneously engaged all three of her major senses.

4 The shape and colour of personality

Margaret Lowenfeld has stressed the importance of close attention to what she has called the Total Response in Mosaic-making, by which she meant not only the process and the resultant product, but also the manner in which the task is undertaken. This attention to the multidimensionality of the response is a key factor in the use of the Lowenfeld Mosaics, especially in its use in psychotherapy. As a result the therapist will be rewarded with a dynamic portrait in miniature of the personality in action and an understanding of a person's style of approach to life. Two examples follow.

Mosaic 4.1
Claire

Claire was a single woman in her late twenties who valued her independence to the extent of always living on her own since leaving her family home in her late adolescence. Professionally, she was already internationally known in her field. She was intelligent and intellectual, and a quick and voracious reader. Languages and communication were her chief interests. In particular, she was intrigued by how language can lead to misunderstanding as much as understanding and the difficulties encountered by translators. She was all for clarity. She was interested in the Mosaics for its claim to being a language and wished to have the experience of doing one.

Although she concentrated on the making of her Mosaic, Claire commented aloud throughout. After my usual demonstration of the Mosaic vocabulary, she began by taking out all the different shapes, each in a different colour, thus virtually repeating what I had just been doing. She said that she liked yellow but not this shade of yellow. However, she decided to start with it, and persisted for quite some time in using this colour in all its shapes, getting more and more exasperated as she did so, until she finally abandoned her attempts and replaced all the tiles in the box.

She started again. She decided to use another colour and chose green. Again she used all the shapes in this colour. There were many adjustments and changes, accompanied by irritated determination; eventually she abandoned this attempt as well.

On her third try, she changed tactics. Claire decided to use only one shape, the diamond, but in three colours: blue, green and red, working steadily from the central pattern outwards. At the end, she quickly added two green scalene triangles to give it "just enough variety". Claire smiled as she looked up to say, "That's it, I've finished."

What you may have noticed so far is her observant and meticulous as well as methodical approach to the task. Furthermore, in going over my demonstration, she seemed to be trying to experience for herself the vocabulary of the Mosaic language and to confirm it for herself through personal repetition. Her Mosaic process certainly deployed her main senses of touch, sight and speech.

In our discussion afterwards, Claire was quite startled by my observation that her immediate response to what was a new situation for her seemed to have been to be drawn first to the qualities which she did not like, to work on them and then to try to weave them into an acceptable form. She thought for a while before acknowledging the truth of my observation by saying that she often did not manage this, because it never quite seemed to work, but yes, she did not give up easily. After another pause, Claire added that she knew she had strong views about everything and occasionally had to accept that she needed to modify her attitude. She was convinced, however, that modification was only a matter of pragmatism. Often it seemed to her like giving in. Claire said she was interested in the "idea" of variety in life, but quickly added "but – in reality – not too much", echoing her gesture and comment when she added the two green scalene triangles.

She acknowledged with some surprise that her Mosaic – her approach to the task, the way the whole picture was built up and the moment when she knew she had completed the pattern – altogether described her attitude to life and how she functioned in reality.

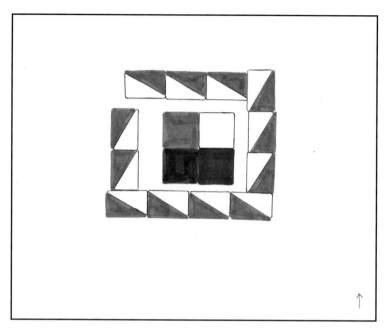

This Mosaic portrait was made in rather different circumstances. When Diane was looking at her friend Edmund's Mosaic, she commented that it did not "look satisfying" and, as an explanation of her opinion, she decided to show us what she meant by doing a Mosaic herself. She began by forming the outer frame of green and white scalene triangles, using all the green-coloured scalenes from one side of the box, carefully placing the pieces more or less at the centre of the tray, beginning from the top left-hand corner of the design and creating and preserving a gap at this corner. She then built the inner square, beginning with the green, then white, followed by the blue and ending with the red square. This was done in silence, without hesitation and quickly. She would not be drawn into saying any more about her Mosaic, except to mention that "the colours were irrelevant" and that it was what she "would call satisfying".

Let us first consider the *Mosaic Process*. Can it tell us anything about the person who had made the Mosaic? You will recall Adam's Mosaic, where my re-enacting of the Process enabled me physically to feel the constriction in the "squeezing", which eventually helped me to understand how Adam had arrived at his own understanding of himself.

Diane's Mosaic, like Adam's, was created inwards, that is, the movement was inwards. Notwithstanding her remark about the colours being irrelevant, the move from the scalene triangles to the squares was linked by the colours green and white. It is as though she was taking those "green and white" elements further into herself, the inner self, and making them "solid", in the form of squares, which developed further with the addition of the blue and red to become solidly four-square. As she later said, "If I don't force myself to take on things, I would never do anything. I need to challenge myself all the time."

As for her *Mosaic Product*, imagine the edge of the tray as forming a border framing the Mosaic, and imagine further the space framing the green and white scalene triangles as also forming a border. You will then see that Diane has created altogether four borders round the solidly constructed central square of her Mosaic: the central square is first ringed by space, which in turn is almost surrounded by a square of green and white; this is ringed by more space, space which is finally enclosed by the tray edge. The central square is thus enclosed by four borders, two of them being made up of empty space.

I have always seen this as a picture of a castle with a double moat. When I mentioned this idea of mine to Diane, she was moved to say that it was true, that people had often told her she was very hard to get to know. However, it is also evident that there is a strong link between the outer and inner self, as shown by the repetition of the green and white. She appeared to be supremely confident in herself, never needing to explain or excuse herself. This gave her an appearance of openness, merely the impression of a person of few words. What words she chose were selected for their exact meaning. Even so, Diane's major senses were also used in her Mosaic response.

Years later Diane asked to see her Mosaic again. She recognised this portrait of herself as a true reflection of how she was then and is now. She felt that the red square represented the core of herself, which she still has to explore. The red square was of course the only one of that colour. Perhaps she had come to realise that the Mosaic was more eloquent and descriptive than her one verbal description – "satis-fying" – and could now be acknowledged as a self-portrait painted with the Mosaic shapes and colours.

Mosaic 4.3
Edmund

The Mosaic that she felt was unsatisfying, her friend Edmund's (Mosaic 4.3 above), was made with white, black, blue and yellow pieces. His pieces were placed mainly in the top left part of the tray. (As if to demonstrate their friendship, the gap in Diane's Mosaic was opened to the space on the tray where Edmund's Mosaic had been placed.) Even so, it is noteworthy that, through that gap in the top left corner, one is still met by the colours of the outer layer of her persona, the green and white squares. The two Mosaics are further linked by one common colour. Whereas the blue is manifested through a square in Diane's Mosaic, in Edmund's it was with a diamond, which has sides of similar length to the square, so that the two shapes could still be perfectly aligned when placed next to each other. Was that the point of contact for the friendship?

The word "satisfying", with which Diane positively described her own Mosaic, thus expressed a completeness of herself at the moment she decided to make her Mosaic. Her Mosaic followed from one made by this particular friend of hers. She was focused on her friend's Mosaic, and perhaps on the relationship between them. This was the original prompt for her to engage actively in doing a Mosaic, but ultimately, it also described her style of approach to life in general. A satisfactory and satisfying expression of herself, she felt, was achieved in less than five minutes.

Conventional psychotherapy recognises the importance of body language as well as the words used between the therapist and the client. In using a projective approach like the Lowenfeld Mosaics, however, both the client and the therapist are anchored by the product that the client produces, and their joint memory of the process by which the final Mosaic is achieved.

The Mosaic language allows all our major sensory modalities, our sight, touch, as well as our voice/hearing, to come into play. In our daily life, this is how we respond to others, to old and new situations alike. We respond with all our senses.

It is the multidimensionality of the expression through our senses, the whole of the personality being engaged, which is the key to our ability to communicate that which we have not been able to express in words. Expressing ourselves in this way, we gradually become aware of the complex strands of our thoughts and feelings.

Through the Mosaic language within the Total Response of the Mosaic Process and the final Mosaic Product, the subjective becomes objectified. Something from within finds expression. Ideas or pictures emerge into a concrete form. There can be no argument about who made the Mosaic and what the Mosaic has been made with. There is now something tangible between the therapist and the Mosaic-maker, something which cannot be denied. It is something on which they can both focus and is a starting point from which to explore.

As you are unique, so will your Mosaic be unique. Even if the product looks the same as someone else's, the meaning of each Mosaic will be unique to each individual. The meaning invested in the Mosaic product ultimately rests with the person who made it.

5 Working therapeutically with Lowenfeld Mosaics

In this chapter it is my intention to describe the Lowenfeld approach to clinical practice in the first part and explain how to introduce the Lowenfeld Mosaics in a therapeutic setting in part 2.

Part 1: The Lowenfeld approach to clinical practice

Adults and children respond differently to the notion of therapy, for external as well as internal reasons. When adults seek therapy, they do so with some idea of what they want, and mainly they want to be relieved of their misery and distress, however that may be achieved. Often they think it involves an understanding of motives within them of which they are unaware. Nevertheless it is a choice adults can make for themselves.

Children, by and large, are referred to a therapist by an adult who thinks they need something called "therapy". Thus children experience the recommendation of therapy as being a solution that is thought by adults to be the right thing for them to receive, not as something they have thought up as the appropriate solution to the situation they find themselves in. Even if a child has some notion of what therapy might entail, I doubt whether they were ever asked to consider the possibility of it being a solution to their difficulties. Therefore, the difference between an adult and a child entering therapy is one of knowledge and of choice. This is why I have found, for instance, that children who have been referred by their school tend to think that they are coming to see me because they have been naughty at school. If they have been referred by their parents, they assume they have been naughty at home.

When an adult wants a child to be different, the child usually takes this to mean that the adult wants them to behave better. The child understands that the adult wants them to change in quite specific ways which are judged as acceptable and an improvement by the adult, but which they do not necessarily regard as the right solution to their problems. For example, if a boy wants to watch a particular television programme but his younger sister wants to watch a programme which is on at the same time but on another channel, he might not find it an acceptable solution if he is told that he should let his sister watch what she wants because, being younger, she will be going to bed before him and he can stay up later and perhaps watch another programme.

My view is that children who are faced with a therapist actually respond differently internally than adults. The response is different from that of an adult client because the therapist is an adult to whom the child is brought, whereas the adult client usually takes the initiative and seeks out the therapist. Thus for the child it is not usually his choice, whereas for the adult it is always his choice.

Adults, because they have a preconceived notion of what therapy is and what it would do for them, assume that the therapist will have the knowledge or the expertise they themselves do not have, to help them find a solution to their difficulties or a way to dissolve their pain. For example, when faced with doing a Mosaic, the adult Mosaic-maker is likely to wonder what the therapist will make of it, possibly thinking that the therapist will recognise the psychological meaning of the Mosaic expression irrespective of what the Mosaic-maker himself thinks and feels about it, that is, irrespective of the Mosaic-maker's own point of view.

When children are faced with doing a Mosaic they tend to expect the adult to know what they are actually making. They do not think the adults will see something else, or a meaning different from what they attribute to it. Since children's common experience is that adults know things and tell them whether what they have done is right or wrong, they have usually come to the conclusion that adults know what they, the children, are doing. Along with "Do as I say!" is the oft-implied injunction, "Whatever you're doing, stop doing it." They do not think of the psychological meaning of what they are expressing, only the subject of their drawing or Mosaic.

Thus adults who go into therapy have an idea, for instance, of a therapist being able to have insights about them which they could not have themselves. Children do not have this second level or sophisticated notion about therapy or therapists. They simply think that all adults know all the facts about them, that is, they believe adults talk to each other about them. If, for instance, a child has been told he is naughty, he will think that is why he is coming to see you, the therapist. Furthermore, he is likely to think that the therapist, knowing all about him, will share the referrer's view of what "being naughty" means, and is going to devise ways to help him stop being "naughty". In other words, he treats all "therapists" as behavioural therapists, which, if one thinks about it, is not exactly wrong. The child accepts his point of view as irrelevant to the treatment and that the accepted view is that adults know best. What adults and children seem to have in common is that neither think the solution is in their own hands. They are both looking to the therapist for a solution to their problems.

Actually both adults and children have their own points of view and, just as people of all ages have their own idiosyncratic ways of responding to similar experiences, they also have their own unique way of resolving similar problems (for clinical examples, see Chapter 11).

Thus we all love in our own way, we all express our feelings in our own way, and our friends or children each love us in their own special way, not only because we appear differently to each of them, but because they actually see us through their own special lenses. This means that it is not only possible, but quite probable, that something which makes one person irritated could actually be found endearing by another. So if you make a Mosaic portrait of your/a mother, it follows that another person, seeing this portrait of your/a mother (whether that person knows your mother or not), will not have the same thoughts and feelings about this image as you do. And this is true also of the ways people try to solve problems. When asked to formulate a solution to the problem of finding the numbers which would add up to one hundred in total, people are unlikely to come up with the same figures.

This also means that when a child "talks" (here we have to take into account the non-verbal as well as the verbal communications of the child) about their personal experiences, whatever thoughts and feelings these arouse in the listener, whether it is pleasure or distress, humility or disgust, alarm or revulsion, these feelings may not be what the child attaches to their experience at all. I remember the occasion when I realised that it was possible for a young child to love the man who had abused her, because the abuser was the only person in her life who had shown what she considered kindly attention.

The Lowenfeld approach to clinical practice thus needs not only to be seen in this light, but takes this as a primary basis of working therapeutically with people, with children, adolescents and adults. Therapists can only facilitate adults and children in finding their own solutions. By providing ways of accessing their own thoughts and feelings, people may be enabled to express themselves to understand themselves, and so to reach for their own internal resource and find their own solutions. The approach is therefore one of *facilitating the child's, adolescent's or adult's own understanding of himself in his own terms in order that he can change in a way that makes sense to him, and of finding a solution which is possible for him to effect*.

The Lowenfeld approach is underpinned by a theoretical perspective which is one of *function*. Lowenfeld was interested in explaining *how* children relate to the world around them and not primarily in a general explanation of why.

In Lowenfeldian work, the explanation, the evidence for this "why" is supplied by the client, whether it be child or adult. This is the real acknowledgement of the individuality, the uniqueness of the person with whom you are working.

To illustrate Lowenfeld's approach, let us take an example from ordinary daily living, food for instance. She would be interested in "how digestion works" instead of providing a general theory that would give a general psychological explanation of a preference for fruit and a distaste for chocolate.

The treatment methods which work from the general "why" approach do have a "how" element: for example, Freud's notions of repression, denial and resistance. These seem to me to be derived from his "why" explanations and not from the client's perspective.

The main difference, therefore, between a theoretically driven psychotherapeutic technique and the Lowenfeld approach is insight derived from the "why" theory held by the therapist (making interpretations), in contrast to the insight which is derived from the "why" theory evolved by the client, from which he could then find his own solution.

The Lowenfeld approach, especially in therapeutic work with children, thus tries to take into account the Whole Person: the external circumstances as well as the inner world of the child, adolescent and adult. And in order to do this, you must put aside your own preconceptions, not because they are of no value or that they are wrong, but because they are your own and not the client's, be it a child, adolescent or adult. This is not as easy as it sounds. To do it, the therapist has first to become more self-aware. We all have our preferences, our prejudices, our point of view, this is inevitable, not because we are wilfully ignorant, but of necessity.

Preferences and prejudices are the result of discrimination and are two sides of the same coin. Discrimination is the tool we use to satisfy our absolute need to make sense of the continuous stream of our personal experiences so that we may master the world of our existence. Any pre-judgements are, by their very nature and viewed within the perspective of ordinary living, temporary, a matter of personal hypothesis. They form the basis of our earliest personal beliefs. For throughout our infancy and young childhood we need to make judgements about the world around us to ensure an appropriate response for our continuing existence. We need them to tell us what is "good" or "bad" for our *individual* survival. Having the ability to form preconceptions is part of our survival kit, and *in themselves* they are neither bad nor good. It is what we do with them, it is the action you take which would determine the moral judgement; the ethics lie solely in the action.

Preconceptions inevitably bias us towards certain preferences, they make our likes and dislikes. In later life, these preferences may be expressed as tastes, good or bad as contemporary fashion dictates. They may also become personal beliefs, expressing for us unassailable universal truths, the "isms" in our personal vocabulary. However, such basic beliefs remain unless or until our own life experiences show us a different way of seeing things. We sometimes say, "I wouldn't do that," imagining ourselves in a situation which we have heard about in the news. In fact of course, none of us can truly say whether we would actually do or not do this or that in a situation of which we have had no personal experience yet.

Let us take skin colour as an example of how we sometimes divide people into groups. We call certain people the Blacks. We have in the past referred to the Chinese as the Yellow races. Also in the past, native North Americans have been referred to as Redskins. Here colour has been generally used negatively, denoting not simply something different from the Whites, but something inferior. In the world of reality, in the world of nature, colours arise from the dividing of white light in the world of earth in its orbit round the sun. What value we place on each colour is a personal and/or cultural preconception or personal preference. Thus black is only an emotive issue because it has been thought of, by certain cultures, in essentially negative terms, used particularly to characterise the negative attributes of a whole group of people. People's skin colour is entirely determined by characteristics that have nothing to do with their moral nature. Moreover, we may think or feel that one skin colour denotes a moral superiority, or greater beauty, over another, but it is whether and how we act as a result of this feeling, this thought, that determines the morality of our action and not our particular notion or feeling about skin colour.

As a matter of interest, our views about animals are not exempt from calumny. For instance, why have pigs attracted so many negative epithets in the English language? We call people "stupid pigs", but in fact pigs are known to be clever animals. We label some people as "dirty pigs". Actually, pigs in their natural habitat are very clean. People, in domesticating them for our purposes, have taken them out of their natural context. Pigs have thus to survive in circumstances imposed by the exigencies and economics of the farming community, where occasionally they have also been known to become beloved pets. Perhaps it is not a coincidence that pigs were the subject of George Orwell's political allegory, *Animal Farm*, as well as vehicles for social comment such as in an Australian film entitled *Babe*.

In this context, Lowenfeld has found the twin principles of homeostasis and epistemology complementary to her theories of E and Protosystem Thinking, which will be discussed more generally in Chapters 15 and 16 and which I have used as the basis to the Lowenfeld therapeutic approach. To achieve an internal sense of psychological equilibrium, we need to keep our own view of the world mostly intact. If our world becomes destabilised, we get disconcerted by too much difference. When we are thus discomforted by too big a change to our mental concept of the world around us, our instinctive response is to try to make sense of what we apprehend through our own understanding of how the world works. In order that you as a would-be therapist do not unconsciously place your own meanings upon your clients, some personal experience of making your own Mosaics is essential for you to get to know the meaning of your own Mosaic language of self-expression. Gaining greater self-awareness enables you more easily to put aside your own pre-judgements.

Now why would you be likely to view your client's work through your own lenses? It is because of the human need to assess the situation one finds oneself in and thus an immediate need to form a judgement. Let us take a hypothetical example. Just suppose a client uses only red pieces to create an image of his mother, and you the therapist, thinking that the colour red usually means "anger", assumes that the client is possibly thinking about his mother, perhaps in relation to feelings of anger. However, the client goes on to tell the therapist that he remembers her as always feeling embarrassed, and hence he has portrayed her in red.

One of the ways of circumventing this dilemma is for the therapist to provide herself with opportunities to observe someone else making a Mosaic. In doing so, she will be alerted to her own, the observer's, need to find meaning in what they observe. As in real life, in this endeavour we are instinctively guided by our own sense of meaning; we will see similar meanings to or find satisfying elements in certain kinds of picture or pattern, and this should not be gainsaid. A therapist will need to treat this absolute and instinctive need of theirs with the utmost respect.

With experience, the putting aside of preconceptions will become almost instantaneous when one is the observer. It is essential to acquire this skill as the ability to do so will determine how well a therapist can pay attention to the client, whether they be child, adolescent or adult, in order to learn the client's language, the client's way of expressing himself, and thus to learn about the client's point of view.

With children, the therapist is likely to have much more background information, so she will have greater opportunity to take into account the child's external history and circumstances – including the personal history and present circumstances – as well as the child's inner world. It is also necessary to record from whose point of view this background history has been taken, being mindful of the fact that the view expressed is that of an adult informant close to the life of the child, one who certainly has an effect on the child, but is not that of the child himself. It is essential that the child's point of view remains the central focus for the therapist. With adolescents and adults, the therapist will be able to see their view of their own past, what to them is critical to their present dilemmas. It may arise from their verbal communication or through your exploration of their Mosaic with them. And as the therapist gets to know the client better, she will also take into account the client's temperament and personality.

The therapist needs to bear all this in mind every time she sees the child, adolescent or adult, and to update this information as new facts come to hand. Make time to do this before and after the session. This is not simply because of the need to practise, it is actually good practice. I have found that the best time to think about the session is whilst I am drawing up the client's Mosaic[6] before writing up the session. It facilitates the recreation of the flow and feeling of the session.

Part 2: How to introduce the Mosaics in a therapeutic setting

When you yourself are first presented with a box of Lowenfeld Mosaics and a tray covered with a blank piece of paper, questions come unbidden to mind, questions such as "What is this all about?" or "What does she want me to do with this?" or "What is expected of me here?" This may very well be what all our clients feel, although often people are simply drawn by the bright colours and the blank white piece of paper inviting a response.

You are about to introduce a client to a new language. How do you begin?[7] If you wish to try this out for yourself, start by *laying the opened box of Mosaics above the tray which has already been fitted with a blank piece of white paper, both in a land-scape position*, with a space between the box and the tray so as to allow the box and/or tray to be rearranged if desired.

This is usually done for the first time so as to make it as convenient for the right-hander as for the left-hander. At the same time let it be known that the tray

---

6 From my own clinical experience, Appendix 2 describes the way of thinking about a client's Mosaic during the process of recording it.
7 See Appendix 1 for the guidelines for using the Lowenfeld Mosaics with individuals.

or the box can be moved to a more convenient position if desired. If one begins always in the same way, then it is easier to observe the individual response. Similarly, the colours are usually arranged in the same order (red, blue, yellow, black, green and white) as at first presented. This arrangement, alongside this placing of the tray and box, allows for a consistency of presentation, and aids the therapist's observation of changes through a series of Mosaics. This facilitates clarity and easy familiarity both for the therapist and for the Mosaic-maker, and allows the therapist to make proper comparisons with future responses.

Accompanied by the appropriate gestures, you say something like this: "*Here is a box of coloured pieces. The box is divided into two sections each containing the same type and number of shapes. There are five different shapes. Each shape has its own compartment.*" Indicate where each shape is by pointing to each compartment separately. "*Each shape has six colours and all the shapes have the same colours.*"

To show the mathematical relationships as well as to demonstrate the colours, you use pieces from the box. *Lay down all the shapes, one at a time, beginning with a red square, followed by a blue rhombus or diamond, a yellow isosceles triangle or half-square, showing this by laying it on top of the red square, a black equilateral triangle, ending with a green scalene triangle* (see Figure 3.2). At this point, mention that "*all these shapes are also available in white*".

Having shown the shapes and colours in the way just described, and whilst putting the pieces back in the box, the therapist then says something like this: "*I would like you to do something, anything you like, with some of these pieces on this tray. Use as few or as many pieces as you like.*" If it is important to you, here is when you give a time limit. And you end your introduction with: "*Tell me when you have finished. . . . Would you like me to repeat that?*"

A form of wording such as this was devised by Lowenfeld so that people are as clear about the task as they can be without being directed in any way. If asked, the instructions can be repeated exactly, for the same reason. Sometimes, with people who are a little apprehensive, particularly nervous children, it is helpful to be able to reassure them: "*This is not a test. There is no right or wrong way to do it. Everyone does something that no one else can or will do.*"

This is not simply a device to reassure, it also happens to be true. Our Mosaic response is indeed unique to us and to no one else. When I was in China doing a piece of cross-cultural research (which will be discussed in Chapters 13 and 14), using the Lowenfeld Mosaics with twelve-year-old children, officials from the Education Department asked at the beginning of the project what my predictions would be. I replied that I did not know what would happen, but one thing I could predict was that all two hundred Mosaics would be different. Believing in the high level of conformity amongst Chinese children, they were politely sceptical. One official followed the project closely and accompanied me to all the sessions. By the time the one hundred and ninety-sixth Mosaic was being done, she came to me and remarked that my prediction was now unlikely to be proven wrong.

Whilst doing a Mosaic, some people might make comments. These comments naturally form part of the Total Response, as does their silence, if they do not speak. Of course, our observation of the rest of their behaviour is of the same importance. Everything is part of that Total Response. The Total Response is a dynamic multidimensional flowing process. The way a person approaches the Mosaic-making, the behaviour towards the Mosaic material, the attitudes expressed, the comments, the actual process of making it, the hesitations, the changes and the final picture or pattern – all go to make up the Total Response.

To quote Lowenfeld, "For successful use of the [Mosaics], emphasis must therefore be placed on a detailed knowledge of the [Mosaics] itself and extensive practice in reading the responses, rather than, as with many other Tests, upon statistical evaluation of large numbers of Designs" (Lowenfeld 2004a: 106).

6 Mirror, mirror on the wall: the psychotherapist's response

How should the psychotherapist respond to the Total Response? In thinking about this, it is important to acknowledge one's own preferences. As our response is unique to us, so is what we think of what we see being made. But that is unlikely to be what the person who made the Mosaic thinks and feels about it. We have our own thoughts about either the subject or pattern that we see, so knowing your own Mosaic response is a huge help towards being able to use this projective instrument with other people with success.

Doing a Mosaic yourself is the best way to learn about your own feelings about the colours, the shapes, and how the shapes and colours interact with each other. This alerts you to your own uniqueness, your preferences and biases, what you find pleasing or dislike, what makes it satisfying or unsatisfying – a whole range of thoughts and feelings that describes your own Mosaic Response. There is no substitute for personal experience. This experience will certainly enable you to appreciate the multidimensional nature of the Mosaic response.

This familiarity is important. It enables you to realise the basic requirement for the psychotherapeutic stance, that is, that we should not endow our own likes and dislikes with general application and mistake our own perceptions of the world around us, our personal beliefs, for universal truths. In other words, we must be able to respond with an open mind to our clients' perspectives, their view as shaped by their own likes and dislikes, their own personal experiences, their own background and history. For this to happen, you must not only be aware of your own Mosaic response, but consciously put it aside at the start of any Mosaic work with a client.

Just as our personal experience of making Mosaics will have raised our own awareness of our way of seeing colour and shape in relationship to some inner directive, this in turn enables us to appreciate that the client will be coming from another perspective, one different from our own. This very act of doing a Mosaic thus creates a climate whereby you, the Mosaic-maker, could also raise your own self-awareness of the workings of your inner world.

To understand the uniqueness of our Mosaic response, it is imperative to adopt a stance of true ignorance towards the client. You are about to meet someone for the first time. You know nothing about this person. No theory will show you what this person is truly like. Like you, he is unique. Adopting this attitude will enable you to concentrate on the Total Response, watching and taking in the whole process of the Mosaic-making. Never suggest you know what they are doing or what they have done or the meaning of their Mosaic. The greatest pitfall is to prejudge what you see, so you must always check every part of the Mosaic, to ensure you have the picture the Mosaic-maker intends. For example, if it looks like "a flower" to you, you must suspend judgement until the Mosaic-maker confirms it is "a flower". After that, you will need to check which part of the Mosaic is the flower and the different elements which comprise it so that you can get the full flavour of this particular flower, their flower. With practice, you will be able focus on the Total Response, which allows you to explore a Mosaic from the perspective of the Mosaic-maker. To show you what I mean, let me suggest some practice:

Mosaic 6.1
Florence

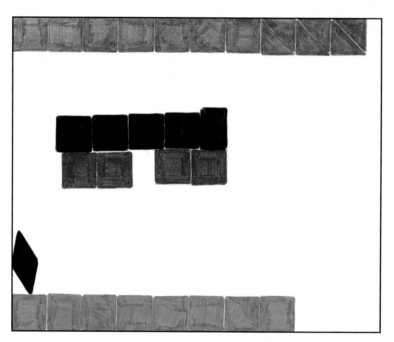

Before you read what the Mosaic-maker told me about Mosaic 6.1, it would be interesting for you to note your own reaction to it. What do you think it represents? Indeed, is it representational? If so, what does it represent? Is it a concept or a scene? Or is it an abstract pattern? Is it even a pattern? Would you say that it was made by a child, a young person or a mature adult? Is there a difference between chronological age and emotional age? Can you tell whether it is made by a male or female? Might there be differences between age, gender or even cultural background? Jot down all the thoughts and feelings you have about the above Mosaic.

If I had said in my introduction to this Mosaic that it was made by an English girl of seven, would it have made any difference to your guess? This Mosaic was made by Florence in the spirit of play. She exclaimed with delight at the opened box of Mosaics and set off without waiting for my explanation to finish. I went with her flow.

The most common "reading" of the above Mosaic is that it depicts a scene with a blue sky, a garden with a black tree, and a red house with a black roof. I have heard it described as many other things as well, but never as what it actually is, with all the elements correctly named. In fact it is a scene with a blue sky and a green train puffing black steam out of a red station with a black roof, and the platform is to be imagined in the white space between the station and the train.

What do you now think about this scene? Do you feel that the black steam is significant? Is the blackness of the roof connected with the steam in some way? Why is the platform only an imagined space?

In reality, telling me about all this prompted her immediately to ask to do a second Mosaic. For Florence, the use of colour in this first Mosaic was her first exploration of the Mosaics, but the actual subject was more pertinent to her thought process. Like the train, she had only just started on her Mosaic journey. She now explored the colours and shapes with a more serious intent, and finally made a totally different kind of Mosaic, one which was "more artistically satisfying". It was a rather unusual pattern and was the Mosaic where her thoughts and feelings were in harmony, one she felt was more expressive of herself.

Mosaic 6.2
Florence's second Mosaic

Here you have a glimpse not only of the importance of the total commitment to the client's view of his own Mosaic, but the fact that the process carries on after the completion of a Mosaic and has a deeper dynamic of its own. In this case, it enabled Florence to continue the exploration through a second Mosaic, which elicited access to some fundamental part of her nature. A well-adjusted and self-possessed individual, Florence was to become a fabric designer, finding inspiration in her many travels around the world.

With the next Mosaic (6.3), I would like to explore with you in greater depth, your own response to the Mosaic process and product. It also was made in playful circumstances, of exploration and challenge, in the spirit of "What have you got here?" and "What can I do with this?" This time I suggest that at this point you allow your own imagination to roam; make a note of your own reactions, feelings and thoughts about this Mosaic.

Mosaic 6.3
Gareth

Now, a brief description of Gareth's Mosaic Total Response, along with my own response at the time.

Gareth began at the centre with the blue square and, radiating from it in all directions, eight blue diamonds which he immediately but purposely removed, "because I don't want to make a cross". Gareth continued along the bottom edge, making a "field", from which arose a "flower" to the left with the "sun" above it, followed by a "tree" to the right, rising almost to the top edge, and linked by the green and white diamonds which had formed the stem of his flower and the trunk of his tree. Gareth sat back and indicated that he had finished. He shook his head to denote dissatisfaction, before voicing in confirmation, "It's stupid, isn't it?"

As you can see, the Mosaic still ended up with a "cross" pattern at the centre, albeit skewed, and no longer integrated through the unity of the colour blue, as it would have been if the blue diamonds had not been replaced. The Mosaic took some time to produce. All blue shapes were repeatedly fingered but never used again. This Mosaic became a composite picture: at the centre is a "Pattern".

From these very meagre clues (so far I have given you only our verbal exchanges concerning the Mosaic at the beginning of our conversation) I wonder what impression you now have of Gareth. Can you give an age? Can you tell anything about the "personality"? Would you expect your response to the Mosaic and mine to be the same? If we were both present at the Mosaic-making, would you expect our reaction to the total process and the resultant Mosaic to be the same or even similar? What makes the difference? Would the difference be the individuality of our perception, investing the whole process with our own sense of what "cross", "blue", "flower", "field", "tree" and "sun" might mean to us? What of the process, how the Mosaic flowed from one concept to another?

How would you now actually respond? How would you explore with Gareth what his Mosaic has evoked in him? Write down your own thoughts of how you, as a therapist or an ordinary reader, felt about this Mosaic and then describe how you would proceed. Reflect upon your observation of this process.

This Mosaic was made during my own training, so I was at the beginning of understanding the use of the Mosaics as a therapeutic technique. My own inner response had at first been that this was a rather childlike Mosaic, given that Gareth was already a professional man. So what did this disparity mean? Aware of my lack of experience, I was interested to see what would happen if I simply went through the Mosaic process with Gareth and reflected his Mosaic process back to him. It was an eye-opener. The meaning emerged alongside the description Gareth gave for his Mosaic, and it was a revelation to us both.

Gareth began by talking about the flower and the sun on the left of his Mosaic, and he smiled at the double meaning of the sound of the word "son/sun" as he said it. It was a constant pleasure to him that he was able to be an active father to his five-year-old son. He wanted to give his son what he could now feel he lacked – a father's care. But he was also reminded of his own happy though materially improverished childhood as an only child with a widowed mother, a time when he thought the sun did indeed shine for him.

As we talked, he became more expansive, yet more serious. He then looked across to the tree on the right of his Mosaic. He saw this as another aspect of a contemporary picture of him: we were reflecting upon the tree pressing up against the top edge, not being able to grow further. Gareth mentioned that he was in further education, but for various reasons he was unable to complete the course he had embarked upon.

We then moved back to the heart of his Mosaic. I referred to his wish not to make a cross, removing all the blue diamonds. I alluded to the fact that I had noticed that he had continually fingered other blue shapes but had not actually used any of them, leaving the centre of his Mosaic with a solitary blue square. I asked about this "centre of yellow, red and blue". Could he tell me about this? Gareth was silent, seemingly deep in thought, for a long while. He finally murmured, almost as though he was speaking to himself, that the "cross" was hard to bear. Blue, and the "cross" pattern, had something to do with his relationship with his wife, he felt. She was from a different culture and religion. There was a total contrast in social background and cultural aspirations. They were constantly at cross-purposes. They seemed to have nothing in common. He felt also that she had overtaken him in her professional status. This seemed wrong to him. It should be he who was providing for the family. He was concerned that his son should be in the midst of such disharmony, a disharmony he had had no experience of in his own childhood. Like his constant fingering of the blue, he now decided that this disharmony had been impinging upon his life for some time. Only now could he see it clearly. Perhaps he could now act.

What astonished him was the ease with which his playfulness had given him access to the centrality of his inner dilemma. There seemed no necessity for inter-pretation or a transference relationship, even if I had known how to do either. Gareth left feeling empowered to act on his own behalf, if not also on his son's.

From then on, with practice, I came to understand that in its therapeutic use, the importance of focusing entirely on the manner, process and product, of concentrating on what emerges from the ensuing dialogue, and of reflecting back the Mosaic in a way which allows the meaning to emerge for the Mosaic-maker and be seen as truly emanating from the self so that it can be owned and acted upon. I discovered in this process of learning over time that the Mosaics is truly a personal language, a vocabulary with a unique meaning for each Mosaic-maker, and that is why every Mosaic is unique in every sense of the word. It is thus vital that the therapist should always reflect back in the Mosaic-maker's terms, using the vocabulary of their Mosaic, and not one introduced by the therapist.

The Mosaic is indeed the Personality in Action.[8]

---

8 The phrase Personality in Action will be used by me as a key term in this work. It was originally used by Lowenfeld in a paper she read to the 7th International Congress of Rorschach and other Projective Techniques (1968: 838–43).

7   Lowenfeld Mosaic language development and the personality in action

People often speak of children as developing individuals, as being mature or immature for their age. How do we know this? How do we make judgements about this? How closely do our judgements agree with reality? For us to be able to make that kind of judgement at all, we need to hold in our minds at least an idea of what is the norm, or what is appropriate, for any particular age.

From what experience do we usually form such ideas? Why do we think that there is a norm of behaviour? Are we actually talking about something with objective reality? What makes some behaviours abnormal? Do the same norms of behaviour apply across cultures and throughout history? Is there an agreed body of knowledge about this?

We can perhaps see more clearly how this idea of development came to us from our physiological selves. No one has been known to run before they can stand, for instance, but from what we see around us we judge that every adult can usually stand, and if they do not, we recognise that something has gone astray! This and other similar physiological developments, like that for the digestive system or sexual development present the same kind of picture. However, when it comes to mental processes, like emotional development and the development of verbal facility, the complexities are multiplied.

From the second half of the twentieth century, with the assistance of advances in technology, psychologists and neuroscientists have been able to chart our mental developmental progress with increasing refinement. We can now demonstrate with some confidence that there are indeed stages of development. As in our physiological development, so our verbal language development follows a progressive line. We go from babbling to uttering single words, to putting two words together and then, increasingly with age, we begin to form whole sentences, at first short but becoming longer and more complex as we grow older. Is there such a clear profile with our ability to manipulate the colour-shapes of the Mosaics?

From birth we deploy all our senses to explore the immediate surroundings which constitute our world and to make judgements about these sensations (Eliot

2001). Not all our senses, however, mature at the same age or together. Long before we are born, touch is our primary tool to explore and develop a relationship with the environment (Eliot 2001: Ch. 5). In the womb our skin is our contact with our first external world, that of our mother's womb. Our skin is our first explorer of the world outside of ourselves. From our very first foetal movements, we are gaining knowledge of this world and its effect on us. Already movement is a major partner in this exploration, so our kinaesthetic sense and the development of our motor skills are of prime importance in this enterprise (Ch. 11) – and movement, the Mosaic Process, is an important aspect of the Mosaic response.

It is some time after birth that touch begins to be concentrated in our hands. It is therefore not surprising that our sense of touch through the entire surface of our skin is developed to a more advanced degree at birth than any of our other senses (Eliot 2001: 123). At birth we can feel through touch much better than we can see or hear. Seeing and hearing later join touch as our major senses, these being the main sense modalities employed in the making of a Mosaic.

Since a major part of development is to enable us to comprehend the world we live in as well as to act within it for our very survival, we have to coordinate the information coming through our senses. We have now discovered that the coordination of vision, touch and the movement of our hands is the earliest to develop (Eliot 2001: 279), and this is just the kind of collaboration required by Mosaic-making.

The actual handling of the Mosaic tiles, and the effect of their physical and sensuous qualities, stimulate the imagination directly. The Mosaic simultaneously expresses this experience and develops these particular sensorial abilities. Our ability to distinguish texture and shape gives us our basic knowledge of an object. Time and again, I have noticed that people tend not to comment until they have started doing a Mosaic. When they first pick up a Mosaic tile, the texture and shape of that tile is the quality which they most often remark on. Our primary knowledge is thus based on sensorial experiences acquired through time. And understanding develops through time, through personal experience.

Around the same time as our neuropsychological assessment tools were being developed, Lowenfeld began to collect Mosaics throughout Europe from children of all ages as well from adults. Her principal intention was simply to discover what kind of Mosaics people actually made. Surveying her collection of children's Mosaics, Lowenfeld discerned that their designs go through definite structural changes as the children grow older. There was a subtle but real line of progressive competence and complexity of design. Inevitably, she also found that there were distinctive individual differences in the productions. Each Mosaic was unique, and any series of Mosaics by one child or adult always showed a profile of only that single individual. Lowenfeld summarized her findings in two tables chronologically, by age from infancy to fourteen.

In this book, I propose first to look at the Mosaics in terms of general human development with particular reference to verbal language development. Secondly, I will look at some specific structural elements which clearly demonstrate progressive maturity. Finally, the Personality in Action in the Total Response will be considered. This will be done using examples from my own collection of Mosaics from children and adults.

Let us now look again at what the child is responding to. Even at first glance, the object of interest is not discrete in the way that a single toy is distinct from its surroundings. Already we are asking rather a lot of an infant who can just sit up and reach out with his hands. Furthermore, what strikes adults about the Mosaics in the box alongside a tray is not necessarily what strikes children of that age. Where adults are more interested in the actual colours and shapes of the Mosaic pieces presented, very young children in particular are much more likely to be attracted simply by the brightness in the colours, the smoothness of the tiles. Focusing directly on the rich colours, children of that age are likely to ignore the tray and the differences in shape of the tiles altogether.

Once they get their hands on the tiles, they may randomly grasp a few and push them into their mouths. This is in line with a common observation of a baby's first attempts at exploring the world around them, of groping towards an understanding of that world by putting objects in their mouths. This perhaps could be likened to the stage when a baby seems to enjoy making sounds, but is not yet recognisably babbling.

So, children, particularly very young children, are more likely to respond sensuously only to the sensorial qualities of the Mosaic pieces. Interest in their environment is broadly random but intense, and the Mosaics are highly appealing to their sense of curiosity. Their preferred method of exploring their world is chiefly through their mouths. It is a universal observation that infants explore all objects within reach by putting them into their mouths, using all the three senses which are most informative for them, touch, smell and taste. This accords well with the findings of neuro-psychologists as well as popular experience. So, when presented with a set of Mosaics, the very young child may simply grab handfuls and shove them into his mouth. What we also know from recent experimental research, is "not only can young babies detect different shapes with their mouths, they actually form an abstract perception of an object – a mental image that makes the leap between their tactile and visual senses" (Eliot 2001: 132).

Where we might be more interested in the interrelationship of the shapes, children before one and half years of age may only see these colourful tiles in the box in clumps. A handful is the first and most basic attempt at defining an entity. The infant will grab at blocks of tiles, pick them up and throw or let them drop, a sort of game with objects countless children can be seen playing while seated in their high-chairs, demanding that the game be endlessly repeated. Thus, whilst they still only seem to focus on the bright colours, they seem to have gone beyond the stage of oral exploration to coordinating their hand and eyes in one movement, but objectifying the movement into the external world. This movement enables the infant to add the sound of the Mosaic tiles being thrown or dropped to their understanding of the qualities of the Mosaics. This may be equivalent to the first signs towards babbling, where sound feedback is an important element of verbal language development.

The next developmental stage is when the child begins to pick up the tiles singly and examine each by sight, simultaneously inspecting the Mosaic tile with their hands, usually with great interest and in some detail. Interest now seems mainly focused on single pieces. The piece may then be dropped anywhere or, at a later point of this stage, more deliberately within the tray. The tray may now also be included within the parameters of the Mosaic material and become part of the background upon which the Mosaic tile can be seen. At this stage, however, it seems that the outline of the tray is hardly noticed, if at all. This is an important step forward. It is the beginning of our ability to distinguish one object from another. This stage may be comparable to the time when individual sounds can be distinguished amongst the infant's babbling sounds.

The earliest perception of space comes where scattered pieces, mostly falling within the tray space have been disposed in such a manner as to offer further evidence of an awareness of the separateness of the pieces. This first recognition of discreteness with some sense of the boundary of the tray also marks a step towards an understanding of the distinction between the self and the other within a personally known background. Such a stage of development is also part of human maturation. And from this stage onwards, different lines of development in individual children begin to appear.

I would now like to use some actual examples from my collection so that you can make some visual connections. This is a collection of Mosaics made by different children, both boys and girls, at different ages, from three and a half to fourteen and three-quarters. From my contemporaneous notes, I will try to fill out the picture of the Mosaic process as much as possible. I will only be considering certain aspects of the Total Response.

First I would like to demonstrate this difficulty of disentangling one aspect of development from the rest of a young child's personality, and offer Alan's Mosaic as an example.

Mosaic 7.1
Alan

Alan, at just two months short of four years of age, seemed eager to get his hands into the box, but once his fingers made contact with the tiles, he brought out single shapes and looked at each one as he turned it round in his hand, before solemnly placing it on and within the tray with earnest concentration. At first, after each placement, he would look up at me fleetingly before carrying on to take out the next piece. Very quickly, he seemed to have forgotten my presence. He continued to place each tile with great care, until he had put down the remaining pieces. He looked up and smiled at me as if to indicate he had finished. Alan seemed to know when to stop, so perhaps he also had a sense of the tray space, the boundary described by the raised edges of the tray.

Alan's Mosaic seems to demonstrate the dawning of an awareness of separateness as meaningful entities, savouring the qualities of each piece as he handled them. A strong sense of the importance of the distinctiveness of each of the pieces he had placed on the tray emerged from the manner of his Mosaic-making. His knowing when to stop and having a seeming awareness of the boundary of the tray suggests more than a milestone in language development. Clearly at the age of nearly four he was well able to communicate with words. In reality, whilst he seemed mainly drawn to the Mosaics by his actions, he never really spoke to me at all. I had only just met him and perhaps he was shy. So, to understand fully what Alan's language development was like, I would have had to delve a little deeper. But he was late for a friend's party, and so it was that I was left with a Mosaic and very little other information.

You will have noticed that the shape of the Mosaic tile was for Alan a quality of the tile worthy of particular attention. Each of the five shapes is clearly distinctive. And it is through touch that interest in this distinctiveness of the shapes has been noted whilst assembling my collection.

This next Mosaic (7.2 overleaf) is a good example of how a child, on encountering the Mosaics for the first time, can cross several stages of development through one Mosaic process.

Bella was three years and six months old. A bright engaging child, she nevertheless became absorbed with the Mosaics and quickly put down some pieces. Perhaps seeing the emergence of what seemed like a line, she continued to add pieces, thus extending this into a wavering line of green squares. With increasing accuracy, Bella matched the edges of similar-shaped tiles. Using equilateral triangles and squares, she did not stop until she saw that two white equilateral triangles had a perfect fit. This was the moment when one of the two white diamonds in her hand was dropped across the left-hand edge of the tray (when drawing round the Mosaic pieces, it was only possible to show what part of the tile remained within the boundary of the tray; the overlapping tile is shown cut off from the edge of the paper at that point). She looked up at me questioningly. My smiling response did not seem to have encouraged her to do it again.

Having once seen that the pieces offered possibilities when she accidentally put two blue scalene triangles together near the wavering line, she proceeded later to place a similar wavy line of pairs of red and blue scalene triangles under the line of green squares before finishing. She clearly enjoyed the experience, as she stayed

to watch me draw round her Mosaic tiles and wanted to know what I was going to do next.

Bella certainly demonstrated an awareness of the tray size when her white diamond strayed over the rim of the tray. She also showed the beginnings of ideas of combining shapes to form new wholes and that of separateness within this combination. This discovery through the wavy line of green squares, followed later by seeing that she could put shapes together to form a new whole (the pair of white equilateral triangles), seem to have culminated in new learning in the deliberate pairing of red or blue scalene triangles in a line underneath.

From scattered pieces, Bella created wavering lines – from chance association of pieces, deliberate pairs of different shapes were made. Out of the babbling process, young children begin to be able to produce sounds from their mother tongue and combine them to make words. Speech becomes increasingly accurate and specifically targeted as meaningful words.

Bella's Mosaic process parallels this in terms of Mosaic language development. From the moment she succeeded in producing a perfect alignment of the two white equilateral triangles, it seemed to have enabled her to take the next step and begin exploring other combinations through the scalene triangles. This seems to be the verbal equivalent of going from babbling sound to single distinctive sounds recognisable as words, followed by combining words to form new concepts. It signals the beginning of the ability to express and communicate in language and share one's thoughts and feelings with another.

So far there seems to be a Mosaic equivalent to language development in the Mosaic designs produced by young children. The edge of the tray seems also to have played a part in determining what area Bella felt she should cover and when to stop: her reaction to the white diamond crossing the edge of the tray may have been a clue. This is similar to Alan's Mosaic, where this concept of boundaried space has been expressed differently.

The spatial component is an important element in Mosaic-making, and it is not surprising that using the Mosaics as drawing materials, when the tiles are applied to sketch out the outline of the subject depicted, begins early in their development in children's Mosaics, but seems normally not to be seen beyond middle childhood. Rarely do adults use the Mosaics in this way. I have certainly not come across any amongst my adult collection.

In terms of language development, other factors besides greater and broader life experiences, such as nursery and play group attendance, contribute to its progress. And this is shown through the increasing complexity of the structure of the Mosaics produced by children beyond the age of three years.

Shape, alongside colour, is another major feature of the Mosaic tile. As all the shapes are mathematically related to the square, this allows the idea of relationship to be built into their use. The ideas of separation and connection, as that between our self and the other, are of primary importance to our relations in our external world. It is not necessary for this to be confined to personal human relations. Relationship implies more than social relations. Any one particular shape is capable of being related in many ways to another shape. A Mosaic is essentially a description of the way one relates to our total sensed environment at the moment of making it. Besides objects, ideas and feelings can be expressed through the Mosaic process and its product, all within one Mosaic projection.

An example from an adult follows of how a personal statement of passionate feeling and strong political conviction can emerge through the use of the Lowenfeld Mosaics.

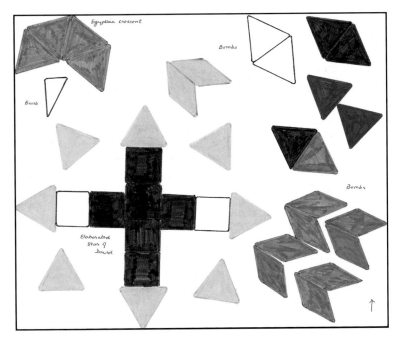

Mosaic 7.3
Charlotte's Egyptian crescent and elaborated Star of David with bombs

Before she began her Mosaic, Charlotte had no clear idea of what she was going to do or make. After a time gazing at the box and tray, however, her first move was decisive. Beginning with the black centre of the Star of David, she quietly mentioned that she hated the colour yellow as she completed the ring round the central cross-like figure with the yellow equilateral triangles. She took a long time to achieve the orientation in the tray for the Egyptian crescent she had in mind. As she added the bombs on the right side of the tray, again she struggled with the placements. Clearly feeling the necessity to explain herself at that point, she told me she was trying to make the bombs less directly attacking. She might also have become aware that she was taking a long time over this when she placed the solitary white scalene triangle under the green crescent. At the time, she explained that she did not want it to seem that all the bombs were targeted at the Star of David.

It was after she had expressed satisfaction with her Mosaic that she expanded on her Mosaic representation. She was struck by the impression that the yellow, that which she hates, is what held her attention. Charlotte now enlarged upon this remark. The yellow represented for her both what she felt to have been unwarranted Israeli attacks upon Egypt, and her own feeling of hatred for this aggression. It described her feelings about the constant tension and hostility between Egypt and Israel. Her chief concern was for her homeland. And she might have summarized it as a representation of her mental and emotional state as she was then. Certainly, Charlotte also wanted me to understand that her Mosaic symbolised a feeling and that this feeling and the accompanying political thoughts expressed are central to her being.[9] Her thoughts and feelings were indivisible and a constant preoccupation in her mind.

As an instrument of exploration, the Mosaics offer the possibility of spontaneous discovery of the different relationships between the pieces. This can develop along two distinct lines: Mosaics which are representations of objects, concepts or scenes, and Mosaics which are abstract patterns. Some people see the potential for representation more immediately than the structural possibilities of patterning, but this seems more a matter of personality than of development. This matter will be touched upon later in this chapter.

Representational designs are Mosaics which by definition represent an object of some kind. This could be a tangible thing, a scene or landscape, an imaginary object like a fairy-tale or mythical figure, a feeling or an idea or concept, like "the road to heaven", so named by a Chinese girl in the sample I collected in China.[10] Mostly, however, representational designs are of common objects, things we see around us, like houses, public buildings, vehicles for travelling in, rockets, persons, trees, flowers, sky and scenes made up of such things. This type of Mosaic design clearly displays a developmental aspect to representational Mosaics. And children

9 A "conceptual design", as in Charlotte's Mosaic, Lowenfeld has defined as the kind of Mosaic "in which representations of objects are used to convey an abstraction which may be either an emotional or a mental concept" (2004a: 65).

10 This Mosaic will be referred to again in Chapter 14.

who use the Mosaics to make such designs may or may not continue to do so. If they do, these tend to be of increasing competence and complexity in terms of the intrinsic qualities of the object chosen, or they may take on a conceptual quality, often infused with personal feeling (see Mosaic 7.3 above).

Abstract patterns in Mosaic designs form a much larger proportion in both Lowenfeld's and my collection in England.[11] These designs have no representational content and are usually simply named by the Mosaic-maker as "a pattern". Together with representational Mosaics, they cover the complete range of Mosaic design types identified so far.

The discovery that putting two red diamonds or triangular shapes side by side produces a new shape altogether is often the first step towards patterning. In her researches Lowenfeld found that certain fundamental shapes are created from the five basic Mosaic shapes (2004a: 36–7). The first three are the enlarged square, the "star" and the hexagon.

The square, being the shape from which all the others are derived, is the least versatile. Using squares alone, only larger squares or rectangles can be made. This corresponds to the first three-dimensional structures made by children. Building towers with bricks is still a popular activity. In ascending order of complexity, the next most common pattern is a "star" configuration, made with eight diamonds. Already there are more ways of achieving the same "star" effect, using other Mosaic shapes, such as the isosceles, equilateral and scalene triangles. Developmentally, the next basic shape to emerge is the hexagon, which is formed from six equilateral triangles, or twelve scalene triangles.

There is, however, one special line of development which I would like to mention here. These shapes can be, and are most often found to be, the precursors to the making of abstract patterns. Lowenfeld has provided us with the terminology for these emerging patterns of abstract form, and I should like to adopt these terms for our present consideration. Lowenfeld has named the "enlarged square", the "star" and the "hexagon" as the more common "Fundamental" designs. An incomplete Fundamental has been called a "Pre-fundamental" and an "Elaborated Fundamental" is self-explanatory. The "Pre-fundamental" is thus the forerunner to "Fundamental" patterns.

Denis's Mosaic (7.4 overleaf) shows how he managed the transition from Pre-fundamental to Fundamental patterns within a single Mosaic process.

Denis was just four years old when he made this Mosaic at my request. Although he had never before seen anything like the Mosaics, he approached the task with clear interest. He began with the squares near the left lower edge of the tray and stopped when he had created the large square with one red and three blue squares. He continued by building upwards on this square, using three red squares. Switching over to equilateral triangles, he carried on adding pieces, extending downwards with white triangles, carrying on with the same shape, eventually ending up with a complete hexagon in a single colour, the blue. Denis seemed

---

11 I will have more to say about the balance between these two types of design in Chapter 13.

unhappy about the blank space he had left on the right-hand side of the tray and began to fill it with a few red equilateral triangles. Quickly abandoning this, he began experimenting with some green and white isosceles triangles, finishing off with the column of white diamonds corralled by red scalene triangles.

Here we can see a child's ability to traverse several stages within one Mosaic process. Denis never attempted to name any part of his design. It might be concluded that his interest lay mainly in experimentation with the shapes and colours, and in creating pleasing patterns. It is, however, noticeable that beginning with the Square and Hexagon Fundamentals, he was drawn to try out further possibilities in new shape and colour combinations.

The Pre-fundamental stage in Mosaic-making may be comparable to a young child's attempts at sentence formation, starting with phrases which convey perhaps a meaning close to what the child wishes to express. The complete gestalt of any Fundamental design could usually be discerned in any Pre-fundamental, just as the meaning of such a phrase in a child's communication could usually be deduced by the words he has uttered.

The Elaborated Fundamental pattern forms the last of this line of development and the beginning of the Abstract Pattern proper. As its name implies, these patterns are extensions to the theme laid down by the basic fundamental shape which forms its core. It can either simply amplify this theme further or change its character. In Mosaics made by children it can also provide a bridge from thinking in concrete images of objects to abstract patterning, as in the case of Ellen.

Ellen, a charming eleven and a half year old, was interested in doing a Mosaic (7.5) and offered to do one for me whilst on a visit to my home. She set about the task in a direct manner and in an experimental spirit. She began with the

Mosaic 7.5
Ellen's Catherine wheel

central hexagon, first placing the three yellow equilateral triangles in their positions, anticipating the black tiles by the spaces she left between the yellow tiles. At the point she completed the hexagon with the black equilateral triangles, she called it a pattern. Ellen elaborated on this basic shape with the addition of blue, red and green equilateral triangles. On looking at this Elaborated Fundamental, she said it now looked more like the sun. Then she took out six white equilateral triangles. Seeing that the resulting design gave it a suggestion of movement, she finally called it a Catherine wheel.

When it comes to Elaborated Fundamentals, as one could see from Ellen's Mosaic, the design could have been designated either as a Representational picture or an Abstract pattern. Ellen was clearly aware of both possibilities. It was her personal preference to name it a Catherine wheel. Furthermore, her Mosaic also shows the beginning of the ability to move freely between concrete and abstract thinking.

Fundamentals are fully recognisably completed gestalts and are comparable to the verbal ability to form full sentences, showing some understanding of the grammatical structure of any verbal language. Here Ellen demonstrates this ability within the Mosaic language. She clearly anticipated the shape of the hexagon when she left appropriate spaces for the remaining equilateral triangles to be slipped between her initial yellow tiles, just as one who knows the structure of a sentence can anticipate the position of the remaining words in it.

The making of Elaborated Fundamentals usually demonstrates some sense of symmetry as well as a more secure understanding of abstract patterning. It seems likely that it is a direct development from the Pre-fundamental through the Fundamental designs. Perhaps the verbal equivalent of this is the beginning of being able to write more complex sentences that convey a greater intricacy of meaning in thought and feeling. This progression in competency and complexity would be expected in a maturing person and accords with our understanding of the growth and development of personality.

The use of colour as part of the Mosaic language is an interesting feature of the Mosaics. As in painting, colour can be used to define the outline of a shape, either emphatically or hardly at all as when a mass of white shapes is shown against the white paper on the Mosaic tray. It can suggest ambiguity or complexity. Just as in language development where the development of vocabulary can be a measure of the breadth of a person's reading, the actual use of colour might also tell us something about the personal experiences as well as the mind of the Mosaic-maker. Already we are into the realm of personality.

So far we have been talking of the use of Mosaics in terms of language development. We have as yet to touch upon how the Mosaic might show us a Personality in Action.

Inevitably the dynamics of personality cannot be fully shown in linear terms. This leads us directly to the Mosaic Process. The movement inherent in this process is the next dimension and extends the picture of a Personality in Action. It is in this respect that the multidimensional nature of the Mosaic Process comes into its own. The whole movement of this process within the tray space will include any dialogue that accompanies this process and encompasses any conversation or discussion which follows. Words and verbal language are linear by nature and thus time-bound, unlike touch and sight, which are immediate and unbounded by the linearity of time.

Any observation of the movement within the Mosaic process encompasses the Mosaic-maker's perception and use of the spatial aspects of the Mosaic and would also add to an understanding of the Mosaic-maker. Where are the chosen Mosaic pieces deployed? Which area of the tray space is left unoccupied? Is the Mosaic centred or is it attached to the top edge of the tray? Are the Mosaic pieces scattered all over the tray space or compacted into a single unit? Do all these differences have meanings beyond the visual effect?

This spatial element within the process adds a third dimension to the Mosaic vocabulary. It adds a third dimension to the two dimensions of the Mosaic product. How the pieces are deployed within the tray space is an important dynamic factor in forming a fuller picture of the Personality in Action. A young man has made a Mosaic he calls "a wheel". It is formed by a loose circle of an odd selection of pieces, a mixture of colour and shapes with gaps between the tiles. It called to mind another person also making a wheel with the Mosaic tiles. That Mosaic was made in a solid ring connected by spokes to a central core, all formed with only red diamonds and suggestive of the possibility of movement. Placed side by side the visual differences would be striking.

Within the spatial element, the thickness of the Mosaic tiles sometimes comes into play. It creates an impression of height when they are piled one upon another. An engineer friend of mine created a rising spiral of different colours, all in one shape, the spiralling effect achieved through his having rotated each tile so that the tips of each tile was clearly visible. He called it "possibly a pattern, or a gear". Sometimes piles are used to represent different objects, a school building, a church, a house or a garage. Occasionally, attempts to stand some Mosaic tiles on edge are made, usually to represent an object. Most recently I came across a Mosaic made by a child of seven who wished to show the fins of a rocket by standing the "fin" pieces on edge. He thought it would be wonderful if he could have done it. Indeed, Lowenfeld had incorporated this feature in one of her first designs of the Mosaics. She had anticipated that some people might wish to use the Mosaic pieces to create three-dimensional designs.

The raised edge enclosing the tray space gives the Mosaic a formal boundary. This boundary is an important part of the spatial element of the Mosaic response. It is the visual representation of the boundary of the emotional personality and can be used in many ways. You may remember the Mosaic created by Diane (see Mosaic 4.2). Her Mosaic was in response to the specific stimuli of another Mosaic made by her friend, Edmund (see Mosaic 4.3). During the making of their Mosaics, they merely exchanged their seats, so they each sat in the same place as they watched the other make his or her Mosaic. They each sat facing the top left-hand corner of the tray. Diane had placed her own Mosaic away from the top left-hand corner of the tray where her friend had placed his. Her Mosaic contained a boundary of its own, and the unused edge of the tray came to highlight her own separateness from her friend. In terms of the spatial aspects of the Mosaics and the use of the edge of the tray, it demonstrates her view of the nature of their friendship, and for Edmund's Mosaic this quality lay in the placement of his Mosaic at the top left-hand corner of tray space, towards where in fact Diane was sitting. It showed perhaps that whereas Diane would have preferred to keep the relationship at a distance, Edmund would have wished it to be closer.

Sometimes movement is incorporated into a Mosaic, as in a representation of a windmill in motion as in Ellen's Mosaic (see Mosaic 7.5). In fact, the movement inherent in the Mosaic Process is the fourth dimension which provides the dynamic quality of the Personality in Action. From my clinical examples, I note that I often encounter blocked movement, which is always a fruitful starting point for discussion. Without a record of the Mosaic Process, our ability to gain the most from a reading of any Mosaic would be seriously impoverished.

Finally, to anyone wishing to study the Personality in Action in greater depth, it is the manner with which the Mosaic-maker approaches the whole process of doing a Mosaic which can give a picture of the style of their approach to life in miniature.

These differences in our various ways of seeing and using the attributes of the tray in relationship to the Mosaic tiles and the differently coloured and shaped Mosaic tiles to each other give a truly dynamic portrait of the Personality in Action and a deeper understanding of the Mosaic Response.

There is another kind of Mosaic response which begins with a spontaneous connection between seeing the possibilities offered by the Mosaic tiles almost simultaneously with seeing an image or idea suggested by these possibilities. I would like to illustrate two dissimilar ways in which this kind of Mosaic can be

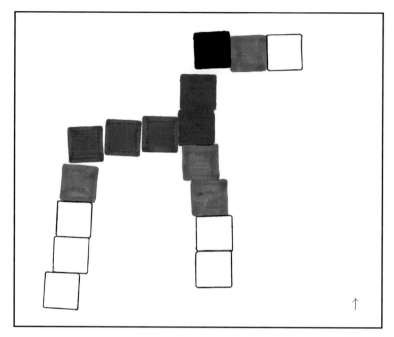

made which demonstrate the two different personalities in action. To show this, I will use two examples from my collection.

Freddie, three months short of four years of age, had been excited about doing a Mosaic, not knowing what it entailed. He had come into the room with smiling expectation. From the quickness of Freddie's reaction and actions, it seemed that no sooner had his eye alighted on the shape of the square than, in a flash, he knew what to do with it. Taking out a few squares at a time, Freddie took less than a few minutes to complete the figure successfully. Before I could respond, he told me it was a "giraffe". The speed with which Freddie translated the image in his mind into a Mosaic picture is one of the key features of this intuitive approach, which is that of a successful lightning collaboration between concept and use of material to achieve its presentation. What Guy did illustrates a somewhat opposite style.

Guy was already a serious boy at eight years old. He approached the Mosaics with a thoughtful manner and took time to obtain the effect he had in mind. He was unhurried. From the first, he seemed to have an image of what he intended to make. Without seeming to experiment with the various shapes at all, he displayed an unusual perception of space in his representation of the letter "a", demonstrating a precise appreciation of the geometric relationships to produce this initial letter of the alphabet. Working methodically, Guy skilfully exploited the geometric qualities of the pieces to accurately depict "a". I could see the immense satisfaction it gave Guy when he looked up from his completed Mosaic (7.7 overleaf).

In case it might be thought that the differences shown between Freddie's and Guy's manner of making their Mosaics were possibly a matter of difference of age, my next example casts some doubt on this conclusion. It is a Mosaic created

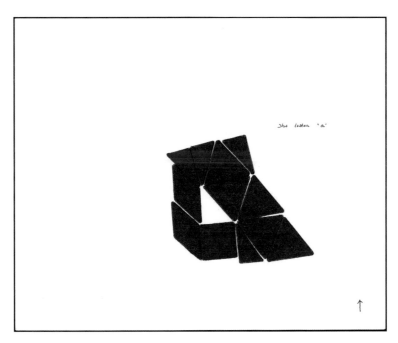

Mosaic 7.7
Guy's letter "a"

by Hannah, a girl of twelve years. She seemed to glide into the room, slipping onto the chair. She seemed to pay intense attention to my introduction, and then with the minimum of hand movements, she executed the following Mosaic. She smiled at me politely and as quickly glided out of the room again. The entire Mosaic process, like Freddie's, took less than three minutes. She had to be recalled to tell me about it.

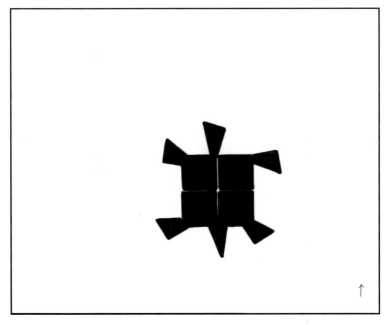

Mosaic 7.8
Hannah's terrapin

The manner in which Hannah looked at the Mosaic material and conceived and executed her terrapin resembled Freddie's approach to creating his giraffe, but there was a striking difference between the two: the terrapin showed a lively complexity when compared with the giraffe. This may of course have been due to their family or educational backgrounds, or developmental differences, given that there was an eight-year gap between them. There was certainly a difference in their demeanour, which may have reflected differences in personality and personal background. However, the extraordinary rapidity with which they each made their Mosaic was the feature in the process which suggested a common style of approach to the Mosaic task.

During puberty and adolescence, within the normal developmental profile, an often-encountered Mosaic pattern is the Cruciform as in Mosaic 7.9. This is a pattern made in the form of a cross or having strong cross-like features. This term was coined by Lowenfeld and suggested itself to her because of the strong association of the cross with the Christian image of Christ's Crucifixion, atoning for the sins of the world. The relation of this form to Christian tradition is perhaps debatable and should be subject to further research, but I find it interesting that over 70 per cent of the Mosaics made by children aged between twelve and fourteen and three-quarters years old in my collection are Cruciforms. Bearing in mind that the period of adolescence in contemporary times is often fraught with internal conflict and doubt and that guilt is often a feeling familiar to those of this age group, contemporary adolescents certainly face a major crossroad in their lives.

Mosaic 7.9
Ian's Cruciform
pattern

However, what is important is the way Mosaics demonstrate the idiosyncratic nature of individual development. This means, for example, that with the

Mosaics a child can demonstrate the particular style of his visual thinking as well as the way he structures that thinking, and give an idea of his ability to perceive space and take account of his surroundings. This dynamic portrait can also reveal the state of his emotions at the time of making the Mosaic.

So, can Mosaics made by children demonstrate growing maturity? Do Mosaic designs follow a line of development similar to that of our verbal language acquisition? Does this line of development mirror an order comparable to general progression towards greater refinement, subtlety and proficiency in our comprehension as well as executive skills? The answer is "yes" to all these questions.

The developing Personality in Action permeates through the entire structure of a Mosaic as it is externalised in the process of being made. It is truly a dynamic portrait of a maturing personality. And through skilful reflection to the Mosaic-maker of meticulous observation of that process, he can be made increasingly aware of his inner promptings.

8 Personality in Action I: working with adolescents

In working with this age group, it should be borne in mind from the beginning that adolescence is not any specific age range but a state of mind.

Most of us who have contact with adolescents are familiar with the fact that often when they are being communicative they either talk non-stop or grunt in monosyllables. The adults round them have had to get used to this type of behaviour. This brick wall of words or silence seems impossible to penetrate.

The Lowenfeld Mosaics are especially useful as a therapeutic instrument of communication with this group. This is because they enable a young person to engage in something that does not require him directly to explain himself. And as he engages with the Mosaics, the therapist is able to see the Personality in Action, to observe the young person's style of approach to life in miniature. But the therapist must first engage his curiosity, thus drawing the focus away from the person, the personal, to an activity. It should then be possible for the therapist to watch at close quarters how the adolescent responds, his actions and reactions in a practical but focused activity, which naturally displays him to the therapist in two ways: first, there is his general manner as well as what actually happens during the process of making the Mosaic, and secondly, there is the final product, the Mosaic.

Inevitably, a person doing a Mosaic will express himself, which will usually include his concerns. The subject of discussion can therefore be naturally shifted away from the adolescent to his Mosaic. This focus on the less intensely personal, makes it easier for the adolescent to respond. Focusing on the Mosaic rather than verbal exchange gives the young person an opportunity to engage, to express himself in novel ways. An expressive statement emerges from his play with the Mosaics, which is sometimes unexpected, is often baffling, but is always pertinent. So careful preparation for a Mosaic session with an adolescent is key to facilitating communication and understanding.

First, the therapist needs to prepare herself to receive the Total Mosaic Response. This is of course usual practice in any therapeutic encounter, the only difference here being the language of communication that is used. This is the moment to recall one's own Mosaic preferences and preconceptions, to value this anew and then to put it aside. This is the moment when the mind is open to a fresh Mosaic response. It is the optimum state of mind for the person receiving the Mosaic as well as the one making it.

The prepared therapist is mentally ready for a therapeutic encounter which is not dependent on words. The adolescent will be shown the building blocks of a new language, the vocabulary of the Lowenfeld Mosaics. Whilst following the usual procedure, the therapist should highlight both the mathematical and artistic qualities of the Mosaics, that is, demonstrating the more adult features of the Lowenfeld Mosaics. This may be particularly appropriate for an adolescent,

Adolescents have a natural reserve, and do not usually display the same kind of spontaneity that is found with a younger person. Although they may not be actually nervous, the therapist should still mention that *there is no right or wrong way of making a Mosaic*. For this age group, it is possibly more important to emphasize the fact that *everyone does something unique to them; that we all have our own Mosaic signature*. As their sense of identity is often in a state of flux and confusion, this reassurance will anchor both the adolescent and the therapist to the seriousness of the therapist's intent and the recognition that the adolescent is an individual in his own right.

When the adolescent has finished, the therapist has a choice of responses. Just as there is no right or wrong way of doing a Mosaic, there is no one correct procedure for the therapist to follow in responding. However, the focus should always be on the Mosaic, the process and its final product. My usual response is to show appreciation of what the adolescent has produced and to ask them to tell me about what they have made. Sometimes, a clear moment in the process offers an opening. If no other natural beginning is available during the silence that follows the making of the Mosaic, it is always useful simply to reflect back your observation of the process. At the least, the therapist will have shown that she has paid meticulous attention, not directly to him but to what he has been doing, and has found it both acceptable and worthy of interest.

My first session with Adam (see Mosaic 1.1) was an important lesson for me. Going through his Mosaic process, using my own hand movements, gave me an unforgettable experience of being "squeezed until I've become invisible". Perhaps my reflecting of this back to him by graphically using my hands may have heightened a remembrance of that movement in Adam, making the space that was being squeezed active again in his imagination. By continuing to follow the process, I felt able to voice what I had seen – the two figures – but this was only after we had explored the Mosaic route he had taken to reach the contracting space in the middle. It was important for me to own the image that I had seen, leaving it open to Adam to respond to my comment. That it seemed to have made a profound impact was neither my purpose, nor my doing. It was what he had made from what he had heard from me which made the difference. What I had done was to raise his self-awareness, heighten his sensitivity to his own actions.

The subtlety of the Total Response was brought home to me in that session with Adam. For Adam, it was through this meticulous exploration of the process that the meaning of his Mosaic emerged for him as a personal revelation. By facilitating and objectifying these thoughts and feelings, through a personal symbolic system of images and patterns, he became more aware of what his experiences meant to him. Thus these thoughts and feelings finally came to be expressible to Adam, and ultimately comprehensible.

For the therapist, the important points here are to do with timing and ownership. My owning of the thought that I had seen that those two groups of shapes looked like two figures was vital. If he did not also see this, or, on seeing it, made no meaningful connection with what I had seen, it could just be dismissed and would have done no harm. The question here is of "timing". My comment could have meant nothing to him, either because it was simply wrong, or because the timing of the remark was wrong, even though the observation may have been pertinent. Unless such observations are recognised as having a resonance at the time they are made, they have no immediate effect. But because they have been voiced and owned by the therapist as a personal view, it leaves the Mosaic-maker free to contradict this view. It may be the case that a point is returned to by the Mosaic-maker later, which would suggest that a connection has then been made in his mind. For an observation to make sense and be useful to the Mosaic-maker, he has to come to it in his own time. Thus it is important from the point of view of the therapeutic task that no more is invested in any observation by the therapist, other than to own the observation as a personal one.

For Adam, that was the moment when he found the words to describe what had emerged through the Mosaic process. The contact, begun so tentatively, was complete. For the therapist, then, the timing of any intervention, the recognising of that moment, is essential for the therapeutic enterprise.

It is certainly true that no two Mosaics are the same, and it is also true that no two Mosaic processes follow the same pattern. Nor is it certain they will bring what might be the expected resolution. I will use two further examples of Mosaics to illustrate further elements of therapeutic responses from adolescents using the Mosaics.

Adolescents are often reluctant referrals. Generally they are struggling to get away from adult values and adult authority to find their own values and their own authority, which makes their reluctance understandable. This is why therapists must be prepared to let them go when they feel ready to stop, unless it is considered unsafe for them to do so. In this, the therapist must balance their own fears about whether they have done enough, and their professional responsibilities, with that of the need to go with the adolescent's attempt at solving his own problems. The adolescent needs to be enabled to take charge of his own life and to take it forward personally, to find his own path, with as little pressure as possible from the adults around him.

This next series of Mosaics from another adolescent is interesting possibly for the light it throws on how the Lowenfeld Mosaics can be utilised by adolescent clients to address their emotional problems entirely through the medium and language of the Mosaics. The following short series of Mosaics was made by Harry, who was in his middle teens.

The referral was couched in vague terms: he was disruptive at school and at home. His behaviour disturbed both the class and the perceived harmony of the home. When Harry first arrived, he insisted that all his problems were to do with "other people", that is, staff and other pupils at his school and other family members; they were the cause of his discontent with the world at large. Things were certainly not of his making, so he had nothing to talk about. It was nothing short of a polite rant, and he went on in this way for half of his session time. A promising beginning, I thought. I had already laid out the Mosaics, so I took advantage of an opening to suggest to Harry that maybe we could do something instead of talking, and then introduced him to the Mosaics. Harry found himself drawn to playing with the pieces and eventually to making the Mosaic below. He worked intently and mostly in silence.

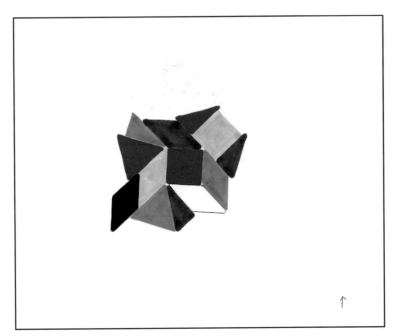

Mosaic 8.1
Harry's first Mosaic: aiming for symmetry

I will now briefly give you the movement of his Mosaic process, including his comments as he went along. In numbered order, Harry's moves in the Mosaic process were: (1) red square; (2) green diamond; (3) blue diamond; (4) yellow diamond; (5) white diamond; and (6) red equilateral. At this point, he said the white diamond was "wrong"; it was "not symmetrical", but he decided not to change it. He continued with (7) green scalene; (8) yellow square; (9) red scalene; (10) blue scalene; (11) green equilateral; (12) blue scalene – note this was the only repeat of shape and colour; and (13) black diamond. Harry then stopped, saying, "It's going to get more difficult to fill up the holes."

I waited. He now explained that he had "wanted to make something symmetrical". Perhaps that is what he meant by "filling up the holes", I thought, but said nothing. He continued the explanation by saying that what he meant by "symmetry" was that the Mosaic must have "sufficient solidity and strength". I put aside my thought about linking "symmetry" with "filling up the holes". I now asked him what would give his Mosaic solidity and strength? He told me that "squares represented solidity, and triangles represented strength".

Harry went on to say that the "separation of colours" was also important.

Furthermore, he did not consider either "white or black" to be colours. These were "shades, not colours". Note, however, it was the white that was wrong, and he stopped with a black piece. Was this a subtle acknowledgement that nothing is black or white? I continued to restrain myself and kept the thought to myself.

At this point we were at the end of our time together. I gave Harry a choice of whether to come again or not. He asked for another appointment.

Mosaic 8.2
Harry's second attempt at symmetry

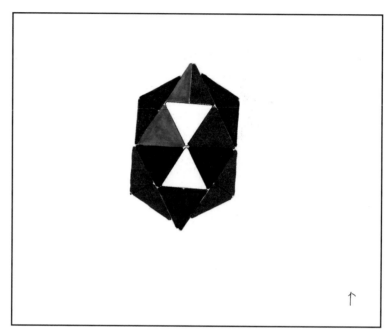

He began with two white equilateral triangles, then promptly expressed dissatisfaction, namely "it's not right", but continued, as he had done in the first session when he had said that the white diamond was wrong but did not change it. Note that on both occasions, it was the colour white which was the common factor, not the shape, when he made the remark. He now corralled these white equilateral triangles with more equilateral triangles – blue, red and green – ending with the scalene triangles surrounding the hexagonal shape in the middle.

He continued to express dissatisfaction with his Mosaic. I noted there were no squares, so, in his terms, the Mosaic had great strength, but would lack solidity. Furthermore, with the placing of two scalene triangles of the same colour together, the separation of colours was not as clear as in his first Mosaic, and yellow and black had not been used. Clearly still dissatisfied, Harry immediately asked to do another Mosaic (8.3).

This time he began with a yellow in a shape he had never used before, the isosceles triangle. The Mosaic process now followed a smooth path. There were no hesitations or changes. Harry worked with a quick but steady pace and seeming confidence. At the end, he declared that he was now completely satisfied with the Mosaic. There was, according to him, "a good balance of squares with triangles

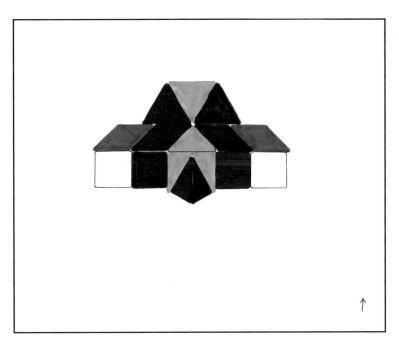

now" – that is, there was now a good balance between strength and solidity – and there was also "sufficient separation between the colours". Indeed, there was an equal distribution of four-sided and three-sided shapes. The green and white colours were evenly balanced between the two sides of the Mosaic, and there were four pieces used of each of the red, blue and yellow colours. Furthermore, the yellow, blue and red shapes were balanced and equally disposed. Having two pieces of the same colour next to each other seemed not to have aroused a negative reaction this time. Perhaps the actual difference in the shapes of the same hue being placed one next to another – thus making a different blue or red shape – made the "sufficient" difference to the Mosaic as a whole for it to be acceptable.

Indeed, the whole tone of this Mosaic seemed different from his two previous attempts. In this Mosaic, Harry had used all the available shapes. My first impression was that he had now eliminated the black but retained two white shapes as in his second Mosaic, this time in squares instead of triangles, thus redressing the imbalance between solidity and strength in the Mosaic. Let us continue to examine the differences.

The first crucial difference may have been how he began this Mosaic, which was by using a shape he had not used before. He had seen a potential in the isosceles triangle that had escaped his attention previously, and thereafter everything seemed to have come together and fallen into place. The isosceles triangle is an interesting shape within the Mosaic choice of shapes. Whereas the square, the rhombus or diamond and equilateral triangle have all their sides of equal length, and the scalene triangle has all its sides of differing lengths, the isosceles triangle is the only shape in which balance and symmetry incorporate difference. It has two sides of equal length, with the hypotenuse, which itself is of a different length to the sides, holding the balance between these two sides.

You will recall that Harry's first critical remarks – "it's wrong", "it's not symmetrical", referred to his choice of the white diamond shape, but he had not removed it. In his second Mosaic, he had picked out two white equilateral triangles at the beginning, and had immediately said, "it's not right", but again had not withdrawn them. You will note that the sides of both these shapes are of equal length. So let us look again in greater detail at Harry's use of the white shapes in his Mosaics.

The white shapes in the first two Mosaics were each surrounded by three colours: blue, green and red, each in slightly different ways. In the first Mosaic, each colour cradled one side of the white diamond placed on the edge of the pattern, leaving the fourth side exposed. In the second Mosaic the sides of the white equilateral triangle were enclosed by one of the same three colours, using three blue equilaterals or a combination of red and green equilateral and scalene triangles. The biggest difference this time is where the white piece is situated. In Harry's second Mosaic, the white was placed in the heart of the Mosaic.

In the third Mosaic, Harry had made a symmetrical pattern, with the symmetry along the vertical axis only. He had reverted to placing the white pieces at the edge of his pattern and returned to using a four-sided shape for it. Now, however, the sides of the diamond shape had been "straightened" out to that of a square; and two of the sides of the white square are now exposed. Each side of this symmetrical pattern has the colours red, blue, green and white, with all the yellow pieces forming the vertical axis of the pattern. There is an interesting touch to this central column. Whereas red and blue flank the top yellow equilateral triangle, the use of four scalene triangles between the squares in the bottom line of shapes allowed Harry an individualistic nicety whilst exploiting the point of contact between the hypotenuse of the isosceles triangle and the scalene triangles.

Thus, for Harry, the transformation of the white diamond into a white square, through all the intermediate changes, was the other major change which rendered acceptable what had been "wrong" and "not symmetrical" in his previous two patterns. In the process, Harry discarded one of the "shades", the black colour, but reclaimed the colour yellow. Upon analysis, his first act in using the yellow isosceles triangle seemed to have been the decisive factor that enabled the adjustments to the remaining shapes and colours used. It was pivotal to his final feeling of satisfaction with his Mosaic production.

At the end of this session, Harry decided that he did not need any further appointments. I agreed and no further appointments were offered. As part of my professional work I did a follow-up on Harry some months later. From the referrers' (his school and family) point of view, Harry seemed to have settled down and was no longer a concern to either of them.

In conventional terms, therapy would have hardly begun in two sessions that were mainly of an exploratory nature. It is perhaps unusual for a satisfactory outcome to be achieved after only two sessions where no major emotional breakthrough has apparently occurred, but let us look at it from Harry's point of view: what was the psychological significance or meaning of "symmetry" to Harry? How do "strength" and "solidity" contribute to his sense of "symmetry" psychologically?

To be sure, it did not take Harry long to make his final Mosaic, perhaps because he had already accumulated sufficient experience of the characteristics of the Mosaics to be able to deploy them with greater knowledge and confidence. Even so, had he consciously built in all the parameters he had specified during the making of his third Mosaic to achieve a satisfactory and to him satisfying Mosaic? Did he have any conscious understanding of its psychological significance to him? These would not have been Harry's own questions; these could only be questions born of the therapist's own curiosity.

I really do not know what happened for Harry. All I know is the sense of satisfaction in his entire manner when he had completed this final Mosaic. Nor did I truly know what the different colours or various shapes meant to Harry apart from what he said, or whether my analysis that the use of the isosceles triangle in his third Mosaic made the crucial difference which led to his decision to end his therapy was right or wrong.

Perhaps there are times when therapists do not need to know what it is that makes the difference, but only to recognise that it has been made. Of course it is entirely possible, and even probable, that the exploration of the Mosaic was only the start of the process of change for Harry. In any case, it is important to support his sense of what he needed and where he should move to next. Trying to insist that Harry continue with sessions because we had not talked about what he had been referred for seemed to me then, and in retrospect now, counter-productive.

Iris taught me a different lesson.

Mosaic 8.4
Iris's first Mosaic

Iris, a girl of fifteen, was referred by her school through her doctor, who was concerned that she might be abusing drugs and was hinting that she might be suicidal. According to Iris, the doctor had told her she should come to the clinic because she was "depressed". Indeed, she said the word sighingly with a gently dismissive gesture and fell silent. There seemed a contradiction in her manner. There was a mixture of childish deference and adult politeness.

I suggested that perhaps she might like to take a look at the shapes in the box and play around with them if she felt like it. I showed her the different shapes and colours and indicated the tray lying below the Mosaic box. I said, "Just pick out some pieces. Play around with them. Make something with them if you like." With a swift and sudden movement, her hand fell on the box, but in complete contrast to this first movement, she was slow but meticulous in her choice of the pieces. As she placed them one by one on the tray, she began to murmur to herself. When I could eventually catch the words, she was clearly going over in her own mind the notion summed up by the word "depressed". She felt "low", had "no energy", "don't feel like doing anything" and was "miserable".

After what seemed like a long while, Iris looked up and said shyly that she had finished, but immediately added in a much more animated voice, "I'm very miserable today. This isn't the real me. It's different when I'm feeling happy. Maybe next time?" Somehow, she felt that the Mosaic had reflected her mood of the day, but more important from my therapist's perspective she had also looked forward to the possibility of a better future. As there was time, I invited her to take a closer look at her present Mosaic. I reflected back the one-sidedness of her Mosaic and she nodded. She said again, more clearly, that she was "feeling miserable today".

Iris greeted me expansively the next time she came. She insisted on doing another Mosaic to show me what she could do "when I am feeling happy and

Mosaic 8.5
Iris's Mosaic at her second appointment

relaxed". Indeed, her whole manner seemed to be infused by a sense of enthusiasm and optimism. She told me smilingly that today she was her usual self – I would see her true nature.

Again I slowly reflected back her whole Mosaic process. She noted with delight that she had covered the entire tray space, in contrast to her previous Mosaic. Clearly she had a strong memory of her first visit. She was pleased there were no black pieces. "Black is a miserable colour," she added. We agreed that the Mosaic gave a bright, colourful picture. This, she said, reflected her normal cheerful self.

Her first Mosaic was to hand, and I now produced it for our joint consideration. We continued to think about the differences. Iris observed that there were more blue and yellow pieces in the present Mosaic. I said that these two colours seemed also to be more obviously connected to each other. She remarked that it wasn't just the black that was absent, there were no green pieces either. That was what made it so much more cheerful. I had a strong impression that Iris had retained a clear image of her first Mosaic. She was pleased to be able to show me the difference her mood made to her Mosaic productions. The positive contrast with the misery of her first Mosaic that was afforded by this second Mosaic was surely proof enough of her assertions.

I wondered what had made her so cheerful at the moment and she seemed happy to tell me. Everyone at school was "off her back" and she didn't seem to mind about the break-up with her boyfriend any more. He had introduced her to drugs, but she did not really like it ("It did my head in"). She felt better off without him and the drugs.

There was a lull in the room until I took the opportunity to make another observation. I pointed to the hollow space at the top of her first Mosaic, noting its position and size. Transferring attention to the present Mosaic, I noted that the space was still there, but it seemed to have expanded with the rest of the Mosaic. Iris did not respond. There was a long moment of silence. Then, speaking as though to myself, I wondered if perhaps there was something deep inside her which felt empty. It was then that her mask dropped. She became serious, and in a solemn voice told me about her life at home, from which she felt she had derived her low self-esteem. We could now move on.

I always find the consistency shown by people's Mosaics truly remarkable in reflecting their Personality in Action. So although Iris's mood had indeed changed dramatically, this was a superficial change and the underlying structure of the Mosaic remained unaltered. Her mood may have changed, but Iris herself was fundamentally the same person. We arrived at this through careful attention to her Mosaic.

For adolescents, an ability in the therapist to give a sense of detached attention to what they do, without focusing directly on them personally, is invaluable for their own struggle through the major physiological, mental and emotional upheavals of natural development. It gives them both the courage and the dignity to come into their own adulthood in their individual unique way.

9 Personality in Action II: working with children

Most referrals for therapeutic work with children are accompanied by some kind of personal history of the child. These may be from brief reports within the referral letter, or direct information gathered from people closely connected with the child, as from parent/s or the head-teacher of the school the child was currently attending.

Is this a helpful beginning? Does having some facts about this child's life help the therapist to be more effective in her work? It could be argued that it is not so much the facts that matter as what the child thinks about himself and his surroundings that needs the therapist's attention. Indeed that is true. But let us suppose that a child has been referred by his family doctor because it was said that the child has been bullied at school. Should the therapist try to check what the facts are, and whether there is any truth in these allegations from another point of view?

In terms of the Lowenfeld approach, it would be argued that this check on the reality of such an allegation should not only be done, but that it is a necessity in all circumstances. It would certainly assist the therapist in this case to decide whether the work needs to be done, or could be done, by the child, the alleged bully or the school. It would also give the therapist some insight into a variety of views about him. These opinions make up a kind of atmosphere surrounding the child. As in the case of Adam (see Chapters 1 and 2), where his parents' belief that he was a lazy boy became an inalterable factor in any decision they made for him. For Adam, this then became not just incidental to his life. His parents' opinion of him became a fact in his life and affected his experience of school as well as that of his parents' treatment of him. This may be a different kind of "fact", but a fact nevertheless in Adam's life.

As the child's point of view is central to the Lowenfeld approach, how is the therapist to disentangle the opinions of those intimately connected with the child, the parents, the teachers and other professionals, from the facts of external reality themselves? And if the therapist does take these distinctions into account, what effect would this have on the therapist's approach to the child?

Children are usually referred to professionals by other adults who feel that some kind of explanation for the referral is necessary. They try to sum up their concerns with descriptions of behaviours, perhaps giving an account of the latest incident, which precipitated this appeal for psychological help for the child. From the beginning, the therapist's view is immediately coloured by those of the adults who are concerned with the child's welfare. If the child's point of view is presented at all, it is mainly through reported conversations with him. A certain bias, by definition, exists. Already we cannot help having certain ideas about this child.

Given this inevitable situation, how would the Lowenfeld approach be applied? Let us for a moment try to see this from the child's point of view. In this connection, I would like to suggest a brief illustrative exercise.

Let us represent the present situation of the child by the number 4 and then find as many mathematical ways as possible to arrive at this number. It does not take long to see that there are many different ways to get to 4, and such lists of equations arrived at would neither be identical nor exhaustive.

Think of the various features of the different calculations as symbols for the facts and opinions accompanying the referral. Now endow the different features with different thoughts and feelings, and it can be seen that it is impossible for a consistent picture of this child to emerge. Furthermore, it cannot be denied that the meaning from any reading of the words is that with which the reader has endowed them. The images seen in the mind's eye are thus likely to be different for each person. Not only will the images not be the same, the reality for the child may be very different.

Perhaps insufficient information has been given in the first place. Add the following information to make up 4: $+ 81$, $- 41$, $\times 31$, $\div 7$. Now a few further reports have come in, and additional information has been gathered from conversations with other professionals involved with the case. The picture seems to be fleshed out. In reality, is there now a clearer picture of this child? Did having more information solve or simplify the problem? Or has it merely demonstrated the fact that there are simply innumerable ways of arriving at 4? It seems to be impossible to be certain what caused the child to be in the situation represented by 4.

Whilst it is clearly important to know something about the child, it is vital to distinguish between the facts (e.g. the child's age and gender and the family make-up) and the opinions (e.g. the child is lazy or bad-tempered) held about them by adults; it has also to be accepted that it is not possible to know which of the facts or opinions surrounding the child holds significance for the child. Nor is it possible to know what important features in this picture have been left out. By virtue of being human, all informants have their own agendas, and their best intentions all have lapses of memory and hold personal views about the meaning of particular behaviours.

In a way, this is what all therapists are faced with when we see a child or family. We are faced with our own humanity. We may have been given certain facts about and particular views of a child, but we still know very little or even nothing of the child's thoughts and feelings about these facts and opinions, nor indeed whether they are the facts that the child regards as significant or pertinent. In fact, this should be the point of any therapeutic contact. The point of departure for the therapist is to find ways to get in touch with the child's point of view and what the child regards as important and relevant to his situation. The therapeutic process is to work with the child towards his own resolution of what he perceives as his problem. This is not simply a supplement to the facts given. It is the Lowenfeld therapist's essential task.

Shall we meet Janet? It is indeed how she perceived her situation which was the point of departure for the therapeutic work. I first heard of her from a colleague who was telephoned by her headmaster with concerns about a pupil newly arrived at the school. The headmaster wanted to consult with my colleague as to whether it would be an appropriate referral to a community clinic. Janet was a puzzle.

Janet seemed to have settled in as far as the teachers were concerned and was said to be no trouble in or out of the classroom. It was noted by many of the adults that her quietness had an air of preoccupation that was unconnected with either the other children or teachers, or indeed the school curriculum. However, she seemed unhappy. Her written work was perfunctory and her participation in class was non-existent. People were reluctant to conclude that she was definitely unhealthily withdrawn, because she did seem to try and participate in unobtrusive ways. She was observed after class closing other children's school desks which had been left open, tidying up dropped paper into the wastepaper basket, wiping the chalkboard clean, all without ever drawing anyone's attention to these acts of helpfulness.

Her mother was offered an initial appointment in order to get a picture of Janet at home. She painted quite a different picture. Her mother had been unhappy almost from the beginning of her marriage, and at the present time had been divorced for some years. Janet was pre-pubertal, and the eldest of three girls by a few years. Whilst her sisters were largely carefree and seemingly little affected by the marital break-up, Janet had been alternately defiant of and solicitous towards her mother, and her father had complained of a similar show of defiance and solicitousness when she was at his house. Her mother had become increasingly exasperated, yet she had to admit that Janet had been a great help to her, caring for her other daughters whilst she gradually came to terms with single parenthood. Though her father was prepared to show patience, his partner was at the limit of her tolerance. The parents' communications between each other were only about the daughters' visiting arrangements. The style of the conversations was confrontational, often ending abruptly. During these exchanges her mother was often aware that Janet was lurking somewhere in the background.

It was decided that I should offer an initial appointment to Janet, that is, time for an assessment from Janet's perspective. As is my usual practice, I began the interview by suggesting that she might do something with as few or as many Mosaic pieces as she liked within the tray provided.

Janet built up this simple figure in a relaxed manner. Beginning from the top, working downwards, she built the central column, putting in the red and blue isosceles triangles simultaneously, then the green and blue. From her actions, she seemed to have some difficulty in knowing what colour each diamond should be, although she was certain that reds had to balance the greens, and that blue would be the common colour. She seemed pleased with the final product. I asked her to tell me about what she had made. By then, experience had taught me not to

presume I knew what it was, even though it had seemed obvious. There might be more in it than the obvious.

She told me it was "a person". "What kind of person?" I asked. She pondered only momentarily: "Hmm. I don't know. Maybe . . . " followed by a longer pause, before she finally said, "It doesn't matter."

"Could it be someone like yourself?" I ventured. "Yes," she replied, this time unhesitatingly, sharply.

I then described how the person had been built up, beginning with where she had started. Janet interrupted me: "Yes," adding, "That's the head." "It's white," I remarked. Without a pause, she explained, "That's because there's nothing inside." I tried to clarify. "So you feel blank inside your head?" "Hmm." After another pause, I continued. "Is that how you feel at school?" "Yes, I don't know what the teachers are going on about. I don't understand a word they say." A note (was it resignation?) had crept into her voice. School had become a kind of refuge. She was content to be left alone and was not unduly troubled by having no close friends.

Another pause and I noted aloud: "The arms and legs have got the same colours as the body, I see. But the blue in the arm and leg is on the opposite side to the blue of the body. And the same goes for the red and green colours."

I was unprepared for her response. Janet burst into tears, sobbing in violent gulps. It was many minutes before she could speak. Without further preliminaries, she haltingly explained: "Mum and I were walking up the High Road. I suddenly saw Dad on the other side of the road. A woman had her arm through his. I thought Dad had gone to a conference in Scotland." It was as though it had happened yesterday.

Janet had been shocked beyond words by this sight of her father with a strange woman on his arm – as was her mother. But they did not talk about it together. Nor did she talk to her sisters, because she had felt they were too young. In any case, she would not have known what to say. It seemed to her that there was no one she could talk to about this and certainly no one had talked to her since that first sighting. This event, however, precipitated an immediate separation between her parents and eventually a divorce. Janet was completely devastated by the turn of events. She had been not only very fond of her father, but had felt her feelings reciprocated. She admired him for the important job he did. He was someone to look up to, an inspiration for her own endeavours. She had been so proud of him. Janet was hurt by this betrayal of the family, of her and her young ideals.

Her father had by now remarried, but the rift between her parents had by no means healed. She and her sisters had regular visits to his new home. Whilst her sisters took these visits in their stride, Janet alone of the three seemed unable to settle in either of the two households. At this point in her tale, she paused and the expression on her face seemed to change. I continued to wait.

Janet sighed deeply, took a deep breath and haltingly explained: "I miss Dad when I am at home with Mum. I miss Mum when I am with Dad. I seem to get angry with Mum whenever I'm at home, and angry with Dad whenever I'm with Dad. I don't seem to be happy anywhere." She agreed that she still wished fervently that her parents were together and she became distressed and angry whenever she recalled what her father had done to the family. Janet had felt that her life with both her parents together had been a happy one, but she seemed to have been unaware of her mother's unhappiness with the marriage throughout her young life. As far as Janet was concerned, she did not experience their marriage as either happy or unhappy but just a fact. She had taken her parents' marriage as a model of marriage. After all, Janet had had no other experience of marital relationships. She seemed unable to accept the present reality of her family situation. It was not possible for Janet to see that her parents may have been happier apart. Life after the divorce was inevitably coloured by her own emotional reaction to the change.

I was now able to see what the blue, green and red of her Mosaic had meant to Janet. And whilst I had slowly reflected back her Mosaic process, she had become aware of the connection between her inner turmoil and her behaviour, her life as observed by others. This self-awareness had crystallised into a feeling. The feeling was released into tears. A self-portrait had emerged which had enabled her finally to articulate the global and multidimensional nature of her situation. Beginning with that singular event, seeing her father with his arm linked to that of a strange woman, and taking in personal history and private turmoil and how she had expressed these in her daily life, she was finally enabled to express all that she had felt through the past few years, which had culminated in her visit to the clinic.

Her Mosaic had for the first time expressed her feelings about herself, and made clear to her, as well as communicating it to someone else, the situation which had brought it about. It described her as she felt herself to be. It was a portrait of Janet's feelings about herself and her family situation, one she could own as being by and of herself.

Janet gained a tremendous sense of relief from this session. She agreed that it would help if her parents were able to communicate with each other with no or less rancour – the first note of realism – and it might also help if the three sisters could have time alone with their father. It was even possible for her to consider that perhaps she wanted this special time with him more for herself. She had not wanted to seem over-demanding, but now there was something tangible to be done.

Whilst Janet continued to be reviewed, her parents were encouraged to improve their communication and to be more conciliatory for Janet's sake. In time, they discovered that their common affection for their children had loosened the knot of their hostility. Janet would also have profited from a change to a less demanding academic environment, but resources were scarce and she managed.

Not all therapeutic stories have such a relatively positive outcome, nor was Janet's adolescence to be an easy passage. But whatever the course of a referral for help, the beginning of all therapeutic work should have in mind the child's point of view and the child's own solution to his problem.

It seems that to help children who are distressed and in difficulties, it is not enough for the surrounding adults to provide professionals with only their own accounts of the child. Thus important facts in Janet's life lay largely buried within adult accounts. The perspectives of the concerned adults are not only from the outside, but are imbued with personal bias. These are also largely retrospective, picking out what seems to them to have been significant behaviours or events. And adult narratives, because they are couched in words, tend to be sequential and time-bound, defining the logic of feelings from the flow of events and from adult perspectives.

From the child's point of view, its life has been lived prospectively. Its response to any given situation is spontaneous, immediate, global and multidimensional. Its thought and feeling are fused with any moment of its life. What is experientially significant for the child could be any single element within that configuration of circumstance, thought and feeling. It is, however, that which makes the greatest emotional impact which defines its significance. And of that it is impossible to predict or select in retrospect from external observation that which has made the most impact to the child.

Keith was a very different personality from Janet. As children are usually brought into the world of therapy by adults, they cannot be seen to be self-motivated. Keith had come with his mother to the initial meeting. It was clear that she had already decided that all her son's problems had originated in the school he attended. On the subject of his behaviour, variously described as "anti-social" or "eccentric", the mother's view was "The school had it in for him." Keith nodded in agreement. He was eight years old and was also said to have produced no written schoolwork during the three or four years he had been at school. His mother reported no problems at home, at least none that she could not manage, and in any case "boys will be boys". He was also said by the school to be emotionally immature and lacking any friends. His eccentric or anti-social behaviour was put down to this immaturity. His mother maintained that the school had victimized him and turned staff and pupils alike against her son. Keith continued to look approvingly at his mother's account of his sufferings. She was, however, prepared to have her son assessed and perhaps given treatment.

So, at his first consultation, I asked Keith to do a Mosaic, to see "what he can do with the coloured shapes in the box". I was uncertain whether it was curiosity that drew him forward, but he did begin and proceeded to make a Mosaic (9.2). The Mosaic was produced quite naturally, without any need for persuasion or encouragement by me.

Given the background of the family interview, I was aware that I had to be fully attentive to his Total Response. At the end I was struck by what close observation of how the particular qualities of Mosaics were being used within the Total Response could reveal and the valuable information it could provide regarding the internal thought processes of the Mosaic-maker.

Mosaic 9.2
Keith: shape versus colour within the Total Response

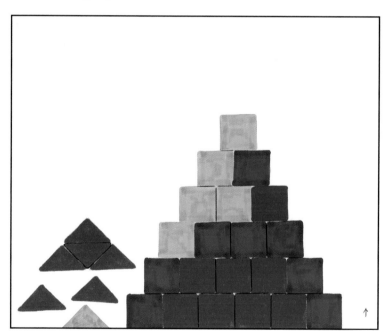

After my usual demonstration, Keith began by picking up all the four red squares from one side of the box, the same compartment from which I had withdrawn a red square for the demonstration. He placed the four squares along the bottom edge of the tray. He told me they were "tiles". He took three more red squares from the other compartment, centred them above the previous row and now told me they were "floor tiles".

As he said this, he took out four blue squares, the next pieces in the row of squares, from the first compartment he had used. He placed the blue squares at the ends of the two rows of red squares. He then picked out three more blue squares, thus repeating his first two moves, but now with the blue squares, and placed these above the second row. He continued by picking out four yellow squares from the first compartment he had started with, thus repeating his first move yet again. After placing a yellow square at the end of the third row of squares, he now thought it looked like a "pyramid" and began building onto this by placing a second and third yellow square onto the two blue squares, to form a fourth row. Keith now paused and said that it now looked like "a house or a wall".

Keith then placed a fourth yellow square to straddle the previous two, and finally decided that it looked more like a pyramid now. He used the red and blue squares, part of the sets of four he had taken out earlier, to "round off the ends" of these last two rows of yellow squares. In the process, he had to adjust the squares in the last two rows before realizing that he needed another square at the top to complete his pyramid. He chose another yellow square for this.

He looked enormously pleased with his production, beaming with obvious satisfaction at his achievement. This seemed to propel him into looking into the Mosaic box once more. He picked out a new shape, a red isosceles triangle. That too was a pyramid. He put it beside the pyramid of squares. Keith became quite excited. He named the next red isosceles triangle a pyramid also. He took out a few more red isosceles triangles and began experimenting with them. Eventually he stopped when he had found a way to make an enlarged triangle. That was to be his one and only innovation, the discovery of how to make this bigger triangle, another pyramid. He began to tell me that there were other pyramids in the distance, waving his hand across the tray. He picked up a yellow isosceles triangle, also a pyramid, and placed it on the bottom edge of the tray. As with his square pyramid, Keith thus completed this set of triangular pyramids with a yellow tile.

Although Keith was happy to end his Mosaic on this note, he seemed puzzled that he had not got the same buzz as when he had finished doing the square pyramid. He seemed a little deflated. He did not look round the playroom to see if there was anything else of interest. At the time, I did not think of this slight detail as having any particular significance. I began to introduce him to the Lowenfeld World (Sandplay) Material and his interest seemed to revive.

During his World-making, the same type of sequence seemed to occur. He started with an earthquake and then he discovered he could actually mould the wet sand to make a volcano, which duly erupted, accompanied by dramatic effects. Thereafter, in later sessions, Keith dispensed with the preliminary earthquake, but the volcano followed the same sequence, erupting repeatedly till the end of the session.

After this first appointment, I began to examine his first Mosaic with greater care, to see if a pattern could be discerned and the thought processes in terms of the Mosaic process and eventual product were shown in any way. It can be seen that he had begun with what I had started my demonstration with, the red squares, and proceeded to follow the line of least resistance through the compartment in the box which contained the squares, by using the four blue and four yellow squares. However, he showed that he knew where to get some more of the same coloured shape by moving across to the other side of the box. (This means that he could and did follow my demonstration quite closely. I thought, whatever it was that stopped him from doing his schoolwork, it was not because he could not pay attention.) But during this building process, Keith repeated short sequences of moves. He eventually broke the sequence and finally was able to complete the square pyramid.

I next looked at the thought process during the building of the square pyramid. Although the actual process of building up this shape required very little thinking, his ideation process moved from one idea to another in rapid succession: from "tiles" to "floor tiles" to "pyramid", "a house or a wall", before reverting to the "pyramid" idea, ending with a yellow square. During this process it never once seemed to have occurred to him that he could try out any of the other available shapes.

This specific act of completion of the square pyramid, however, seemed to have suggested to Keith a new shape he could use. Consequently, he next chose a red isosceles triangle and almost immediately began to experiment with this shape to make a larger pyramid. So he was able to change, and the moment he made the connection between the shape of the isosceles triangle and the shape of the pyramid was the moment when he did. However, as soon as that happened, he seemed unable to take the idea forward. It seemed that the inspiration from this one insight was not sufficient to stimulate further exploration. From then on, Keith seemed to be stuck with both the idea and the shape and remained grounded on the last piece he used, a yellow isosceles triangle, which signalled the end of his Mosaic-making.

What did this say about Keith? Did it shed any light on his inability to produce any written schoolwork? Clearly, as he had managed to produce a Mosaic, he had demonstrated that he was capable of producing at least some work. And, as noted earlier, he must have paid some attention in order to have remembered that the same coloured shape could be found in two different places. He also made a major discovery: how to form a coherent image of the object he had in mind, when he discovered how to make the red pyramid with isosceles triangles.

However, the Total Response of the Mosaic process seemed to show that as the doing and thinking flowed together, his perceptual skills were unable to keep up with his ideational flights. Furthermore, the flow of thoughts was mainly tenuously connected with the colours and shapes he was using, and showed most clearly in the process towards the formation of the square pyramid. Even after what might have seemed a major breakthrough, in the achieving of the red pyramid, he could not build on it and returned to using a single piece. Keith's thoughts were thus tied up with the immediate sensation of how the shape was altered by the new pieces he had added and then became fixated on the shape and idea simultaneously, which ultimately showed his inability to move away from or develop the idea further.

Thus his inability to produce work was the difficulty Keith experienced when called upon to produce something entirely self-motivated. He could maybe find one thing to say, but he could not develop the idea into a narrative or find connections to the next idea. Hence, for Keith, his inability to produce schoolwork of any substance was perhaps linked with his inability to make friends. He found it hard to make, maintain and develop connections, and repetition soon palled, stopping any further development.

Given that I had made the contact through the assessment process, our clinic team agreed that Keith should receive a period of regular psychotherapy with me. He attended regularly. His mother had parallel appointments with a colleague, whilst Keith came to see me, mainly to see if the psychotherapy offered was indeed effective by obtaining a contemporary picture of his life outside of therapy. Throughout this period, his mother had maintained that Keith's inability to do adequate or any substantial piece of schoolwork was because of poor teaching. She now admitted that he could be exasperating at home, and occasionally even she was struck by what she described as "his eccentricities". These were rather "endearing" but she did not elaborate. His company was a little trying at times, but then he was "his own person", so she accepted this state of affairs. In the meantime the school had decided to implement other measures to accommodate his "eccentric" behaviour. This proved adequate in terms of his behaviour, but improvement in his schoolwork was negligible.

After a year's attendance, it was clear that Keith's work with me had not changed significantly. He had continued to create earthquakes which heaved and broke up the surface of the sand, and volcanoes which erupted with increasing extravagance of gesture. He seldom answered any of my queries or responded to what I had intended as thought-provoking musings. It seemed that the sheer sensation of the physical movements of the activity of his World-making gave him the deepest satisfaction. His enjoyment of these were paramount. In my professional experience, this treatment phase did not last long. I was concerned that I had missed a crucial element in the treatment process which had produced this impasse. I decided that I should review the situation at his next visit.

He had not done another Mosaic since his first, and so I asked him to do another Mosaic at the beginning of the review session. I began by asking him whether he remembered doing a Mosaic the first time he came to see me. He was doubtful, so I gestured towards the box of Mosaics and the tray already fitted with the correct-sized paper and said to Keith that I would now like him to do another one.

As he finished making his Mosaic (9.3 overleaf), Keith was greatly pleased by his representation of a speedboat. It could certainly be seen as an advance on his pyramids. Following the process, I noted that he had fundamentally repeated the first approaches to his first Mosaic, that is, using up all the red equilateral triangles in one compartment before picking up similar pieces in the complementary compartment on the other side of the box. From the way he deployed the equilateral triangles, I realised that he had remembered as well as learnt from his previous experience with the isosceles triangles of the first Mosaic. On this occasion, he had liked to pair the equilateral triangles and always put a pair of them together, so he discarded the remaining red equilateral triangle in favour of a pair of blue ones to complete the hull of the speedboat. This seemed another departure from his first Mosaic. The other blue equilaterals were used to depict the rest of the speedboat, the details of which were vague. He could not say anything about these blue equilateral triangles.

I continued my journey of discovery about his speedboat by asking which

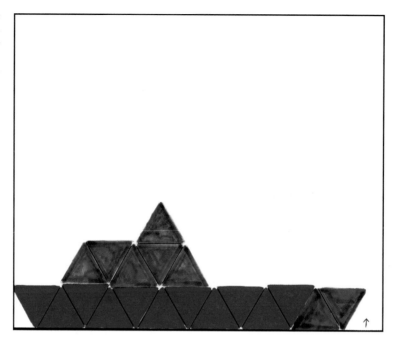

way the boat was facing, which way would the boat be facing if it were to go forward? Keith replied unhesitatingly, "The front is here. It's going that way," pointing to the red piece on the left of the picture, as we looked at his Mosaic together, "and the back is the blue bit." I looked at him and responded, "It's right on the edge of the tray here. Has it just come from the other side?" I said, pointing to the right-hand edge of the tray. Keith nodded. "It looks as though it had moved forward a little way," I continued. "Can it move forward some more? Does it want to go anywhere in particular?" I wished to find out whether Keith himself had any desire to move from his present position or a wish for change. He laughed aloud and answered, "It doesn't want to go out anywhere else. It just likes going out for fun, nowhere in particular."

I then explained about the function of the clinic and asked Keith directly whether there was anything in his life he would like to change, either at home, or at school or in himself. It was his turn to explain himself. He grinned mischievously, his eyes sparkling, and said that he had enjoyed his sessions, particularly making earthquakes and volcanoes in the sand (possibly because he knew I would have to clear up the sand that went all over the playroom floor as the volcano erupted violently at the end of every session). Yes, he would certainly want to continue coming to the clinic. In any case, the school had stopped bothering him, so there wasn't anything else he would want to change.

It was one of the most difficult decisions of my professional career. What if I had made a mistake in taking him on in the first place? Would increasing the number of sessions have improved the chances of Keith progressing? Had I denied Keith the opportunity to work on himself in a different way? This lack of a motive for change after a period of attendance, however, was a clear indication to me that what we were doing was not promoting any change. Perhaps I should have reviewed the situation sooner? What of the reality in his life outside of the treatment room? After a year of therapeutic work with me, the school had not reported any significant change in Keith's willingness or ability to produce more than a few sentences. The only change which had been reported were the changes put in place by the school. I now decided to consult with the full clinic team. It was suggested that perhaps Keith needed more intensive work than I could offer, so he was duly referred to another service, where such intensive work could be provided. From this case I learnt that a more frequent and rigorous review system should form part of the treatment plan. Operating on an open-ended policy is wasteful of everyone's energy and time, and is likely to be ultimately unproductive.

Several years later and whilst he was still in intensive psychotherapy, it was reported to me that although Keith had started at secondary school, he continued to be a loner and had continued to produce a minimal amount of work. I recalled that Keith had not asked for help himself. It had been the adults around him who found his work unsatisfactory and his behaviour unacceptable. Keith himself had not once expressed a desire for change. Looking back now, I wonder whether some other approach, or indeed some other diagnosis, requiring perhaps a different solution might have been more helpful to him. But I continue to believe that personal motivation for change is an essential factor if change of any lasting significance is to be effected.

Even in the era when child and adolescent psychotherapists were able to offer open-ended treatment, once the case had been accepted for therapy, decisions to end treatment were never straightforward or the sole preserve of the professional. As I had worked in the public or state sector, I was always made aware of the inadequacy of such therapeutic provision in proportion to the needs of the children, adolescents and their families who required this service.

In practice I had found that it is often the clients who determine the length of time of the treatment. Their reasons are manifold and I can give no more than a glimpse of the particular course this third case has taken. I have chosen Lawrence mainly because the Lowenfeld Mosaics have made a significant contribution to his understanding of himself, but they also demonstrate how the external circumstances surrounding the life of the person undergoing psychotherapy play a major role in assisting or hindering this process, and more importantly how personal determination and resilience help in constructive adaptation towards a more hopeful future for the individual.

Lawrence was a striking contrast to Nellie, a case I shall be discussing in the next chapter, for despite severe deprivation during his childhood years, he never gave up hope. At his assessment, the use of the Lowenfeld Mosaics seemed to have given him an understanding of himself that encouraged Lawrence rather than deterred him from pursuing the goal he had set himself. I found his case particularly affecting, for I found his personality entirely impressive. It demonstrated for me the power of the Mosaics in portraying a Personality in Action.

Lawrence was nearly fifteen when he came for his assessment interview with me. He was said to be a taciturn boy who kept himself to himself. When he had

Mosaic 9.4
Lawrence's first Mosaic

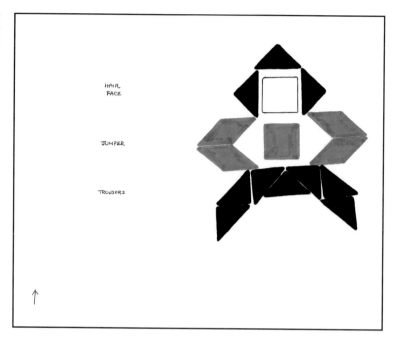

completed his Mosaic, I ascertained from him that the figure depicted featured a white square for a "face" within a frame of black "hair", under which was a green "sweater", and a pair of black "trousers". The words in quotes were the only words he had uttered so far.

I asked Lawrence to elaborate. He told me that it was "a little boy", but after a pause he changed it to "a boy", and then there was another pause before he decided that it was "anybody". He continued to change his mind, saying next that "it doesn't matter", following it by "a person" then going back to "a boy". After a longer pause, he finally decided it was after all "a girl", and he began to change the Mosaic trousers into a skirt, but somehow stopped short of actually effecting the change.

Upon further enquiry, he explained that "he", indicating the Mosaic figure, could be "living anywhere", seemingly having forgotten that he had last said it was a girl. Quietly, without any show of emotion and as though in resignation, he added, "It doesn't matter where he lived really."

Notwithstanding the power of this verbal communication, what he had depicted as a person gave a veritable picture of the absence of a personality. In the image he had created, there was no suggestion of substance inside the clothes. Furthermore, its placement gave the impression of a puppet dangling in mid air to the side of centre stage, or sidelined.

To unpack the Total Response of this Mosaic, I would like to look more closely at the whole process leading to the product, and including our subsequent conversation about it so far. Lawrence's confusion about the gender of the personality seemed quite clear. Equally clear to me from his reversion from "girl" to "he" was the fact that he was thinking about himself. This is not simply a matter of guesswork on my part. Held in my mind at the time was a piece of information from his personal history, which had preceded Lawrence in support of his referral to the clinic. It was that his mother had been exceedingly disappointed that he had not been a girl. The parents had agreed that they would only have one child, but the mother had additionally wished to have a daughter as that single child. So the mother's sense of disappointment was that much greater.

At this point in our conversation, I recalled that Lawrence had mentioned that it "doesn't matter". This came in the midst of his attempt to say what the figure was. So there was not only confusion about his gender, but a certain feeling, possibly one of despair, that it would still perhaps not have mattered regardless of its gender.

I was particularly struck by Lawrence's remark, "It doesn't matter where he lived really." This was also a clear reference to his personal experience. From an early age, at the first signs of Lawrence encountering language difficulties, the parents had begun to seek professional help. When this help did not seem to be having the desired effect, they became increasingly insistent that his slow language development had become intolerable to them and was delaying Lawrence's personal development. This quickly led to their demand that Lawrence should be found a boarding school placement when he was still under eight years of age. Eventually, these wishes were acceded to and the local education authority funded this placement solely on educational grounds, because behaviourally and socially he had not presented any problems either to the parents at home or to the staff and other pupils at the primary school he was attending.

At the age of eight, he was sent to boarding school. This is not an unusual age for some children to be sent to boarding school, in fact, but for Lawrence it seemed to have had an adverse effect. At school, his misery was evident to all who had contact with him and his educational progress was painfully slow and possibly non-existent in some areas. He was at home throughout the school holidays, where, like other children who attend boarding schools, but particularly for Lawrence, it was difficult for him to find any peer group companionship. When it was time for him to return to the boarding school, his reluctance was such as to cause the parents quite regularly to seek help from the authorities to return him to school. It was a difficult time for both the parents and Lawrence.

When Lawrence was rising fifteen, he succeeded in persuading both the authorities and his parents that he should return to mainstream schooling. He had wanted very much to be able to take part in the first public examinations of all children. For Lawrence it would be a mark of his normality even if he could achieve nothing more than attendance at these examinations. To do that his schoolwork had to demonstrate a specific level of knowledge and competence. The secondary school which had accepted him proved to be an adaptable institution and was particularly supportive of him. The staff found Lawrence a determined boy but racked with unspeakable anxiety. They desired above all to relieve him of this anxiety, at least sufficiently for him to succeed in his educational endeavours. So it was that he came to be referred to the local service where I worked.

Clearly the feeling that he was not and had never been wanted at home had weighed heavily on him, and I was struck by how precisely and succinctly this personal viewpoint was expressed in his first Mosaic. Despite the feeling of being a puppet in a relentlessly heartless environment, Lawrence must have found the inner resources to take advantage of whatever nurture the boarding school had provided and to fight his way back to a chance of normal living.

In his Mosaic portrait, he painted a realistic picture of his predicament, and yet, in his direct response to my first enquiries about his Mosaic, I could detect an element of steel in his character not yet evident in this Mosaic portrait. The making and the talking about his Mosaic together had, however, opened up a further, fuller dialogue. He now told me he was considered to be "slow" by normal academic standards. Nevertheless, he appreciated the help the teaching staff was offering him. It was plain to me that he had won over his teachers to the extent that they were prepared to go out of their way to help him arrive at the point of having a chance to succeed in his bid to sit his first examinations and even perhaps gain some academic qualifications. He explained that he wanted very much to use his time at the clinic to make his future viable. Over and again, he explained to me that the school was helping him to catch up in his studies so that he stood some chance of attaining sufficient marks for the school to make it possible for him to retake the subjects, should he not succeed at the first attempt. He needed to believe that it was also psychologically possible. He felt that if he could become less anxious, he could just do it. It was then borne in on me how vital it was to include the ensuing conversation as part of the subject's Total Response in order to appreciate fully an individual personality. It would give the full portrait of Lawrence in action. For my part, it would have been difficult for me fully to appreciate Lawrence as a person at our first meeting without also having the personal background information which had accompanied his referral.

For various reasons, usually due to the amount of school work he had to complete, he was unable to attend regularly or even very often. But we were both committed to this project. On his third visit, he drew a whale; at first it was very faintly outlined, but later, as he drew over the original lines, his pencil marks became bolder. As he drew, I ventured to say that whales were very interesting creatures. They mostly live deep in the ocean and they communicate with each other by means of sounds, but as a whole sentence for them would take a very long time in our way of thinking, they are thought by humans to be very, very, very slow indeed. That, however, is normal for whales. And I added that there are people who are naturally slow, just like these whales. For these people, being slow is just right for them, since that is how they are. I could see that Lawrence had taken in this metaphoric reference to our first conversation about him being slow, and I have never forgotten the smile he gave me then.

At his very next session some time later, his need to spend ever more time catching up on his schoolwork became paramount and we both realised that he would need to discontinue his treatment. The burden of examinations had loomed larger and larger in his consciousness. So we agreed that as he felt he had become already less hampered by anxiety and more able to carry on by himself, he would do a last Mosaic.

SKIER

Lawrence told me that this was a "skier" and that he was happy with what he had made. As a Personality in Action of himself, it had certain pointers to the changes within himself. It is quite obvious that this figure was more centrally placed and looked more solid. The head was framed by a "woolly hat, keeping the head warm". Lawrence was acknowledging the input from external reality in keeping him able to function. The face, though still white, is now more interestingly constructed with a side view, suggesting that the skier was at least looking in the same direction of any possible ski movement. He told me that the body was wrapped up in "ski-gear", which was his term for a ski-suit. He explained that he thought this sort of clothing enabled the skier to ski without putting himself in "danger of freezing". He remarked that "this", pointing to the ski pole in his hand, "was a bit short". I said that I thought it looked as though "this" was an extension of his hand and arm. We agreed that it was not as useful as it might have been. Perhaps I should have added that he has had to extend himself in order to have even a primitive ski pole in his hand, just as he had been extending himself academically throughout that school term. The skis are black, so are at least differentiated from his person, but when activated by the skier would carry him much further and faster than if the skier had had to walk down the snow-covered slope of the mountain. Although it was unclear whether the skier could move of his own volition or the skis were under his control, it seemed an element of hope, realistic or not, had been built into the image.

We were talking as though the skier was indeed a metaphor for Lawrence. To appreciate the precision with which this portrait had been painted, I will now fill in the background details at the time this Mosaic was created. The final report I received from his school related that Lawrence was making progress in his efforts to catch up, slowly it is true, but progress nevertheless. The school was impressed by the way Lawrence had organised his studies. This serious devotion to the task demanded single-minded application. Schoolwork took up all his time, in and out of school, and often he stayed on after school hours for help from his teachers. Thus it was that he felt and finally decided he could not spare the time to continue his attendance, which had already been erratic during the short time he had been coming to the clinic. So although there was progress, for Lawrence it was no miracle. Lawrence himself had largely contributed to his own progress. His Mosaic simply reflected where he was at the time of his making it.

Tragically, he had to leave the area before he could take his first examinations. The company his father had worked for, without any prior warning, transferred him to another branch of the company in a different part of the country, and the school lost contact with him. But that too is Life, and I occasionally still fall to wondering how he has fared since.

I realise that Lawrence does not strictly belong in this chapter. In my mind, Lawrence was neither a child nor an adolescent. He had no age. His personality shone through all the vicissitudes, all the adversities of his life and was for me truly unforgettable.

10   The use of Mosaics as an assessment tool

A ssessment is usually the starting point for a process with diverse possibilities. It is a term often used quite properly to cover the range of available options within the reality of local resources. Within the National Health Service in Britain, where a triage system is emerging, the practitioner will need to have at the back of her mind the kind of expertise available to meet the needs of the community. These may come down to the distribution of a certain number of referrals each week amongst a fixed number of professionals, and the time these professionals have available to take on ever more new cases.

Whilst there is never an ideal system, there is usually a wish for a better system. For the community at large, however, the children and families of it can only think of their own needs, their own pain. Assessment is not a matter of numbers for them. They simply want to be released from pain, to be able to face the future with some hope, for change for the better. Given that children and adolescents are occasionally referred because of the pain they are causing the adults around them, one of the main tasks is to bring the young person to see the point of the referral.

Martin is a good example of a reluctant client. He felt that his world was no different from his friends and contemporaries, many of whom had come from broken homes, some with multiple problems. He was certainly not going to be seen as a sissy, as someone who was not man enough to take life's knocks. He feared he would be a laughing stock if he was even seen near the vicinity of the community clinic, however bland the name the clinic had been given.

On the advice of her social worker, Martin's mother had taken him to his family doctor. His parents had separated when he was quite young, and ever since the birth of his brother, the youngest in the family, his mother had become increasingly physically disabled. Being disabled, she had to rely on all the children to help with the general work around the house, the shopping and cooking. She was now concerned that he was falling behind in his schoolwork and possibly playing truant with what she had heard were neighbourhood louts. Mindful of her inability to keep a parental eye on all that was going on, she sought help. Thus had Martin found himself with an appointment to see me. He was accompanied by his mother's social worker, perhaps the first indignity.

Even before he had seated himself, Martin protested against any necessity for him to "come to see a shrink". He did not want to talk, and had nothing to talk about. This was the kind of beginning I had become familiar with, so I inclined my head and began to introduce him to the Mosaics. He simply looked at me blankly. I started to play with the pieces myself, the very pieces I had used to show him the different colours and shapes. I put these away, whereupon he leant forward and picked out other pieces, quickly building up the figure in Mosaic 10.1.

Without prompting, he told me that it was a person. By then he seemed eager to explain. He said there were shoulder pads in the jacket, that people who wear such jackets feel big and that in turn made them feel great. I wondered whether he or his friends owned such clothing. He replied with a cheeky grin that he would like to. I wondered whether the person he had depicted could be how he would like to see himself. His grin widened.

I then pointed to the space down the middle and said that to me it looked like this person's body was split in half. He protested hotly that "it was a mistake", adding that he would make another one to show me what he had really meant to do. Leaving his first Mosaic to one side of him, I gave him another piece of paper on which to make his second Mosaic (10.2). Without a single glance at his finished Mosaic, he recreated the figure, carefully overlapping some white pieces with the blue.

Whilst acknowledging the difference, I pointed out the fact that the gap between the two sides of the body seemed now to be covered by white pieces and overlapped by the blue jacket; thus the effect was the same and was not affecting the split in the body underneath. Martin looked at his two Mosaics in silence for some time, and when he spoke, it was to ask a question: "Could I come a few times . . . just to see what happens?"

He came regularly and always on time. Though he came for a few sessions only, he used his time earnestly, and it seemed usefully, judging by his continuing interest. In fact his sessions enabled him to realise what his chief dilemmas were and why he was unable to move forward in life. He had questions concerning his personal standing amongst his peers as well as how to balance what he saw as his responsibilities towards his family and his need to become master of his own destiny.

At his very next session Martin raised the issue of the recent "March Against the Bomb" campaign. I was mildly surprised at his solemnity. I had underestimated his seriousness. We discussed the issues at length. Finally, Martin rocked back in his chair and then moved very slowly forward again, pausing before saying, "I've been on the march you know." It was then that I understood why he needed the shoulder pads in his jacket. The family lived in a tough neighbourhood, where the usual way for a young man to prove his manliness was to "act tough". This seemed to Martin to mean only one thing: he felt impelled to be acutely aware of the possibility of the term "sissy" being applied to him, and the overt way to avoid this charge was to behave "tough", to swagger, swear and be prepared to put up his fists. It was not something he could easily reconcile with his pacific nature. This had troubled him greatly. He was visibly relieved that he had now been able to air the issues in confidence. Martin felt then that he could find a way to "sort this out".

Martin's parents had been separated ever since he was a child in primary school. His father had grown impatient with his mother. All this he had gathered from his mother's point of view. Martin was unable to discover his father's reasons for leaving because he had not seen him for some time. He had moved away and had not been in touch with his family.

Not long after his father's departure, his mother fell ill and became increasingly incapacitated and unable to care for her family of two boys and a girl. Martin was the middle child. Nevertheless, he felt burdened with the care of the family. The time was about to come for his mother to go into community care. He felt his responsibilities towards his younger brother keenly, since his older sister was about to enter employment in another town. The family depended upon welfare benefits, but Martin felt that he, being the eldest male in the family, should be the one bringing in an income. It was also the prevailing culture of his neighbourhood.

As he grew into his adolescence, he increasingly felt the absence of his father. In Martin's mind, he was an image of a mature presence, and Martin wished for the possibility of an intimate masculine companionship in his life. They had both shared a love of fishing and football. At the moment he had no one to go fishing with, and none of his present family wanted to watch football. He had no close male relative to turn to for advice or support. To him, his situation seemed insoluble. In what was to be his final clinic session, his solution was modest but at last clear to him. He wanted to find his father and see if they could get back in touch. The split identified in the Mosaic was chiefly to do with his feeling of being torn in two between his sense of responsibility and loyalty towards his mother and siblings and his longing to have a real relationship with his father.

Once he became convinced that his wish to see his father was not in conflict with his ability to care adequately for his present family, Martin was able to see how to go about finding his father and finding help for his family. By freeing himself of the guilt of selfishness, as he saw it, he was finally able to pursue actively help for his family and ways for finding his father. Once he had seen what his task was, he had no need for further sessions. He felt he could manage his life by himself. Like Harry, he knew when it was time for him to stop. He knew then how to take the next step in his life.

Until Martin was convinced by evidence that he could not deny had come from himself, he did not feel free to seek help, and he would not have been able to take advantage of any help which the community had to offer. His own Mosaic was for him that evidence.

Readiness to face the problem is another feature which forms part of any assessment. This is where I have found the Mosaics to be invaluable. It was Nellie who brought this home to me.

Nellie was referred because to her parents and her school teachers she seemed to be an unhappy girl. Why else would she argue, complain or moan all the time? Nothing seemed right to Nellie. All the adults impressed upon me the fact that Nellie could be an attractive girl if only she could lose some weight; it might give her a less dour outlook on life. Although her parents were divorced, her mother considered that she was providing her three daughters with as good a home as any other single parent. Nellie admitted she got along reasonably well with her sisters, although they could be a pain. She got on less well with her father. Access was erratic, and she did not care for her stepmother. At school Nellie found her classmates friendly enough, and the staff seemed sympathetic. What then could account for her discontent?

From her point of view, however, she felt unhappy in herself and was at a loss to understand why. Our first meeting began with an exchange of words about the reason for her referral. After a short pause, she admitted that maybe she did have a bit of a weight problem, but it was not something she could not change if she wanted to. Anyway, she "doesn't really like boys that much". Nellie mentioned this as an afterthought, seeming thus to find a connection between her weight and an interest in boys. She could certainly be said to be "plump", but there were none of the signs of pubertal development; she was then nearly twelve years old and already in a secondary school, but her manner and behaviour were that of a much younger child.

Nellie seemed happy to do a Mosaic, however, leaning forward over the tray while taking her time to choose the pieces for her design.

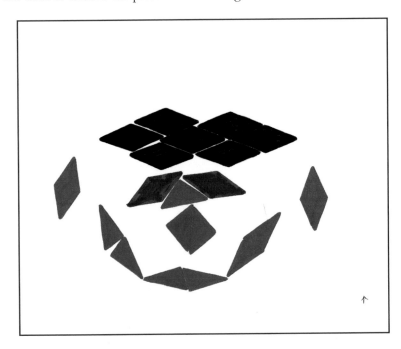

Mosaic 10.3
Readiness is all: Nellie's first Mosaic

She beamed over her "happy face", agreeing with me that it correctly reflected how she would like to feel about herself. I noted the hope rather than a fact. I wondered whether the face had a body attached. Nellie looked at her Mosaic for a moment before answering, "Yes". "There's no space to do the body," was the reason she gave for its absence. Without pausing, she went over the features of the face, showing me which shapes formed the eyes, the nose and the smiling mouth, and the black hair that framed them. "They were earrings, not ears," she said, in answer to my query. And "Yes, that's her, smiling, well, more like a broad grin," she clarified. I noted the change from a hope to a statement of fact. I wondered to myself about the absence of ears. Nellie was clearly communicating something about the ears. Since the face was now her face, was she at that point not wanting to hear anything I might have to say?

Before I could think of how to broach this issue, Nellie went on to tell me about the contents of her wardrobe, which sadly lacked all the sorts of clothes she would have liked to have. She described these missing garments in great detail, which took up the whole of the remainder of the session. She waved a friendly "goodbye" before leaving.

A further two meetings produced similar happy faces. There seemed no way to advance. I wondered what besides time could make a difference. After all, there was a long waiting list at the clinic. And I had not forgotten my experience with Keith. I suggested to her that perhaps it was time we had a review, to see if we were doing the right thing for her. Maybe she did not need to see me so often or even at all? Well, she was adamant, she was now quite content to get out of attending school and come to chat. Nellie did not seem to understand that she could do anything to ease her own unhappiness. I explained that this was a place for children who wanted things to change in their lives, who were unhappy with their lot in life, but who thought they would like to be helped to make the changes for themselves. The options at this point were to stop, continue or be referred for a different treatment, but I suggested that I could keep in touch, to see how she was getting on and she agreed to be reviewed at three-monthly intervals. The three-monthly interval was her choice.

Six months later, at our second review, Nellie wished to continue using the Mosaics and produced another "happy face". This one lacked any hair and had acquired some yellow eyebrows. She lingered in her Mosaic-making.

Mosaic 10.4
Readiness is all: Nellie's Mosaic at her second review

After a few minutes, but before we could look beyond the fact that it was another happy face or note the differences, Nellie decided we should go on to play a game of "Hangman". It was clear that she was not interested in the game as such. She seemed unaware of her limitations, nor was she interested in winning or losing. It became clear too that it was a way to pass the time. The choice of game was of interest to me, of course, and I had a thought, indeed a concern. And so this session passed, but it was necessary to put in place some safeguards. I explained the situation to a colleague and asked her if she could continue regular contact with Nellie's mother. I also contacted the school to ask the staff to keep a close eye on Nellie, to note and report any changes at school directly to me or to our service.

Since the heading for these faces had remained the same, clearly it was expressive of something important for Nellie. Perhaps she was trying on different masks for herself, assuming other personalities. Was she expressing a discontentment with herself, or had she come to a point in her life where she was wishing to explore other possibilities for herself? Was Nellie, whilst not willing to admit she wanted to change, actually not ready to look at what might have made the adults around her refer her to the community clinic? Was the Hangman game suggestive of something more sinister? As Nellie wanted to continue as agreed and did not want to change the frequency or times of her appointments, the case for reviews with alert external support was stronger than ever.

At the next review meeting, she began with a Mosaic as usual. At that point, neither her mother nor school had reported anything untoward. Nellie departed from her "happy face" for the first time. She took out some Mosaic pieces and made vertical strings of loose shapes down from the top of the tray to the bottom across the Mosaic tray surface. These were suddenly brushed aside, forming an untidy pile to the side of the tray. She wanted to do another Mosaic. This was clearly a new but dramatic departure.

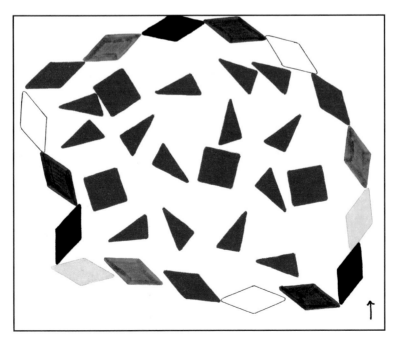

Mosaic 10.5
Readiness is all: Nellie's Mosaic of tears or love and happiness

This second Mosaic had begun as another "happy face" whilst she made the frame for it with some diamond pieces of different colours, but already there had seemed to be a different atmosphere in the room. I now began to look more carefully at her appearance. It looked as though she had hurriedly thrown on her clothes. Nellie now tried hard to settle down to her Mosaic as though there had been no interruption to her sequence of happy faces. For the first time, she lost her sure touch. She shook her head but continued putting pieces inside the circular frame. All the features of the face were made with the same colour, red, but in two different shapes, diamonds and squares. She continued to add more red pieces inside the ring of diamonds, and the circular frame itself expanded with extra diamonds, the colours carefully chosen to display the available range in the Mosaic box.

Nellie was unhappy about what the face had become. "An untidy mess," she muttered. I was unsure whether she was aware that this comment also reflected her appearance. She maintained that it was still a "happy face", but admitted that it "had gone wrong". She tried to smile her usual smile. I asked where it had gone wrong? To my surprise, she said she didn't know "how it had gone wrong" or "what had happened". She wanted to do something else, but could not think of an alternative activity or subject of conversation. Abruptly, she volunteered that her dieting was not working and whatever she did, she did not seem to be able to stop eating.

Gently I enquired whether it was now not a face at all but had become something else? I wondered what it might have become. Almost without a pause in the flow of the conversation, Nellie said that it looked like a "stomach". I responded by asking whether the red Mosaic pieces could be the contents of the stomach? Nellie nodded slowly but solemnly, then doubtfully pronounced the word "food". There was a long pause before she quietly added "tears". "Like the lines of Mosaics you brushed aside," I said and I pointed to what remained of her first Mosaic, the pile of Mosaics lying by the side of the one under present consideration. I then described to her the process of her first Mosaic, how she had made the strings of Mosaics down and across the tray, brushing them aside as one might have brushed tears aside.

I asked her whether she knew what symbols were. I explained, using my wedding ring as a symbol of marriage. She quickly grasped the idea. I then wondered what for her each of the six colours stood for, in particular the red. Her response was immediate. "Red is for Love and Happiness." I asked if she could imagine the outer ring of her Mosaic as a picture of her stomach and that there was this big space in the middle. At this point, she exclaimed, "That's it, it is like that." And I continued, saying, "All these red pieces are like the food you eat, all muddled up with your tears. Perhaps you eat because you feel unloved and feeling unloved makes you unhappy." As we continued to talk, she began to remove the red diamonds inside the frame of multi-coloured diamonds, replacing them with the much smaller shape, the scalene triangle. She left the session thinking that this time she might be more successful with her dieting, seemingly forgetting that she had only mentioned it for the first time during this session. She now seemed to me to be ready, but ready for what exactly I could not have predicted.

Despite an earnest desire to persist in her diet regime and to look further into herself, Nellie returned to playing out stories of happy families. It became evident to me that she had arrived at another impasse in herself. Outwardly she appeared to be progressing in the reality of her life. Schoolwork was beginning to claim more of her time. To be sure, the family and school had become accustomed to her moans. Her weight, however, stayed the same. Even she saw she was not really using her time profitably. She was now entering fully into her adolescence. We therefore agreed that perhaps she should stop coming. After all, she could always come back to the clinic if she felt we could be of further help. Some years later, by chance I learnt that she had indeed referred herself to a clinic for older adolescents, but this too had failed to engage her and after a short attendance she stopped attending there as well. This pattern was to be repeated, for as a young adult she continued to refer herself for therapy, but discontinued soon after starting.

Clearly I had something to learn from Nellie's case. It was now obvious that the presence of readiness was not all. Perhaps my skills or my judgement had been lacking, but then why had things gone in exactly the same way with other professionals using entirely different techniques? After reflection, I concluded that I had not considered fully one of the other features of the therapeutic use of the Mosaics, the Total Response. The recognition that the Total Response could give the observer a glimpse of the Mosaic-maker's "style of approach to life in miniature" had been missing in my thinking about Nellie. Using it, I eventually concluded that maybe Nellie had found it difficult to continue after an opening had been made. This start-stop style of approach to life seemed to characterize her, and perhaps become a way of life. Perhaps, but perhaps not. In the final analysis I could not rule out the presence of a blind spot in myself.

11   Two contrasting styles of working through similar presenting problems

In this chapter I would like to discuss the use of Lowenfeld Mosaics with children and adolescents in psychotherapy from the point of view of temperament and personality. The treatment of mental illness, including childhood mental illness, is usually processed through a diagnosis from the presenting symptoms. Diagnoses are normally categorised in terms of discrete syndromes, each with its own defining character. The temperament and personality of the referred child or adolescent seem not to be considered as an important dimension for the choice of treatment, or as an important factor in determining the success or failure of any given therapeutic treatment. In Britain, the decision for psychotherapy often hinges on the culture and variety of skills within the clinic team. So whether the clinic offers behavioural therapy, cognitive therapy, psychotherapy, drug treatment or a combination of these depends largely on what the team can collectively bring into the service. It has seemed an eminently sensible approach.

However, it will be evident from the Mosaics made by individual children or adolescents so far discussed that a uniqueness of personality is invariably displayed in their Mosaics and may have had a decisive impact on their eventual therapeutic outcome. Remembering the lessons that Keith and Nellie had taught me, I now wish to use two other examples to pay closer attention to the makers' distinctive style of Mosaic use in resolving similar problems during the course of their treatment. I shall focus mainly on their Mosaic work to illustrate their differing personalities in action. Of course, just as personalities are unique, no two circumstances can be exactly the same. So here I am merely referring to a broad category of distress caused to a child by being in the midst of family strife which is centred on the difficult marital relationship between the parents.

The first series of Mosaics was made by a fourteen-year-old boy named Oliver. Before being referred to me, Oliver had been seen at another clinic for family therapy with his parents and younger sister. He was the subject of that referral. He had felt increasingly picked on during the family sessions and began asking for individual psychotherapy for himself. Eventually, and after much pain and frustration felt by all during their family sessions, the family sessions ceased and he arrived in my consulting room full of grievances, saying the family had made him depressed.

As usual I presented Oliver with the Mosaics. The very first piece he picked out was a yellow equilateral triangle. A selection of red shapes was followed by some black and white pieces. He moved these about the tray space. Gradually, a pattern emerged which left certain pieces unused. He now declared that he had finished.

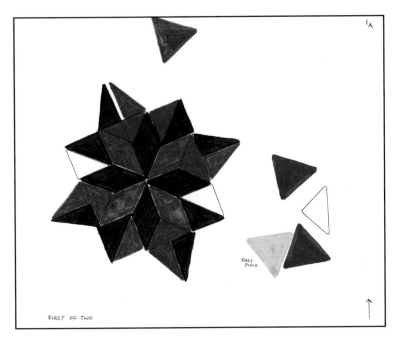

Mosaic 11.1
Oliver's first Mosaic

I asked Oliver to tell me something about his Mosaic. He said that he had noticed "a cross" in the middle of the pattern. In fact it was a red and black cross, intertwined within a square block. Using the vocabulary provided by Oliver, I wondered aloud what a cross reminded him of, if anything. His reply was imme-diate: "Jesus." I remarked that I knew that Christians believed that Jesus was cruci-fied on a cross, that He had died for the sins of the world and that He was considered to be the Saviour of mankind. This produced an astonishing explosion of anger from Oliver. When he could finally speak more calmly, he said, "I'm blamed for everything at home." "What sort of things?" I asked. He gestured expansively before answering: "For things disappearing." After a short pause, he rather sheepishly admitted that he did sometimes take things, but had not done so on all the occasions of which he had been accused. I responded with another ques-tion: "So you feel a little like Jesus, being blamed for everything that disappears or maybe even for all the things which go wrong at home?" His back straightened as he emphatically agreed.

At this point, I referred back to his Mosaic. I said that I remembered his first piece had been this yellow triangle there. "Oh," he replied, "that doesn't belong in the pattern." I then drew his attention to the gap between the two scalene triangles, one black and the other red, asking him to tell me about this part of his Mosaic. (I had noted that Oliver had carefully created this gap.) "They look like horns," he said softly, as though to himself, but loud enough for me to hear. I now pointed out to him that he was dressed in red and black, the same colours as his pattern. He grinned at me and added, "It would have been better if there had been more colours." "Would you like to do that now?" I asked, deliberately leaving it vague as to what he was to try to do.

He hesitated for a moment before asking to have "another go". Given a clean piece of paper on a separate tray, he began with a yellow equilateral triangle, the very colour shape he had said did not "belong". He began to build on this triangular piece, using first three black isosceles triangles followed by four black diamonds, then three yellow diamonds. Oliver elaborated on this design further with a few blue and green pieces, finally ending with some red and black shapes.

Mosaic 11.2
Oliver's second Mosaic in the first session

This design began almost at the exact same spot where Oliver had started his first Mosaic, and he had again picked a yellow equilateral triangle as his first piece, but this time he was able to integrate it into the heart of his design. This was elaborated into a yellow and black three-sided figure, which extended outwards at the three points created by a pair of yellow and black diamonds. Without any prompting, Oliver told me it was "a face with horns; in other words, the Devil". I replied that it seemed that using all the colours had changed Jesus into the Devil. Oliver continued to enlarge upon his description of this Devil. Pointing to the black and red equilateral triangles enclosed by the two red scalene triangles at the bottom of the figure, he said there were also some "bared teeth". He now confirmed that the yellow, black, blue and green colours comprised the face, whilst the horns and bared teeth were in red and black. Thus black was the common colour for all the features named so far. I had noted that Oliver was dressed all in black that day, but before I could say anything, he went on to say he had "not succeeded in integrating the colours very well". At this point, he stood up as the clock on the wall was indicating that the session had come to an end.

Oliver had been reported by the school as a bright pupil, if rather argumentative at times. He was perceived to be the kind of pupil whom teachers find "challenging". He tended to dissipate his intellectual energies in producing obscure but erudite witticisms which entertained his classmates and occasionally severely embarrassed his teachers. Although he was doing quite well at school, he was likely to be one of the pupils of whom teachers would write "could do better" on his end-of-year report. It had crossed my mind that Oliver was beginning to have a sense of himself as lacking in something, which for the moment was being identified as having "not succeeded in integrating the colours very well".

On his next visit, before he was fully inside the room, Oliver asked if he could do another Mosaic, "to try to integrate all the colours". This had clearly been in his mind since the end of his first session and had now become his main aim.

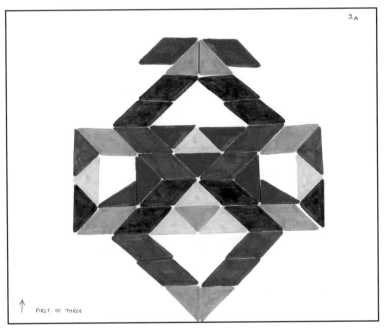

Mosaic 11.3
Oliver's second attempt at integrating the colours

Starting with a red and a yellow isosceles triangle as the centre of his Mosaic, Oliver built up this design in a deliberate attempt at symmetry, whilst weaving the inverted squares through an oblong in the middle of the design. A Cruciform pattern had subtly surfaced again. I also noted the flattened effect of the two red diamonds, in contrast to the "horns" of his previous Mosaics. Before I could comment on this, Oliver said he was dissatisfied with what he had just made. A pause ensued. Since the major puzzle that Oliver had set himself to solve had been to "integrate the colours", I now suggested that he might like to explore each colour in turn and see what happened. He took the idea up with some enthusiasm.

I asked which colour he would like to begin with. Without a moment's hesitation, he said, "Red," and proceeded to make a "red heart".

Mosaic 11.4
Oliver's red heart

Oliver's face was suffused with a softness I had not seen before. "Could you tell me something about this red heart? What does a red heart mean?" I asked him. He replied that it meant "caring for people; people I'm very close to; [and] people I love". I asked him to write these phrases on his Mosaic. I wanted him to savour this moment of a feeling, a feeling that I felt had not often been publicly expressed by Oliver, and so I asked him to write the three phrases on this Mosaic of his. I had thought that writing these words would help him physically to integrate the moment, that feeling with the Mosaic picture of a red heart with all the resonance this image had for him. As he was writing, Oliver began to enlarge upon those three statements, speaking with warmth and affection about his family and his new girlfriend.

There was a brief pause before he told me he would like to use "black" next, and with that remark he made the "skull and crossbones", Mosaic 11.5.

For him, this Mosaic in black, signified "death, pirates and danger". He looked quite startled by his own words, and when we began to explore the meaning of this representation, he seemed ready to mention that he had often thought of death in association with danger. The excitement of facing the ultimate danger seemed a thrilling notion, and he had imagined himself meeting the challenge of potholing, of not being buried in death, but alive to all the dangers below ground.

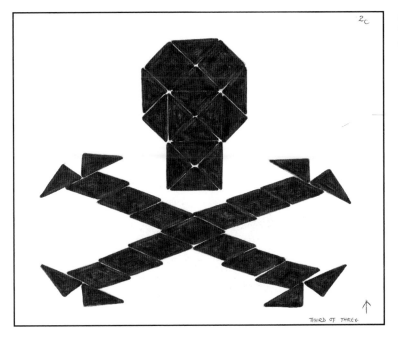

He was not certain how "pirates" came into this idea. Eventually, I referred to his confession of having taken things from members of the family.

The expression on Oliver's face changed suddenly. He looked as though he was about to protest at what he later termed my "accusation", but remained silent, perhaps remembering that I had said no more than what he had himself confessed to during his first visit. At a later session, it emerged that he had been aware of the tension that had existed between his parents for a long time, but there seemed no way anyone in the family would or could acknowledge this deepening pain. He felt the frustration turning into anger, which often led to what amounted to unnecessary provocation in a family situation. This was the real cross he felt he had to bear.

On this occasion, he decided he would use "yellow" for his next Mosaic. He remained still for a while before his right hand began to hover over the box in an attempt to choose the particular piece to start his yellow Mosaic. After a while these hand movements slowed to a halt and we both sat and waited. The minutes ticked by. In the end, I broke the silence with a suggestion. Perhaps we could try some other way of working? It was time to end the session in any case, and we agreed we would start differently on his next visit.

After some sessions of working through the medium of the World Technique or Sandplay, during which one of the main issues explored was the pain caused to him by the discord between his parents, he announced on arrival one day that he thought it was time for him to stop attending the clinic. He thought he could now manage on his own, that if there was any further work to be done, he could do it by himself.

I said that in that case perhaps he would do one last Mosaic for me? He did, and Mosaic 11.6 below is the result.

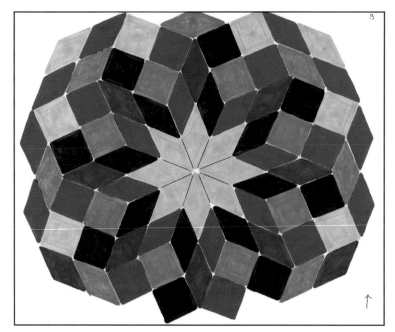

This Mosaic showed me that indeed he was ready to stop. Recalling his first discarded yellow equilateral triangle, which he had said "did not belong in the pattern", and his subsequent inability to use it at all, the solid yellow centre round which his last Mosaic was built was all the confirmation I felt I needed. He had felt he was in a triangular tussle between his parents. Perhaps this was why the yellow triangle could not "belong in the pattern". Oliver had now found a way to step out of this triangle. Being able to disentangle himself from his parents' problems with their relationship, but feeling also more confident that he could have the possibility of a steady relationship with his girlfriend, had finally enabled Oliver to make his own life centred on himself. He started his last Mosaic with a four-sided figure, the yellow diamond, and created a yellow centre that radiated towards the edges of the tray.

This Mosaic conveyed both an outward movement and a firm anchoring to the centre. It took full advantage of the tray space. It also demonstrated Oliver's ability to tolerate the fact that he would not be able to complete the gestalt of the pattern if he did not want the design to overlap the bottom edge of the tray. Oliver preferred to omit the green diamond so that the pattern could not be truly symmetrical, thus favouring containment within the tray space. Smiling with quiet satisfaction, he looked at me as though he knew I would understand. Perhaps I did, but I did agree that he could stop attending the clinic.

Peter, whose chief problem also lay in the disharmony between his parents, was both younger than Oliver, being only ten years of age at his referral, and came from a personal background where, at the time, his parents were already physically living apart. Since their separation, the parents' relationship had continued to be acrimonious, and Peter persisted in being the subject of their quarrels. Like Oliver, he was the eldest in a family of four, but his sibling was a boy who seemed to do no wrong in his parents' eyes. Both the mothers in these two families professed great concern for their sons, and it was their fathers who seemed to have been most angry with their respective sons. Both fathers had perceived their sons to be a primary cause of the discord in their marital relationship with their wives. In fact, Peter's father had gone so far as to lay the major blame for the breakdown of the marriage and his consequent dislike of Peter on his "soiling".

The father's treatment of Peter was harsh in the extreme, attacking the very core of his son's dignity. He used to get so exasperated with Peter that he would rub his son's face with his soiled pants. Naturally Peter was reluctant to visit his father, and the issue of access was becoming a serious matter, and was likely to lead to court proceedings. The father suspected Peter's mother of denying him access because he thought she did not like the idea of Peter seeing this very disagreeable man, who might unduly exert the wrong kind of influence on her son. The mother meanwhile believed that her husband was trying to use Peter's "soiling" as a way of excusing himself from his responsibility for his son. No one seemed to be able to see Peter's suffering. Both parents believed they were doing their best to promote Peter's welfare.

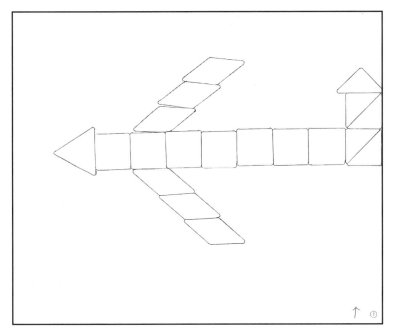

Mosaic 11.7
Peter's white aeroplane

On his first visit to see me, Peter made an all-white aeroplane. The only shape he did not use was the scalene triangle. It was a recognizable representation of an aeroplane. Remembering Keith, I noted the position the aeroplane occupied on the right side of the tray, leaving space for the possibility for it to move forward. When I asked him to elaborate on his white aeroplane, Peter told me that this reminded him of a story involving a murder on a Boeing 747 aeroplane, connecting this detail with a recent trip abroad his grandmother had made in a similar aeroplane. There was just a hint of fear in the feeling of this description, and I was also left in doubt as to whether this aeroplane would indeed want to move forward, although the possibility of it being able to do so remained.

On his next visit a week later, Peter created a "freight-carrying steam train" with a carriage attached to a truck, both with black wheels standing on the rails. Despite its freight-carrying status, Peter hastened to let me know that there were passengers inside the train, with luggage piled high on top of the carriage. I was to imagine both the people and the luggage in the picture. It seemed clear that although it was not obvious to the outside world at large, Peter had wanted me to know what the train was really carrying inside, a burden of people with all their baggage. It immediately set up a psychological resonance in my own mind. Was Peter telling me in this Mosaic that the portrait of himself he had painted showed someone who was having to carry other people's burdens within him?

Although he had used several colours in the squares to depict the train and rails, he had instructed me to colour all the train carriage squares in red, and all the squares used for the rails in blue. In reality, he had used a selection of differently coloured squares for the train and track, and no reds were actually used for the track, but blue squares did go to form the body of the carriages. This was the first indication that Peter had a sense of independence beyond what he was yet prepared to show. After all, by his use of the four white isosceles in his previous picture of the aeroplane, he had shown he could have made further red squares using isosceles triangles. By getting me to colour the carriage and the truck red, the final image gave a strong coherent picture, especially the solid nature of the steam train.

Furthermore, he had felt able to make use of me, to use me to help him achieve his aim. Within a week of starting therapy, Peter had begun to move.

Mosaic 11.9
Peter's passenger ship

On the next occasion, a week later, Peter depicted a "passenger ship". It was the first Mosaic in which he used all the shapes, but he stayed with the three colours of red, blue and black. Since the very first Mosaic, Peter had demonstrated an increasing awareness of the possibilities in the Mosaics. Inevitably it was a very idiosyncratic view.

This third form of transport completed a range of carriers which covered movement on land, sea and in the skies. It was of interest to me that Peter had not as yet shown a mode of transport which was more usually self-directed, like the car. The aeroplane, train and passenger ship were all built to carry large numbers of people. Although luggage was mentioned, this was clearly associated with personal use and only tangentially with commercial goods.

Referring to the solid ring of red scalene triangles in the present Mosaic, Peter told me it was "a wheel to save people who might have fallen into the rough ocean", so singling out the safety feature of the passenger ship, with the implication of care and thoughtfulness from those whose job it was to look after the passengers. This seemed to reinforce the notion I had in the previous week, that Peter was depicting himself as "someone who was having to carry other people's burdens within him" and to ensure that they were protected from suffering.

He did not offer any further information before going off to play with some miniature cars housed in the toy cabinet. This had been his activity following the making of his first three Mosaics, but it was not an organised activity. At the time, his play with these cars had no comprehensible sequence. It was the play of a much younger child. When Peter had left and whilst I was reproducing his Mosaic, I realised that Peter's use of the colours blue and red, had specific meanings. The significant features of his Mosaics were always highlighted in red and referred to in our discussions, whereas the blue remained a colour to be manipulated to give the picture a particular image. It was this aspect of the carrier of passengers that needed to be rearranged. Did the colour blue refer in any way to the people whom he felt might need to be emotionally bolstered up? These thoughts remained in me, requiring further evidence that would either contradict or confirm the idea, which could ultimately only come from Peter himself.

Mosaic 11.10
Peter's first symmetrical pattern

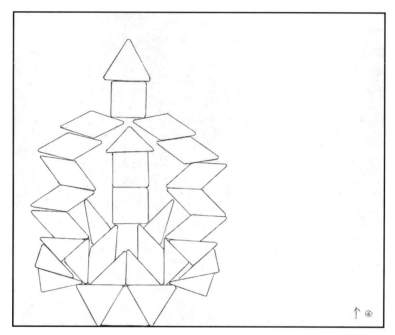

The next sequence of four Mosaics occurred after a gap of six months, during the sessions of which Peter also developed his play with cars. A new theme emerged. He departed from representational Mosaics and began to create what he called "symmetrical patterns", usually ones round a vertical axis. Like his very first Mosaic, Peter used all white pieces, but this time in all its forms. This was to be a strong indication of the link between his first and this next series of Mosaics.

To ensure the symmetry in this Mosaic, Peter always picked up a matched pair of shapes and placed them both simultaneously down on the tray. The Mosaic (11.10) was built up from the bottom edge of the tray, resting on the points of two white equilateral triangles. It can be seen that his very first Mosaic of this sequence was firmly on the left side of the tray, leaving a blank space on the right side entirely unmarked as well as unremarked. I only realised that he had not spoken until he had moved on to playing with cars again. The process was reminiscent of his very first Mosaic, that of the white aeroplane. A new phase had undoubtedly begun, marking new developments in the therapy.

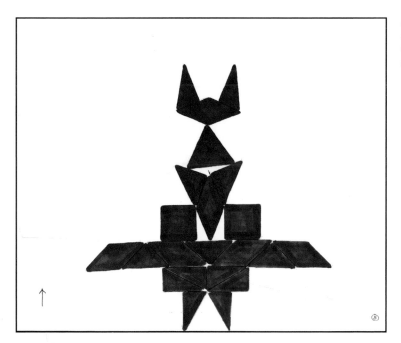

Peter's next Mosaic (11.11), which was done at the session following the white symmetrical pattern, was also said to be a symmetrical pattern at first, but was placed centrally and again rested on the bottom edge of the tray, this time on the points of two scalene triangles. It was all made with one colour, blue, but again Peter had used all the five shapes to create this design. He now introduced the idea of the possibility of two points of view. From one side of the tray in its landscape position, the side he had built the Mosaic (11.11) from, Peter explained to me, one could see a picture of "a plane" flying straight up, and here (indicating with his hand) was "a cat" perched above, on the plane's nose. It looked to me as though the cat might have blocked the pilots' view.

If it was looked at "upside down" (Mosaic 11.12), Peter continued swiftly, turning the tray round for my benefit, what had been the cat was now "a man" and the plane had become "a boat". The plane was carrying the cat in the first view, and the man was up in the air carrying the boat.

Retrospectively, the two sides had been prefigured in the previous Mosaic by its position to one side of the tray, the blank side being perhaps suggestive of a vacant space awaiting occupation. The blank side was perhaps even "whiter" than the aeroplane. From the Total Response perspective, the aeroplane seen from another point of view became a boat. This was a further reference to his first series of Mosaics where these two modes of transport had first been depicted. We now had an expanded notion of the meaning of the boat and aeroplane. It had first been a passenger ship, carrying people and luggage. And in all the first series of people carriers, the people were never seen, thus now the blank space to the side of the pattern had an added meaning. In this Mosaic, a man was pictured as carrying the boat. Furthermore, the man in midair is unsupported, whilst himself supporting

the boat. It gave a very powerful image of the reverse of what the first ship was said to be doing. Here the safety feature of the red wheel is also missing, pointing up further the contrast to the precarious position of the man in this Mosaic.

Coming to the cat, in the first point of view of Peter's Mosaic, the cat had now become a man. The cat had been carried at the head of the aeroplane as though it was the driving force. Now the cat had become a man, in a supportive role but from an unsupported position. If he was the driving force, it was from behind or below the boat. His task was made that much more difficult for his force being exercised from behind or below instead of leading from the front. Peter had depicted a truly upside-down world to the one first presented. Perhaps Peter was beginning to realise that nothing in his world was quite as straightforward as it at first might have seemed. In this Mosaic, Peter seemed to be exploring his inner self, the meaning of energy as a force which leads from the front or drives from behind, and the meaning of energy as used in support and whether the supportive force required support in return.

Nevertheless, it also heralded the first introduction of living creatures into this world. Viewed from above, in an aspect of the Total Response, all four subjects can be seen simultaneously: the aeroplane and the boat, the cat and the man. I had now been vouchsafed a deepening sense of what the colour blue meant to Peter. Viewed from this perspective, the simultaneous presence of all these elements, which were so clearly pictured in this Mosaic, and the multidimensional nature of the five Mosaics in terms of ideas and the use of colour and space across the space and time of the making of them, suddenly illuminated a rich picture of Peter's Personality in Action.

Peter's third Mosaic of this series was again a symmetrical pattern. It was a deliberate attempt to reproduce a totally centralised symmetrical pattern, the base of which continued to be anchored by points. Having expressed the complexity involved in giving recognition to the presence of two points of view within one symmetrical design, Peter now felt the need to reconcile the two sides. This was dramatically demonstrated in his very first action. Faced with the tray in its usual landscape position, with a sweeping gesture he firmly turned the tray round from a landscape to a portrait position, emphasising for me the idea of the Personality in Action in Mosaic-making. For the first time Peter was active in changing a given external circumstance. Previously, in terms of his Mosaic-making, he had always asked me to achieve the changes, as for instance in his asking me to colour in some pieces in another colour than the actual Mosaic piece he had chosen. This had the effect of reducing the flamboyant multicoloured nature of the actual Mosaic he had produced, but enhanced the meaning he wished it to convey. He had the idea or the wish, but external circumstances had prevented him from achieving them. Peter needed help to effect those changes. Now he could do it for himself.

After this striking departure from his norm, Peter embarked on introducing an entirely new colour, yellow, into his Mosaic vocabulary. His expressive repertoire was expanding in several dimensions. At the same time, his play with cars had become more coherent. Using the whole of the playroom floor space, Peter had been developing a tale depicting a chocolate-making factory that delivered its products by boat down a river that wended its way to the sea, encountering all manner of adventures and obstacles. On this occasion, the boat had somehow become destabilized, capsized and discharged the load prematurely. The load was scattered and carried along by the current into the sea, spreading the chocolate far and wide. This enabled me at last to make some reference to his soiling. It had already been reported to me that his soiling had become less frequent, and generally his mother was finding him less difficult to manage after his regular visits to his father. At last he was beginning to be able to articulate a problem that had been central to his expression of his thoughts and feelings regarding the bitter relationship between his parents and the way he had been blamed for having caused this rift.

It was not a simple matter of using first the cars roaming around unmarked routes along the playroom floor, then graduating to this very graphic image of the passage of faecal matter from the body into the external world. It was also the timing of these stories in parallel with the work with Mosaics, revealing the whole complex nature of his problem being worked on simultaneously using different expressive materials. Peter was beginning to integrate those earlier experiences, their meanings and their consequences in his personal life.

In his next Mosaic, Peter returned to the theme of two points of view within one Mosaic, continuing to flesh out this idea. For the first time he was able to use all the colours in one Mosaic, and to let those colours stand. He took time and care to create this Mosaic.

When he had finished, Peter began by telling me that this Mosaic represented two points of view, which he acknowledged he had done once before. On this occasion it would be different. In this Mosaic, each half of the Mosaic would

Mosaic 11.14
The theme of two points of view in one Mosaic again

represent one view, but only when it became the top half, so that when the picture was turned, the top half would then represent the second point of view. So in the Mosaic (11.14) as first constructed, the blue and black part alone would represent one view. It was a picture of a face framed with long blue hair. Peter pointed out the facial features, all delineated with black scalene triangles, the eyes, the nose, ending with the "black earrings, like Mummy's". All this accompanied by a smile. I had noted the absence of ears, but Peter would not be drawn into further discussion or indeed provide any more information about this half of his Mosaic. Peter did, however, explain that his mother seemed to be mostly enjoying life with her new partner and that she liked to look pretty.

Mosaic 11.15
The theme of two points of view in one Mosaic again inverted

Before we could develop a dialogue about this, Peter swiftly turned the tray round as though to change the subject. From this second point of view (Mosaic 11.15), Peter told me, the yellow and red depicted two birds on a branch with blossom. Again he would not be drawn into further conversation about this half of the Mosaic. I did not even get a chance to find out which Mosaic tiles had been used for the birds, and which for the branch with the blossom. Peter was clearly in charge of the conduct of the session, for he got out of his chair and went to draw on the chalkboard, and then suggested he used the World material instead. His play with cars or stories about the chocolate factory had now moved on. But no new theme had yet emerged. We were to be in this state of uncertainty for a while.

Four months later, the first Mosaic (11.16 overleaf) relating directly to his own reality appeared.

This Mosaic, Peter told me, showed an aerial view of a passenger boat on its way back to England from the Isle of Wight, which in reality was quite a short

Mosaic 11.16
Peter's aerial
view of a
passenger
boat on a
short trip

journey. At least we were now back to the familiar territory of a passenger boat. One of the blue scalene triangles was "the Captain", but Peter could not be specific about which. "It was an aerial view, so things were seen from far away," he explained. There were people talking, and the black pieces represented falling rain. He further divulged the fact that he had been on holiday with his father in the Isle of Wight a while ago and this Mosaic was a pictorial representation of their return journey. This idea of an aerial perspective was a neat device to put a distance between him and the feelings that that journey now evoked in him. For the first time he brought his father into a conversation with me.

I asked Peter whether I could start to draw round and colour his Mosaic rather than wait until after the end of his session. He replied by asking me a question. Could he give me a hand in colouring his Mosaic? I readily agreed and used the time together to converse beyond the Mosaic, to talk to him about his father.

Whilst helping me to colour his Mosaic, he had introduced some non-Mosaic features. Peter had altered the image imposed by the Mosaic shapes. He was showing me that he was no longer entirely subject to the will of others or his environment. This simple acceptance of his request to help had given me an important insight into the strength of his character as well as his present state of mind. I thought that it augured well for ending treatment in the near future.

I was to be proved wrong yet again. Peter had another idea. He was not ready to stop his clinic sessions. During the next year, Peter began to tell me more about his school life, how he was now enjoying his lessons and able to keep up with his schoolwork. He had also developed a new extra-curricula skill, having acquired a skateboard for his birthday. It was a joint present from his parents. He told me that his access visits had become more amicable, that his father seemed to be more interested in him and what he had been doing in and out of school. His father seemed to have stopped quizzing him about his mother and what happened at home. He now also had a new partner, who seemed to Peter to be at least pleasantly tolerant of his presence. Clearly the emotions surrounding his external circumstances had greatly changed. Consequently, Peter's energy had been largely freed to get on with the job of living, to explore the twin worlds of work and play.

But this was not quite enough for Peter. At the end of this year, he asked to do another Mosaic.

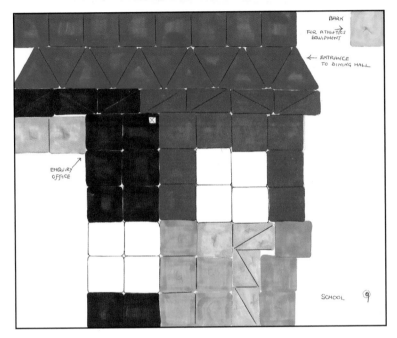

Mosaic 11.17
Peter's plan of his school

Peter started with the black square, here marked with a cross, and worked downwards, adjusting the pieces so that the black and white column of squares rested firmly on the bottom edge of the tray. In total silence, he worked round this column, filling almost the entire tray. Peter had not told me what he was making, and I was imagining that it could be a picture of a house, but naturally I put this idea aside and hoped I would be enlightened later. Peter ended with a yellow square in the top right corner of the tray. The sun, I thought, but wisely continued to keep my own counsel.

Peter looked up and announced that it was a plan of his school. He insisted that I should write down verbatim his descriptions of various features of the school which had special significance for him. It was again an aerial view, this time of the school building set in its grounds. He took me on a tour. He started with the first black square, the "*enquiry office*" in the angled corner of the school building, which led into or out from the school building to the school yard immediately in front of the entrance into the school. The different coloured squares were the classrooms separated either by corridors or screens. The blue equilateral triangle was the entrance to the "*dining hall*", here represented by all the blue Mosaics. And lastly, the yellow square was the "*barn where all the athletics equipment was kept*". So much for my ideas of what it was all about.

Nevertheless, it gave us an opportunity to talk over his Mosaic and its meaning to him. The "enquiry office" was our point of entry. He had come to the clinic not only because he was troubled, but because he was also curious about himself as a person. His school was Peter's first point of entry into a world radically different from that of his warring parents. For the first time he had a point of reference that contrasted in important ways with what he had known about adults and children. This revelation had given him hope as well as a dilemma. How to reconcile these two worlds? When the parents finally became physically separated, and their animosity continued between them, Peter had an additional irreconcilable puzzle in his mind. He now had two contrasting worlds, the one between the different worlds of his parents, who could not seem to cooperate so far as he was concerned, and the world where adults and children seemed largely to agree about the aims of their life together, the adult to teach, the child to study, in an environment (the school) where both could learn together.

The nurturing aspect of his school life was expressed through the entire Mosaic. Peter specifically singled out the aspects of school life which he felt were important for him: the classroom, where his mind was enriched (depicted first in his Mosaic); the nourishment of the body, here specially pointed up by "entrance to", and then the "dining hall"; and lastly the "barn where all the athletics equipment was kept". The "dining hall" symbolised the food that maintained and sustained personal growth, and the barn the possibility of exercise to maintain physical health. These were all the things he had found to be in stark contrast to how he experienced his life in the two parental homes. Now that the situation between his parents seemed to Peter to have improved, he felt he was able to take a more dispassionate look at what it was at school that was missing at home, his two homes, where other adults seemed to view the nurture he received as the norm. I now recalled that the colour blue had been earlier associated with the man and the boat as well as the cat and the plane, and also the hair that framed his mother's face. And the yellow was the colour Peter had used to achieve a fully balanced symmetrical pattern.

Some time after making this Mosaic, it was reported to me that a family friend had asked Peter why he came to see me; he had replied, "I went for *me*, for *myself*." And indeed it was not until this was achieved to his satisfaction four months later, as demonstrated by his last Mosaic, that he felt he was ready to terminate his visits to the clinic.

Peter strode confidently into the room and requested to do a Mosaic. He began by folding the Mosaic paper into two halves. He then built the two figures from the paper join between them, each figure holding the other's hands. He only had to make minor adjustments at the beginning of the process to accomplish the perfect balance between the figures, both in terms of the space each occupied and in relationship to the centre of the tray. Without any prompting Peter told me that it was a picture of "Me, myself". He felt he now could be himself wherever he was,

Mosaic 11.18
Peter's self-portrait entitled "Me, myself"

at home with his mother, at home with his father, and at school amongst his friends. His "soiling" had ceased by then and Peter was reported to be enjoying his visits to his father's household whilst feeling secure at the home he shared with his mother and brother. His academic achievements had proved enduring, and he had been welcomed into the school's athletics team. Peter knew it was now time for him to stop coming to see me. How could I argue with his Mosaic, or indeed with Peter himself?

Oliver's and Peter's differing ways of working through what they perceived as their problems, whilst unique to them as individuals, also demonstrate some common features. Throughout the whole of their treatment process, the contrasting ways in which Oliver and Peter handled the Mosaics in structuring each of the Mosaic products, along with the dissimilar ways each had perceived the treatment task, have been noted. Having analysed each of their Mosaics in some detail, I would now like to conclude with an analysis of their Mosaics through their use of shape and colour in their singular ways of portraying how the conflict between their parents had impacted on them.

From the very first Mosaic, Oliver and Peter each expressed the conflict caused by their parents' unresolved marital problems through both their use of colour and shape. Oliver used the four-sided red and black diamonds in his portrait of himself as Jesus, with all that that implies, being blamed for his part in disturbing the equanimity of the family of two parents and two children and for the points of view of the family of four, with just a hint of the devilish horns, cleverly using the three-sided red and black scalene triangles (with three unequal sides) to suggest not only his part in a triangular relationship with the parents, but also the fact of the three different personalities involved.

Peter, however, began to depict an aeroplane with a single colour, white, and cleverly exploited four of the five shapes (leaving out the scalene triangle). His subsequent representations were also transport carriers of people, and his internal image was massed through the colours red and blue, although he was to use all the colours in his construction of the steam train and passenger boat. Thus Peter's use of colour over the Mosaic's shapes was a definite statement to create a sense of mass rather than a lack of ability to exploit the relational aspect of the shapes of the Mosaic pieces. It was also clear that he wished to create pictures of people-carrying vehicles on land, sea and in the air. In the first series of Mosaics, Peter had also identified three as an important number. However, after the first Mosaic, the reference to three is more comprehensive, in the number of transport carriers pictured, in the colours black, red and blue as being the colours 'used' to be placed on record for these images which, unlike the aeroplane, were grounded on the earth. The white used for his aeroplane in his first Mosaic bore a different significance. White used on a white background suggested in his case an as yet unknown personality. That was his first question, "Who am I?" that was only answered with his final Mosaic, also in three colours, that of red, yellow and black.

Oliver dealt with the issue of the threesome by using the equal-sided equilateral triangle as the first piece in his second Mosaic, starting with a shape and colour he first said "did not belong to the pattern" and which subsequently he could not use at all, the yellow equilateral triangle. The equilateral triangle is the only three-sided figure which has all its sides equal in length. It was his way of showing the equal tension, the tug of war that existed in the relationship between himself and his parents. Oliver eventually resolved this by accepting the colour yellow fully into the heart of his final Mosaic, using the four equal sides of the diamond. Oliver continued to move more directly between the family and the triangular contexts until his last Mosaic, where all the Mosaic pieces used were now four-sided. This time, the equality of length signified the equality of balance. He achieved his own equilibrium by placing the relationships firmly in the family of four, or in the balance between the parental pair and that of the bond then existing between his current girlfriend and himself.

All this had been prefigured in Oliver's very first Mosaic. The Cruciform he produced there, noted by Oliver as a "cross", had summed up this intertwined conflict (the intertwining of the red and black crosses encased in a solid square at the centre of his Mosaic had joined these two issues in his representation of the "cross" and the reference to "Jesus") as the nub of his problem. Oliver's solution was unique to him but his expression of it in a Cruciform Mosaic was also a common expression in adolescence.

Being pre-pubertal, Peter's solution was also age-appropriate. He was much more clearly the child between his embattled parents, fearing that he might indeed have been the cause of his parents' marriage breakdown. Peter not only had to tread more carefully, but he felt a stronger need to understand each parent's point of view and how that might have impacted on him and the present unhappiness amongst the three of them. His brother hardly seemed to figure in his thinking and feeling. Additionally, Peter's view of his world sharpened with his entry into school and the subsequent separation of his parents. The contrast between the worlds presented to him of home and school escalated into one particularly painful crisis for Peter, a moment of utter humiliation and indignity. This may be why it took Peter longer to be confident that he had now found "Himself", which was also a sign of his self-belief in his own worth. He now felt assured that he could be "Himself" in any situation that he found himself.

I find the most striking features of their two personalities to be their distinct character and temperament, which were displayed from the moment each put down the first Mosaic piece on the tray. Each displayed an individual style of approach to their Mosaic-making during the Mosaic process and each resolved their problems through a series of Mosaics with a recognisable personal signature.

Lowenfeld's distinctive contribution was her belief in the utter uniqueness of the individual, their personality and their feelings and thoughts about their personal experiences, so that the defining meaning of the communication lies with the communicator not the listener. It is that view, the meaning of the statement to the communicator rather than its interpretation from someone else's theory, which needs to be heard. And a helpful and usable solution has to be something the communicator finds possible to adopt, which is what defines it as a solution.

12   The touchstone of experience and expression: Mosaics made by two pre=lingually deaf persons

When my children were infants, and long before they could utter any recognisable words, I was intrigued by their intense curiosity in the world around them. Their eyes gazed keenly at any new object, their hands waving busily towards it, and later grasping it with eagerness. This was so with both my daughter and my son. Although in other ways they were clearly very different personalities, they had this in common.

At the start of my child and adolescent psychotherapy training at Lowenfeld's Institute of Child Psychology, those images returned to me as I watched the children handle the toys when making Worlds or manipulating the coloured shapes whilst making a Mosaic. There was the same intense concentration and eager absorption in the task, one involving mainly their eyes and their hands. The similarity was unmistakable. This observation was so striking that I began to wonder whether there were any underlying principles that governed both the developmental phenomena and my observations of these children using play techniques in their therapeutic work. I re-read Lowenfeld's *Play in Childhood* (1991) and her theoretical work, now partly gathered in her *Selected Papers* (2004b). However, it was only after many years of clinical practice that I understood more fully that it was by using our senses, our sensorial experience, that human understanding of the world within and without us is achieved.

Quite early on in my work as a therapist, and whilst continuing to collect Mosaics from ordinary people,[12] I had an inkling that the physical qualities of the Lowenfeld Mosaics were integral to the therapeutic process. It was Quentin, however, who finally convinced me that these physical qualities could also be an essential element even if used as a research instrument. I had wished to do research into the possibility of using the Mosaics therapeutically with people with profound

---

12 I have been making my own collection of Mosaics from the normal population of all ages from when I began my child and adolescent psychotherapy training. These occasionally included developmental profiles from young people as well as adults who gave me permission to keep my drawings of their Mosaics.

hearing difficulties. I also had a piece of cross-cultural work in mind. Both became possible around the same time, but it was Quentin who finally clarified for me the importance of the physical qualities of the Lowenfeld Mosaics as a basic therapeutic and research instrument.

It had been suggested to me that to minimise the cost of producing Mosaic sets, the Mosaic vocabulary (box of Mosaic tiles with the tray on which the chosen Mosaic pieces are manipulated to create a Mosaic) could be put on a CD-Rom to be used on a personal computer. Within the research context, this had the advantage of making the Mosaic-making process more private and not requiring the presence of a reflective observer, which might be seen as interfering with the process and the final Mosaic product. I thought this distance between the researcher and her subject of study created by these means might make the Lowenfeld Mosaics a better research tool. The drawbacks were that it would require the research subjects to have the use of sophisticated computer equipment and would deprive the user of direct contact with the research material.

I now mentioned this to Quentin. I was astonished by his reaction. He was not only shocked by the idea, but he actually spluttered and shook his head vigorously at such a suggestion. Quentin was a highly regarded researcher and original thinker in his own field, with many ground-breaking publications to his name, and so I asked him to explain what in his personal experience of the Mosaics had led him to react in this way.

He described his own experience of doing the Mosaic in detail and then emphasised the crucial importance of the physical qualities of the Mosaics to the totality of that experience: in particular, his sense of touch being used simultaneously with seeing the effect created by his own manipulation of the Mosaic pieces as a means to achieve the complete expression of his own feelings and thoughts. He emphasised that it was the touch combined with the simultaneous sight of the Mosaic piece that determined exactly which was the right piece to use next, as well as where this piece should be placed in the tray. Seeing the Mosaic set and manipulating the tiles only on a computer screen would deprive the user of a fundamental quality of the Lowenfeld Mosaics as a projective research instrument. Furthermore, he regarded the presence of an interested but neutral observer who was motivated by an impersonal curiosity as the other important element in his experience.

I then felt emboldened to seek out research opportunities on the two subjects I was most interested in finding out about. One was to use the Mosaics therapeutically with people with profound pre-lingual hearing difficulties;[13] the other was to see whether the Mosaics could elicit cultural differences in a people whose mother tongue was not English (a project I shall describe in the next two chapters).

After some years in clinical practice, an opportunity arose whereby I thought I might be able to combine my teaching with a research element. I was invited to

---

13 Guidelines for presenting the Lowenfeld Mosaics to subjects with profound pre-lingual hearing difficulties are detailed in Appendix 3.

set up a working group of hearing professionals who wanted ways and means to facilitate their own communication with the deaf people with whom they have professional contact. Fortuitously, at around the same time, I was given the chance to go to an area in south China to do the piece of cross-cultural work I had thought I might be qualified to do by virtue of the fact that my ancestral family came from the vicinity of the area, so I might have an emotional as well as a linguistic connection with the culture of my potential subjects. It was also my hope that I might find the local organizers more sympathetic to my project. Quite clearly, these ideas were highly influenced by my own hybrid cultural background.

This chapter is concerned with the first subject of my research interests. It was an attempt to assess whether using the Lowenfeld Mosaics with a specific group of deaf people, whose additional difficulties encompass a range of mental health problems (autistic spectrum disorder, special learning needs and challenging behaviours) and who often experience difficulties in communicating and using language of any kind, would be helpful to their ability to express and convey their feelings and thoughts.

The Lowenfeld Mosaics have specific properties that have particular relevance to its possible usefulness to deaf people. Each tile stimulates two corresponding aspects of sensorial experience: the sense of sight and that of touch. These are the very senses which deaf people use for their own language, Sign language. So it seemed to me that the Mosaics would have a natural affinity with deaf people. And if the Mosaics together with some form of Sign language were used as a means of communication, contact between the deaf prople and their carers might be more easily achieved. More importantly, the Mosaics might also enable the deaf people to express themselves by using their two main receptive senses, which is in any case their normal mode of communication. Such was the hope.

A research group was set up within a small centre catering for around thirty places.[14] This centre offered total care to people who had profound hearing problems and aspired to the eventual rehabilitation of as many of their clients as possible into the larger community. The staff came mainly from the hearing community, and for some time they had been looking for a means of communication that did not rely on words or signs, since most of the centre's clients were unable to make use of these means in any case. Intensive training in Mosaic work with the deaf was developed by this group.

After an introductory day with the staff of the centre, I was invited to begin a training group. What had persuaded some of the staff to do this training was what they saw as the potential of the Lowenfeld Mosaics as a medium of expression for this group of clients; in particular it was the calming effect of using the Mosaics on clients whose only means of expression for their frustration had been through acts of violence and tantrums.

---

14 For reasons of client confidentiality I am unable to thank staff of the centre personally, so I would like to extend my gratitude anonymously to the staff of the centre for their dedication to this project.

During the period of about fifteen years that the project ran, many subjects passed through the centre, some for assessment only, some for residential care or tailor-made educational courses, whilst others attended a day unit on a daily, weekly or occasional basis. Very soon after the beginning of the project, it was hoped that the Lowenfeld Mosaics could be embedded into the routine working of the centre. It could thus be said that the eventual number of deaf subjects using the Mosaics came to more than thirty long-term cases,[15] and many others with a shorter contact. Out of these I have chosen two cases who so impressed the group of the usefulness of the Lowenfeld Mosaics as a means of communication between deaf persons and their carers that it was no longer doubted. As a research project, we all felt the Lowenfeld Mosaics had proved its case.

Ryan was normally a sweet-natured young man in his early twenties, usually full of exuberance and affectionate playfulness, but he was nevertheless capable of sudden flashes of aggression. Apart from his profound pre-lingual deafness, he exhibited a number of regressive behaviours, and at these times his moods became unpredictable, often escalating into uncontrollable violence. He seemed eager to participate in the Mosaic sessions. Reviewing the first few Mosaics of a series made by Ryan, it became evident that a theme had emerged and was clearly identified in them (Mosaics 12.1 and 12.2), and therapeutic measures were put in place.

I shall now present two consecutive Mosaics made by Ryan to demonstrate the nature of the theme that Ryan was working on.

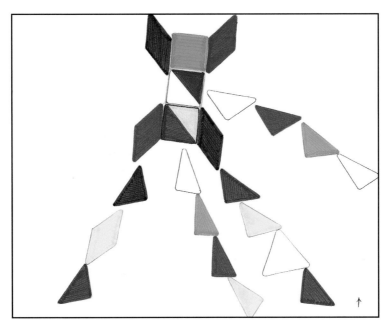

Mosaic 12.1
Ryan: interrupted work 1

---

15 These cases can vary from less than a year to more than ten years.

According to Ryan, this Mosaic represented a "type of rocket". Two doors (the yellow and blue isosceles triangles overlaying a yellow square, which gives it the three-dimensional effect) open into the cabin where the aeronauts oversee the flight of the rocket. The black and red diamonds at the top of Mosaic 12.1 were the antennae which received messages from space and were also used to guide the rocket through its journey.

Mosaic 12.2
Ryan: interrupted work 2

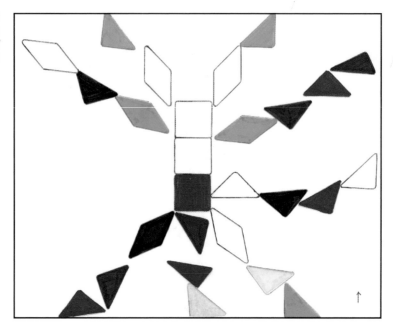

Ryan's next Mosaic (12.2) saw some variations to the same theme. He was now able to say that the three lines which extended from the cabin (now white squares because there were no people inside) to the bottom edge of the tray could be the steps up to the cabin. However, he did not offer any explanation as to why there were three pairs of steps. And the most notable differences were the addition of two lines just below the antennae which seemed to be tenuously attached to the cabin of the rocket.

Some seven months later, Ryan's Mosaic had suddenly altered, both in terms of subject matter as well as in appearance. Even a casual look at the Mosaic (12.3) would have shown that something unusual had happened in the meantime. What had caused this Mosaic to be so radically different from the first two? For an explanation, we have to go back to what happened six months before this Mosaic was made. Soon after the making of the second Mosaic (12.2), Ryan's key-worker was involved in a fatal accident. The centre's staff thought his behaviour had deteriorated markedly as a result of his key-worker's death and the heavy emotional atmosphere which had overhung the centre. The staff naturally made allowances for this, but after six months they were beginning to wonder if he was taking advantage of their tolerance. The Mosaic training was in its early stages and I now

advised them to ask him to do another Mosaic, and Mosaic 12.3 above was the result.

Ryan said that this Mosaic depicted a "giraffe". Ryan calmly but meticulously pointed out the various features which made up his giraffe: the red square at the top of the Mosaic was the giraffe's head; the white diamond to the right of the head was simultaneously its neck and its "horn"; the yellow scalene triangle just below the black diamond (another horn) on the left was one of its eyes; the other eye was represented by the red scalene triangle to its right; the red isosceles triangle just below the eyes was the nose, which was directly above the black isosceles triangle (in the middle of the Mosaic) that was the mouth, which lay over a blue isosceles triangle which was the giraffe's body. This was some distance from the white square which was another part of the body. The legs were in a tangled mass below the body, although the "arms" were appropriately placed just above the upper part of the body, and it could be seen that these limbs were also in tangled masses.

It can be seen that all the parts that made up Ryan's giraffe were not in their proper place. This Mosaic was also clearly nothing like the two Mosaics shown before it. Ryan had nothing else to say, and contrary to his usual ebullient self, especially after he had completed a Mosaic, he sat glumly, looking down at his shoes. Ryan's style of approach and manner, as well as his choice of subject and how he depicted his subject matter, were totally at variance from what he had previously produced. Although he had no way of knowing what had actually happened to his key-worker, it was as though he had known about the injuries his key-worker had sustained. On the strength of this evidence, and without any prompting from me, the staff understood that he was still suffering from the effects of the trauma.

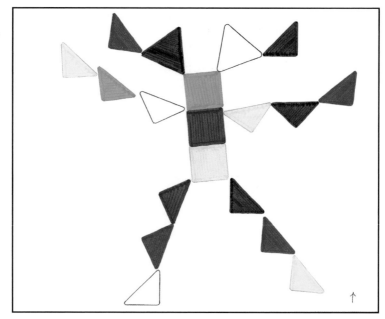

Three months after Mosaic 12.3, Ryan made another Mosaic (12.4). It can be seen that he had now returned to his original themes, but with some changes. One month later, he was faced with the departure of a much-loved tutor. But Ryan had been prepared for this eventuality, and it was hoped that he would not be too much affected by her leaving. Mosaic 12.5 was made for his beloved teacher on the eve of her departure.

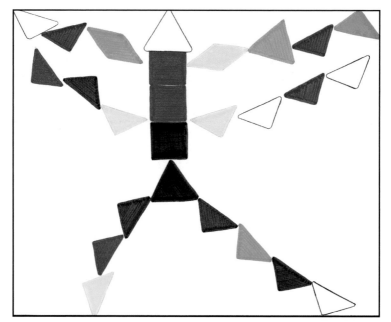

As can be seen, Ryan was continuing to work on his personal preoccupations, but in a gesture of acknowledgement to her, he replaced a second black square with a black equilateral triangle. He shyly indicated this to his teacher, saying that this was now a "skirt" and then pointing to her. He wanted her to keep this Mosaic of his.

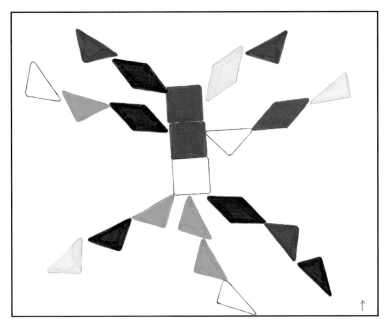

Mosaic 12.6
Ryan:
interrupted
work 6

Four months later, the work originally expressed in Mosaic 12.1 continued (Mosaic 12.6). Whilst the look of the Mosaic itself had hardly changed, the meaning given to each shape and colour used had now given him and his key-worker greater insights into his thoughts and feelings about himself and his predicament. From this series, Ryan was enabled to communicate through the use of the Lowenfeld Mosaics, both to himself and to his carers and teachers. This is not simply because his command of verbal language was impoverished by his hearing loss, or that his facility with words was inadequate to express his state of mind. It was because multidimensionality characterised that state of mind which the sensorial aspects of the Mosaics made more readily accessible. This is a state of affairs which is common to all humanity. Our normal mode of expressing ourselves is through our actions, through the use of all our senses. Thus, notwithstanding his lack of the usual communication skills associated with hearing loss at birth, using his other two major senses allowed Ryan to express the turmoil of his feelings and thoughts and to work on certain conundrums of life he found puzzling. Ryan found his experience with the Mosaics ultimately helpful as well as satisfying.

The Lowenfeld Mosaics is as much a self-communicating tool as a means of communicating with others. It has been said about words that "I cannot know what I think until I hear what I say". It is in this sense that doing the Mosaic can be self-communicating. In this context, it would be a case of "I cannot know how I feel until I have seen with my own eyes what my hands can show me". Thus the Lowenfeld Mosaics is capable of expressing more than thought; it has a way of also expressing our personal feelings about our total situation, with all its complexities and ambiguities. Most of our words for feelings are usually nuanced through the use of general terms, like "love" or "affection", "hate" or "dislike", "quite interested" or "rather interested", and the listener is just as likely to misinterpret as to understand the nuance implied by the speaker. With the Total Response of Mosaics, the interpretation is based on the Mosaic-maker's personal understanding of his own process and product, and there is less danger that a projection of its meaning by the observer could be mistaken for that of the Mosaic-maker. It is in this sense that a Mosaic provides a rounded dynamic self-portrait of the Personality in Action.

The training in the use of the Mosaics with people with hearing loss at this centre had required not only that detailed personal histories be taken regarding each client, but that the entire Mosaic process be videoed because of the necessity for the observer's hands to be used in communicating with the subject, so it was not possible for the observer also to record the process at the same time during the Mosaic session. Watching the video replay enabled the staff to see the process unfold and to chart its movement by numbering the pieces during the Mosaic-making. The next example is intended to demonstrate what care and attention had to be taken in order to understand better what has been expressed through the process of Mosaic-making, which may be hidden by the Mosaic structure. It also powerfully demonstrates the subtlety with which important aspects of the Personality in Action can be conveyed.

Stephen was in his late teens when he entered the centre as a boarder because his mother needed respite time. Up till then his needs had been mainly catered for by his mother. He was the elder of twin brothers. In their early childhood, their mother had suspected that something was profoundly wrong with her children. At the hospital, his brother, Stuart, was diagnosed as "partially deaf"; the paediatrician who saw Stephen decided, however, that he was simply "mentally retarded". It was not until he was aged four that he was further diagnosed with profound pre-lingual deafness. However, the earlier label had persisted, and he was not placed in an appropriate school until he was eight years old, where, despite early promise, he lagged seriously behind. The twins' temperaments were distinctly different: Stuart was more active and responsive, whilst Stephen had seemed to his mother to have been a difficult child from the beginning. Naturally, his mother found Stuart's company the more rewarding of the two. Nevertheless, Stephen's mother cared deeply for him, so his world was mainly limited to these two positive relationships.

By the time he came to the centre, Stuart had started work as an errand boy in an office but had not yet left home, whilst Stephen continued to fall behind in all areas of his life. He shared little of life's experiences with Stuart, nor Stuart with him. There was clearly none of the kind of closeness between Stephen and Stuart that is so often seen between twins. Stephen seemed to have had no other peer relationship. Thus it was assumed that any good experiences of personal relations were limited to the one he had with his mother. In time, in his relationship with her, he became increasingly in turn petulant and anxious to please. He was always either seeking her approval or sulky, and occasionally he was even aggressive towards her.

By the time of his referral to the centre, his mother had become weary of being at his beck and call, but she felt guilty when she demanded that he some-times did more for himself. It brought on a "yes but, no but" kind of atmosphere in their home, one that was often tinged with anxiety and a sense of the possibil-ity of sudden erupting violence. Finally his mother decided that he should spend some time away from home. She had heard that the aim for their clients at this centre was for them to become "self-reliant and independent".

At first Stephen seemed bewildered by his unfamiliar surroundings and the routine of the centre, where nothing seemed to make sense to him. Often his behaviour seemed bizarre. He also seemed to be in a state of permanent weariness. Everything was "too much" for him. He hardly knew how to communicate with either staff or other members at the centre. He seemed increasingly solitary. He could only ask for help, and it seemed to others that he expected them to do things he could very well do for himself. He did not seem to consider other people, their needs or their views. He was a caricature of a self-centred "Mummy's boy" or "spoilt brat". Yet it could be discerned that these epithets did not quite fit the bill. He was always anxious to please, constantly searching for approval. Often he was impulsive, or his actions did not match what was the required response. Occasionally he could be very destructive to personal belongings or explode into unexpected violence, but mainly he was a puzzle to the staff. He seemed to be in another world. It was difficult to grasp the nature of the problem that Stephen had created for the members of this small community. So, at the earliest opportunity, a Mosaic session was arranged for him.

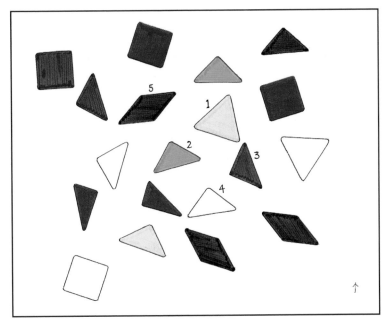

Mosaic 12.7
Stephen: structure and process

Stephen's very first Mosaic (12.7 above) seemed to reflect his sense of confusion, where nothing seemed to connect to anything in ways he could understand or indeed make out for himself. At first glance, randomly scattered pieces characterised this first Mosaic. But by going through the process from the numbered moves between 1 and 5 it can be discerned that Stephen's Mosaic process was like a weaving movement: it swung up and down as well as from side to side, as though he was being pulled between two moving poles. And this movement had characterised the entire Mosaic process.

The disconnected nature of Stephen's first Mosaic enabled the staff to understand that perhaps what Stephen required was to have his new environment explained to him, and they put in place a plan to have all their actions around him explained to Stephen by whoever was on duty. Besides giving him reasons for why he should or should not do anything, they would also give him reasons for their expectations, with the hope that he would then be in a position to make the connections necessary for his cooperation. They hoped this would assist him towards a greater sense of independence and a more self-reliant way of life. At that point, the weaving motion of the process was merely noted. It was not clear what other meanings it could have, nor its relative importance.

His next Mosaic (12.8) was made twenty-seven months later. During this time, the staff were actually quite gratified by the seeming improvement in Stephen's understanding of his environment. They were used to very slow progress from a large number of their clients, as most of them have multiple problems, but they thought that he was now more able to connect with others. His companions were usually the ones who smoked, and they could often be found smoking together, "chatting" whilst they puffed. It was not clear at the time that it was the others who did most of the "chatting". He did seem to be making other connections: he seemed more able to follow the centre's routines. But again it was not noticed that this had been in only selected areas of activity. Nor had his bizarre behaviours abated; it was simply that they seemed to come and go without rhyme or reason. The origin of any specific trigger could never be traced. What had become apparent, however, was that he would regress a little every time his mother visited or before and after any weekend he spent at home. His mother interpreted this as Stephen missing his home, her and their time together, and she thought that the solution was to increase his home visits and began to argue for more frequent contact. The staff tried to discuss this possibility with Stephen, but he seemed reluctant to make a decision.

Although it was also clear that Stephen had now become a much more active and cooperative member at the centre, the staff was baffled by the pattern of his behaviour which seemed to underlie much of his actions. For instance, although he seemed readily to understand the need for certain actions, there seemed to be an inner battle before the action could happen; they could see signs of an internal struggle flittering cross his face. This struggle sometimes ended with some act of aggression. This aggressive behaviour had become more generalised and less predictable. His other-worldliness began to be more noticeable. He began to be obsessed with violent fantasies and displayed odd gestures, and this became a matter of increasing concern to the staff and other clients at the centre. This was the particular reason for asking Stephen to do another Mosaic. The staff wanted to know whether they could learn anything from the Mosaic that could help with their work with him.

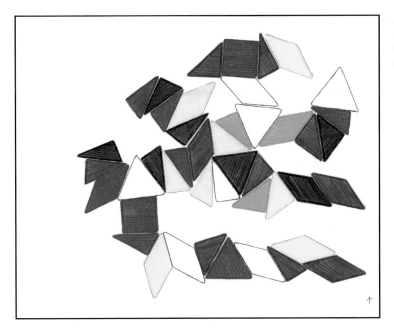

Mosaic 12.8
Stephen: structure and process

As can be seen, all the Mosaic pieces were now connected and structured into a whole, albeit a whole without a pattern or any sense of pattern. Stephen seemed to have placed pieces regardless of shape or colour. This kind of pattern-less structure can have a special meaning if made by an American (2004a: Ch. 10), but in European terms it would be classified as "incoherent" and would be deemed by Lowenfeld to be a "Slab". According to Lowenfeld (2004a: 99), Slabs made within European culture have a special but uniform significance. They "represent either a stage in the development of normal children, or are . . . diagnostic of the presence of emotional disturbance or psychosis[16] in the maker".

Stephen was referred to and subsequently seen by a psychiatrist, but psychosis is an extremely difficult diagnosis to be certain of, even amongst the normal population. Without the benefit of the centre's Mosaic findings, the psychiatric opinion suggested a tentative diagnosis of "autism". With someone who had the profound learning and communication difficulties which Stephen clearly showed, no firm diagnosis was ever reached and this became a matter of continuing psychiatric review.

---

16 The diagnosis of psychosis for this type of Mosaic was arrived at by Dr Margaret Lowenfeld, who besides pioneering this form of therapeutic treatment, was also the founder and Psychiatrist and Physician-in-Charge at the Institute of Child Psychology, a psychiatrist in private practice and a founding member of the Royal College of Psychiatry in Britain.

Furthermore, Dr Henri Ellenberger,[17] in Chapter 9 of Lowenfeld's Mosaic book (2004a: 241), stated that the Lowenfeld Mosaics "can supply more information about the stage and severity of the condition than about its nature". And an analysis of the process (Mosaic 12.9) did reveal an interesting detail.

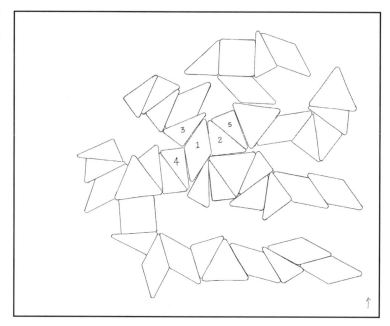

Mosaic 12.9
Stephen: structure and process

It was that Stephen's Mosaic process in this Mosaic was virtually identical to that in the one he had made before when he first came to the centre over two years ago (Mosaic 12.7). It seemed that there had been no underlying change in him. And of greater significance was the fact that what was originally seen as a "push and pull" process could also have been viewed as a mood swing, that is, a change from his noted deeds of unaccountable aggression and destructive behaviour to the calm but often obsessive and repetitive acts. But these swings in the Mosaic process were not always large and it could be argued that whatever the meaning or meanings, these were subtle. It could be that the mood swings were not so severe as to denote a clear and irreversible manic-depressive response, or, if it were as originally thought, that it was a "push and pull" response to his mother's ambivalent feelings towards him, that this was not an irretrievable situation in the face of which the staff at the centre need feel helpless.

So the staff began to review Stephen's history, to see if a programme could be devised which would bear sensitively on these issues. They began with the idea that

---

17 Dr Henri Ellenberger was one of her collaborators in her study of mental illness. He was the co-author in her work (2004a) and wrote Chapter 9 on the use of the Lowenfeld Mosaics in the study of mental disorders (2004a: 28–9).

the Mosaic process had indeed been masked by his Mosaic product. From this point of view of Stephen's behaviour, that which made it seem as though he had grasped the idea of connections now seemed on the surface to have been confirmed by a Mosaic where all the pieces had been connected. Now the Mosaic training group reviewed Stephen's recent history again to see if this offered any further clues.

The subject which had been most often raised by his mother was his continuing residence at the centre. She had recently confided to the staff that although she still found his weekend visits tiring and his behaviour tiresome (there was hardly any change to his demanding behaviour at home), she nevertheless missed his presence in and around the home. Since Stuart was now leading an independent life, caring for Stephen had become more and more her preoccupation, and had lately become her sole purpose in life. She was now bereft and lonely.

Rightly or wrongly, the staff now wondered whether her explanation for his difficult behaviour at home defined his relation to his mother. And the staff concluded that so long as she continued to feel the same towards him, partly rejecting and partly needing him, the "push and pull" effect, the process as identified in Mosaics 12.7 and 12.8/9, would probably continue to underlie his response to the external world. The movement within the process clearly portrayed Stephen's ambivalence and indecision when it came to any action on his part. Perhaps the "push and pull" view was part of a complex pattern, and it was not a question of an "either/or" situation, of "autism" or "psychosis", or a portrait of Stephen's relation with his mother, but that both views could simultaneously be true.

In this respect, however, the tentative moves Stephen was making towards a positive contact with his external world were ineffective, at least, not until the home visits were limited to the weekends, and at a time determined by Stephen himself. This pattern took some years to establish, but after it had become an accepted and stable arrangement, and although the impulsive, obsessive, aggressive and somewhat bizarre behaviours continued to wax and wane, Stephen's energies were eventually sufficiently freed for him to explore the subject of his own identity, as one of a twin.

Many long years later, Stephen made a series of Mosaics within one session. This in itself was quite a dramatic change. From the very beginning of his attendance at the centre, he had been reluctant and bemused by the whole process of doing a Mosaic. However, his relations with his mother had now stabilised and he had been on an educational programme using drawing as a means for him to communicate. Lately, his pictures of his weekends at home conveyed a real sense of fun. Eventually the exchanges became a conversation between him and his Mosaic observer, and the back and forth accompanying the Mosaic-making was mainly based in the reality of his world. By the time this series was done, Stephen had decided to take the lead.

Stephen began by making a definite and symmetrical shape. This was to be only the first surprise. He signed "butterfly" and seemed pleased to be rewarded with lavish praise. With a sweep of his left hand, he brushed the pieces to the side of the tray and reused certain of them to make something which looked like the figure of a person with a white centre but no head, but he was unable to say what it was or anything about it. As he continued to gaze at it, and with some gentle prompting, he added a red diamond above the white square. Moments later, he began to change it again signing that it was to be a "dog". He discarded one of the "limbs" and moved what might have been the head to where the dog's tail would have been. Thus it was that the complete figure of a person was deprived of a limb and become a dog. Again he brushed these pieces aside and made the Mosaic below (Mosaic 12.10).

Mosaic 12.10
Stephen:
Mosaic not
discussed

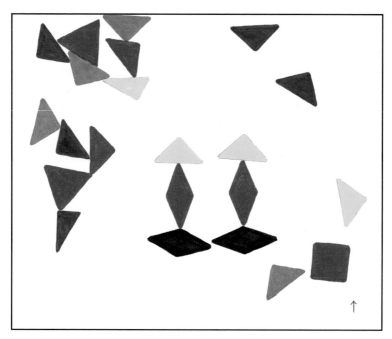

Stephen closed off the session by standing up and announcing it was now "Teatime". Despite this lack of discussion, it was clear to the Mosaic training group that he was now raising the subject of his identity as a twin. In future Mosaics he explored this idea in depth, beginning with Mosaics depicting two identical people, who shared a single leg, or who had only one leg each. Other Mosaics portrayed twin figures, one somehow damaged, or more damaged than the other. In reality, his strange, obsessive and aggressive behaviours had long contained better periods of relative quiescence, but they never quite disappeared. In reality, too, his twin brother Stuart had been promoted at work, was now married and the proud father of a daughter, thus, in Stephen's eyes, clearly leading a more successful and independent life than himself.

Thus although it was important to have a psychiatric diagnosis such as "autism", that should not be a once and for all defining factor in the care programme. In both the case of Ryan and Stephen, by careful assessment with the aid of the Lowenfeld Mosaics, the staff was enabled to see which steps taken by them had proved helpful to Ryan and Stephen and which had not.

Working with people with mental health problems like autism or regressive behavioural difficulties cannot be easy at the best of times. Compounding these difficulties with one of communication requires utter dedication on the part of professionals. The staff at this centre certainly did not withhold such commitment.

Ryan and Stephen taught the training group invaluable lessons: first that for the therapist using the Lowenfeld Mosaics, attention to the Total Response is essential to the therapeutic enterprise. In response to the client's Mosaic, the therapist's own commitment must also be total. And secondly, the group was to learn how every aspect of our lives is affected by the context in which we live, and for therapists, it was essential to have ongoing contact with this context as well as a detailed and frequently updated personal history for each client.

In the midst of this work with the deaf, I came across Oliver Sacks's account of his "journey into the world of the deaf" (Sacks 1990) and was impressed by his observation that people construct their own personal reality from the given contextual reality in the world around them. He tells of two deaf children: Joseph and Charlotte. Joseph (pp. 38–44) was very like many of the subjects at the centre where Sacks's project was carried out. His deafness was undiagnosed until he was four years old. Following a sequence of diagnoses familiar to the staff at the centre, including that of retardation and autism, Joseph started at a school for the deaf at the age of eleven. It was clear that Joseph longed to communicate, and the school soon discovered he possessed a remarkable talent for drawing. Sacks surmised that "Joseph saw, distinguished, categorized, used; he had no problems with perceptual categorization or generalization" (p. 40). He was able to pick up, follow and play games like tic-tac-toe. It was clear to Sacks that "thought and language have quite separate (biological) origins, that the world is examined and mapped and responded to long before the advent of language" (p. 40).

Like Joseph, Charlotte was congenitally deaf, but otherwise a very different case. Oliver Sacks met her with her family when she was six and half years old. Unlike Joseph, she was full of fun, liveliness and more importantly, full of questions. In his contact and conversations with her parents, their observations very much complemented his own impressions of Charlotte. It seems that Charlotte employed predominantly visual thought patterns to construct her world. Specifically he was "struck by the graphic quality, the fullness of her descriptions" (1990: 74). Furthermore, he noted in her signed conversations that "it was not isolated facts that she wanted, but connections, understanding, a world with sense and meaning" (p. 72). In one of her letters to Sacks, her mother had written, "I feel our experience bears out the idea that early exposure to visually coherent language develops *complex* (my italics) conceptual thought processes. Charlotte knows how to think and how to reason. She uses effectively the linguistic tools she has been given to build complicated ideas" (pp. 71–2).

It was of course Steven Pinker who showed us that thought indeed precedes language. Furthermore, I agree with Lowenfeld that not only does thought precede language, but that from the very beginning people need a useful way of thinking about their world. Their world is not arbitrarily constructed, self-generated without reason. The logic of this reasoning, however, is commanded by our singular and overriding need to survive. This style of reasoning will be discussed in Chapter 16, with the exposition of Lowenfeld's theory of Protosystem Thinking.

13 Cross-cultural research with Mosaics

My first moment of consciousness of culture in the shaping of personality came when I least expected it. I had always wanted to come to the land of Jane Austen and George Eliot (two novelists whom I did and still do admire), but who had together shaped my idea of English society. I was excited when the plane landed at Heathrow Airport, but almost at once I became discomforted by the sight of English men and women working in the more menial posts, scrubbing the floors, serving in cafes and portering luggage. No "white" person should be doing such lowly work, would be a fair summation of my thoughts and feelings about that sight which greeted me at the airport.

I had been unprepared for ordinary life in Britain. For the first time I realised that I had fused what I had seen of English life in Hongkong, then still a British colony, where all English men had positions of authority over the indigenous Chinese and most English women led lives of leisure or did voluntary work for charity,[18] with those aspects which were consonant with my favourite reading from English literature. I had clearly ignored or dismissed the picture of life as depicted by Charles Dickens and George Orwell as irrelevant to that same society, simply because I had preferred the writings of Jane Austen and George Eliot. It was partly to be explained by where and when I was born and brought up, the kind of education that was available to me, as well as a view of the wider world that was idiosyncratic to myself and my prejudices at that time of my life.

Lowenfeld had speculated "that the varieties in the traditional forms of folk embroidery and design in Europe might reflect and might have developed from essential differences in the cultural structure of the countries in which they occur" (2004a: 16–17). And by the time her book was published in 1954, an extensive chapter on the expression of cultural differences through the Mosaics had been included (ch. 10). Lowenfeld had identified two distinct cultural features in the process of Mosaic-making from her collections of Mosaics gathered from round the world, which had often been presented to her by anthropologists in the field

---

18 In the late 1940s and early '50s, no Chinese was permitted to head any department in government, the civil or public services. These heads were all recruited from the United Kingdom. This included the head of the Chinese Department at the University of Hong Kong.

for comment.[19] In this chapter she made specific references to the differences between European Mosaics and those made by descendants of Europeans, from the United States. Hitherto Lowenfeld had used the structure of a Mosaic as the main feature for analyzing and understanding Mosaics. She now began to see that the Mosaic process is also a cultural phenomenon. And through her extensive contacts with people from the United States (notably Margaret Mead, who had used her Mosaics as an anthropological research tool), Lowenfeld also came to recognise that the cultural background of the observer of another's Mosaic process and product was an important aspect of Mosaic-making and impacted upon any analysis and grasp of the results.

The idea that the Lowenfeld Mosaics might be the kind of personality projective instrument that would be appropriate to use for cross-cultural studies had occurred to me during my child psychotherapy training. It was my good fortune that I was asked to assist in sorting out Lowenfeld's collections of Mosaics from around the world, including Asia and Africa (Woodcock 1986: 25–31). Furthermore, by then I had been introduced to Dr Rhoda Metraux and her anthropological work among the Iatmul people in the East Sepik District of Papua New Guinea, using the Lowenfeld Mosaics (Metraux 1975: 293–308) and had made my own assessment of Metraux's Mosaic collection (Woodcock and Hood-Williams n.d.). By the early 1980s, I began to see a way by which I could at least study my own cultural differences. I thought then that it may be possible to look beyond my own Mosaic and see how much of my ethnic nature is now visible through an upbringing in a British colony. I hoped eventually to examine what changes might occur in the Chinese diaspora through being educated within another cultural background.

This was the original context in which I set out to do my cross-cultural research. I was thus fortunate to be able to build upon the insights of others. In addition to the Mosaics made by Chinese-Malaysian children (Thornton 1956), I had also made a brief study (Woodcock 1986a: 25–31) of a collection of Mosaics from Tanzania (formerly Tanganyika) in Lowenfeld's archive collection, and began to use these insights both in my clinical practice as well as in my cross-cultural research endeavours. In this chapter, I shall outline the main subject of enquiry through the three pieces of research in London, Guangdong, a province in South China, and in San Francisco, on the west coast of the United States, and examine some of the findings. In the next chapter, I shall be reflecting upon the implications of the findings in relation to cultural differences between the Guangzhou,[20]

---

19 Lowenfeld had herself acquired extensive experience by using the Mosaics with a large population of subjects in various settings. Besides mental health colleagues, she had also collaborated with people in other fields of study, including anthropology, education and clinical psychology. Other professionals using the Lowenfeld Mosaics would also send her their collections for comment. Thus the collections accumulated in the Lowenfeld archives were extensive, although not all are housed at or have survived the transfer to the Centre for Family Research at the University of Cambridge, and lately to the Wellcome Library in 2005.

20 Guangzhou is the capital city of Guangdong Province in South China. I had also collected a sample from the rural district of Panyu in Guangdong. For the sake of comparison, only the urban (Guangzhou) sample will be referred to in this work.

formerly known as Canton, and San Francisco samples, using the detailed analysis made by Ames and Ilg (1962) of their very large sample taken in Connecticut, on the east coast of the United States, for comparison, and end with the case of an Asian child whose Mosaic illuminated her plight. A fuller statistical analysis of the three samples is tabulated in Appendix 5c.

Before undertaking the research project abroad, I felt that a pilot study with Chinese-British children in London, might give useful clues as to how to go about designing the protocol for taking the next stage of the project to the city of Guangzhou.[21] Using the analysis of the sample collected by Thornton of young Chinese boys and men in both urban and rural districts of Malaysia (also in the Lowenfeld archives) as a kind of base line, in 1985, I collected 31 Mosaics from what was assumed to be second-generation Chinese-British children who were attending extra-curricular Chinese language classes whilst being educated in the state schools in their own neighbourhoods in Greater London. The Chinese Community in London had recently opened up a community centre. From there, I was introduced to a new Chinese language school that had been established to help second-generation Chinese children maintain their mother tongue. Classes were held only on Sunday mornings. I was given permission to invite the children to participate in my Mosaic project. So that their education would not be interrupted, the Mosaics would be done during the short break between classes.

All this meant that I could not plan the pilot study in any systematic way nor place a time limit to this part of the project. I also did not have time to collect more than the briefest of details except for the date of birth; it was assumed that all the children were from the second generation. It took me more than half a year to collect these 31 Mosaics, and the children had a much wider age range than I would have wished. At this point, the results were consistent with those obtained by Thornton (1968), and were sufficiently encouraging for some meaningful conclusions to be drawn for the larger project I was proposing to do in China.

I was then advised to prepare to apply to the educational authorities in Guangdong for a base sample in mainland China. Using the Thornton protocol for samples from an urban and a rural area, I had chosen Guangdong Province because both the Malaysian and London samples were taken from children whose parents mainly came from that area.[22] My application was eventually successful and early in November 1986, my son, who accompanied me as an unpaid assistant,[23] and I

---

21 Appendix 4 contains brief guidelines for using the Lowenfeld Mosaics in crosscultural research. Appendix 5 contains the research protocols and response forms used for the research in China and the United States. For the London sample only brief and anonymised details have been recorded for each Mosaic.

22 Personal thanks are owed to Lynn Pan for her assistance and advice in the eventual success of my application to the Foreign Office and Education Department in Guangdong. I am also grateful to Professor Martin Richards for his assistance in my application as well as advice regarding the gathering and analysis of the research data. And I am indebted to the Dr Margaret Lowenfeld Trust for providing travel grants for this and the subsequent research project in San Francisco.

23 I am indebted to my son, Ian Sebastian Woodcock, for his invaluable assistance in this work. Whenever I have contemplated our joint work in Guangdong since, I know that the task could not have been accomplished without his help. In many ways, he was the technical collaborator in this piece of research.

were met with immense courtesy and obliging support from the personnel[24] in Guangdong. I was given all that I had asked for (200 twelve-year-olds in total; 100 from the city of Guangzhou, 100 from the rural district of Panyu; 50 boys and 50 girls from each area) and, because of the interest expressed, more assistance than I had anticipated or expected.

Five years later, after a period of long negotiations, up to and after my arrival in San Francisco, I was finally able to complete the third and last phase of this research project.[25]

The project had begun with a pilot study in London to see if the results I had identified in Thornton's work in Malaysia could be confirmed for children who had been educated in a similar background, that is, where the Chinese children were being taught in English, but continued to have contact with their mother tongue in their daily life. With this confirmed, I felt it was time to attempt the research to discover whether these rough criteria could be sharpened into a specific enquiry. Early in 1986, I wrote to the officials in Guangdong, saying that my research sought "to establish whether Chinese upbringing and education creates a common perception of the world. Moreover, it is concerned to discover whether there is a link between the common perception of the world and the language used in children's education."[26] With the results from Guangzhou analysed, I was emboldened to attempt to try to answer a further enquiry. In San Francisco, in 1991, I had four main objectives.[27] The most important of which was to see if there were further dimensions in the Mosaics which indicate that, several generations on, there would be greater acculturation between the host culture and the descendants of Chinese emigrants. These results will be more fully discussed in the next chapter.

I will now use examples from all these three samples to show the commonalities as well as differences. First, it must be accepted that the pilot sample is in no way comparable to those collected from Guangzhou or San Francisco, so data relating to, for example, preferred shape or colour, for which there is no information, will only refer to that from Guangzhou and San Francisco, and not to the London sample.

The first discovery I made from looking through Thornton's collection was the disproportionate number of representational Mosaics made by the Chinese in

---

24 My appreciation to all the Chinese Foreign Office and Education Department officials, staff and pupils of the schools in Guangzhou and Panyu for their affability, ready helpfulness and unfailing efficiency in expediting the whole project so smoothly and pleasantly. It was, for me, an entirely happy experience.

25 I am grateful to Dr Roger Brindle for his tireless efforts to secure the cooperation of a school which would largely satisfy my research needs. I am equally grateful to all the staff and pupils of this school who so freely gave up their time for what must have seemed to them an exotic but tedious enterprise.

26 See Appendix 5a for the full protocol.

27 See Appendix 5b for the full protocol, including the ancestry form provided by the school where the children personally identify which generation they belong to. This form was completed by each child without any general explanations from myself. This information had thus to be taken on trust.

contrast to the English children who made a similarly large percentage of abstract patterns in Lowenfeld's collection. Representational Mosaics, including scenes of objects, continue to dominate by a large margin through all three of my Chinese samples. For the London and Guangzhou samples, the percentage is over 90 per cent. For the San Francisco sample, it was just over 70 per cent. The San Francisco sample was thus about half way between the figures for London and Guangzhou, on the one hand, and the Ames and Ilg figure of 47 per cent for the Connecticut twelve-year-olds. Perhaps there is evidence after all of a subtle acculturation of the Chinese-Americans in San Francisco.

All Mosaic examples from the London, Guangzhou and San Francisco samples will be chosen with their cultural background in mind. The order in which examples from each sample has been presented is based on the order in which the sample was collected. The unifying criteria for my assessment of all these Mosaics is based on the written descriptions given by the children themselves. I will begin with the representations of objects. Mosaic 13.1 is from the London sample and it is "a shape". This is not a term I have come across as a category in either Lowenfeld's collection or Thornton's sample, or indeed in Ames and Ilg's records, but was to occur again and again in the Guangzhou and San Francisco collections. Perhaps it is not too fanciful to imagine that "a shape", in the eyes of the Chinese children, was similar in meaning to "a rectangle", and was seen as much as an object as "a page of a book" or "an A4 piece of paper". And within all the three samples, such Mosaics as ones entitled "three blocks" or "triangles" appeared.

Mosaic 13.1
"A shape" made by a Chinese girl from London

A SHAPE

The second representation of an object was also made by a girl, but from the city of Guangzhou, and is of a very common object in the Mosaic collections under consideration. "This is a house," she had written, and she then described it as being "situated in a village which is powered by solar energy". Indeed, it will be noticed that the house has two white equilateral triangles on an otherwise colourful roof. Furthermore, the description made it clear that her Mosaic was in a setting that was located in the future. Since the Guangzhou sample have many Mosaics displaying ideas for the future, it might be said to belong to the sense of optimism expressed there, especially in 1986, not long after the then British Prime Minister, Margaret Thatcher, had visited Guangzhou and other parts of China, when it had seemed to the Chinese officials that China was at last opening its doors to the outside world.

Mosaic 13.2
"A house" made by a Chinese girl from Guangzhou

The third Mosaic of a representational object (overleaf) was made by a Chinese boy from San Francisco. He had written of his Mosaic, and I quote, "This is a Gromet [*sic*] without wings." I understand from one of the school assistants that it was a character from a computer game from the Dungeons and Dragons series, popular in 1991. Indeed, there seems to be no examples of Chinese Mosaics from San Francisco that refer to artefacts outside of American culture, or thoughts and feelings beyond the United States or the present time. However, it is always possible for this to be a coincidence, a matter simply of sample bias or a blind spot of mine.

The next classification of Mosaics from these three samples that seem to be distinct from any of the other collections mentioned in this book is the number of scenes made by the children.

The first Mosaic example I have chosen is one made by a Chinese boy from London (13.4). It depicts a landscape, which was how he described it to me. In the

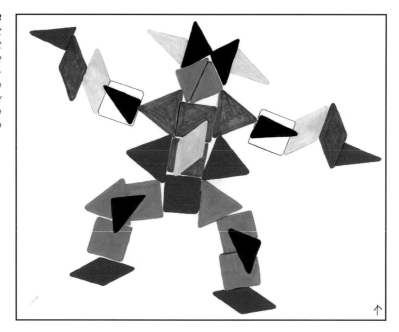

foreground is a red Chinese junk, some green land and a blue sea, with yellow mountains behind; in the distance are high green mountains topped by trees, with blue clouds and a red and yellow sun above. He had, successfully in my eyes, tried to create a complex three-dimensional effect that is almost poetic in its visual effect, not unlike that which can be seen in traditional Chinese paintings.

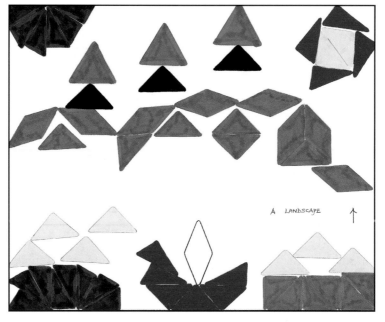

The next Mosaic (13.5) was made by a Chinese girl from Guangzhou. It was meant to be an amusing allegorical scene depicting the pettiness of two chickens

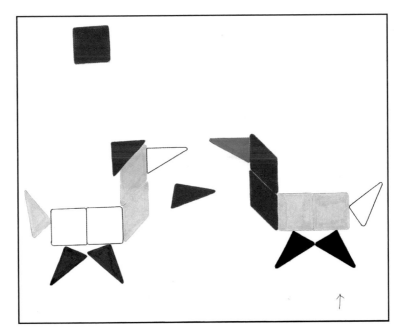

quarrelling over a trivial matter. It is a scene showing a green-beaked chicken quarrelling with a white-beaked chicken because the first chicken has annoyed the latter by putting a red hat onto the second chicken's head. Imagery is often used in Chinese poetry or painting as an analogy for an abstract point or idea, and it is perhaps fanciful of me to imagine that this girl had such an idea in mind. My idea derives from the fact that when her text was being translated for me, the interpreter was amused by what this girl had written.

The next one is a Mosaic (13.6 overleaf) made by a Chinese boy from San Francisco. It is a dynamic scene of an ongoing basketball game. He informed us that it was "Michael Jordan playing basketball vs the Celtics." It was clear that Michael Jordan was his hero. The title implied that Michael Jordan was playing the game single-handed against the Celtic team. It is a typical and quintessential masculine activity according to Ames and Ilg (1962: 77–9), and the topic of sport was a popular theme amongst the Mosaics from the boys in her sample.

Collectives of representations of objects is the next large category to be included. Lowenfeld mentioned in Table 2 of her book (Lowenfeld 2004a: 126–7), that at twelve years of age, mixtures of abstract patterns and representations of objects begin to appear, but mostly the collectives are of abstract patterns, not of representational objects. Given that the percentage of all English representational Mosaics was less than 10 per cent (Stewart and Leyland 1952: 246–8), this type of Mosaic is unlikely to be common in England. Collectives of representational designs are not mentioned as a category in its own right, but more of a difficulty in Ames and Ilg (1962: 87), and separate items in a Mosaic were usually considered as components of a single design or a scene (p. 82), or a spaced design in terms of compactness (p. 87). So as far as such designs from San Francisco are concerned,

Mosaic 13.6
A scene of "Michael Jordan playing basketball vs. the Celtics" made by a Chinese boy from San Francisco

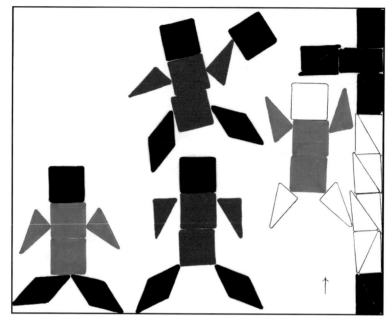

I will attempt to provide examples both as defined by Ames and Ilg and of those which conform to ones I have found in London and Guangzhou, including a Mosaic example from my collection from English children as an illustration of Lowenfeld's classification.

Again I will begin this group of Mosaics with an example from London. As

Mosaic 13.7
A collective Mosaic consisting of a cuckoo clock, a bird and (two) shapes made by a Chinese girl from London

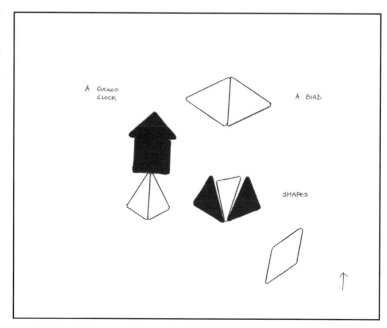

it was such a small (31) sample, I was not surprised to find that there are no sure examples of collectives of representational objects. For the sake of completeness, however, I am including the only collective in the sample which could either be a collective of a mixed representation of objects and abstract patterns, if what was said to be "shapes" were considered as abstract patterns, or it could be classed as a collective of representational objects if a "shape" was considered to be an object. This collective (Mosaic 13.7) consists of a cuckoo clock, a bird and two shapes. The Mosaic-maker did hesitate over what to call these shapes by saying first "Don't know" before changing her mind and saying "Shapes". These may or may not have been surplus pieces, but when asked to write something about what she had made, she also may have felt she needed to be able to say something about all the pieces in the tray. The cuckoo clock was the only design I felt confident was intended. The so-named "bird" and the "shapes" may have been more a product of identification after seeing the resultant figure at the completion of her Mosaic.

In contrast to the previous Mosaic, the next Mosaic, made by a girl from Guangzhou, was clearly intended to be a collection of objects. She numbered each object in the order that she had made them, suggesting that together these did not form a scene in her mind.

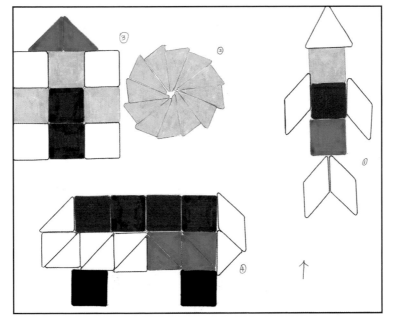

Mosaic 13.8
A collective Mosaic comprising (1) a rocket, (2) a flower, (3) a house and (4) a motor car made by a Chinese girl from Guangzhou

Three Mosaics from San Francisco are included here to demonstrate a fact about this collection of 70 Mosaics. Two of the designs seem to approach the definition of collectives given by Lowenfeld, except they are representations of objects. The last conformed to Ames and Ilg's classification of separate designs of forms within the tray space that constitute a single design. But these were the only kinds of collectives in the entire collection from San Francisco. I thought it was worthwhile to include all three to give what I have come to call a flavour of a San Francisco Chinese-American Mosaic not found in the other two samples.

The first Mosaic (13.9) was made by a boy and is rather like the Mosaic from Guangzhou shown above (Mosaic 13.8), but had an element of ambiguity much like the collective Mosaic from London. To explain what I mean, I will have to quote his description in its entirety, including the punctuation: "I use 1 square and a couple of triangles for the sun /[28] I made clouds, a flower, rabbit, bird, fish / grass, water out of different shapes." It is not so much the lack of appropriate punctuation, but the lack of a sense of a totality that the description conveys. Visually, however, a sense of a scene became obvious when the different objects had been identified and when one could see how the forms were disposed over the tray. This boy was nearly fourteen years old.

Mosaic 13.9
A Mosaic made by a third-generation Chinese-American boy from San Francisco

The second of the three Mosaics from San Francisco was by a Chinese-American girl who described her Mosaic (13.10) thus, "My mosaic has many different colors green, yellow, red. I used a trangle [*sic*] and a diamond for my wheat and my sun: my sun has yellow and red and my wheat has yellow red and green." This is similar to the previous Mosaic, except that she laid greater stress on her use of colours than on her use of shapes. Clearly these were the principal qualities of the Mosaics that attracted her. This Mosaic, however, also exhibited the same kind of ambiguity as the previous Mosaic (13.9). She did not seem to be mainly concerned with the distinction between a scene and a collective of objects.

---

28 My use of the forward slash / indicates the end of the line, with no punctuation dividing the two words.

Mosaic 13.10
A Mosaic made by a third-generation Chinese-American girl from San Francisco

The third in this series of collective Mosaics from San Francisco is one made by a second-generation Chinese-American girl. She had described it (13.11) as "a design. One part was all different shapes and colors. The other part was all black and green with different shapes." It will be noticed, however, that, although she had ascribed the Mosaic as a single design, the emphasis was on the shapes and colours. This may have something to do with an attitude identified by Lowenfeld as a cultural trait in Americans; she refers to these as Am-type Mosaics (Lowenfeld

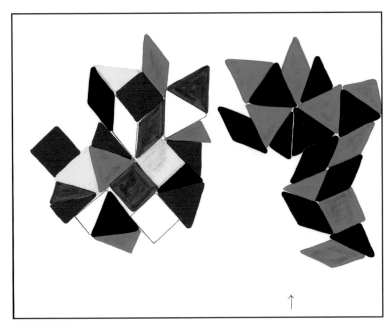

Mosaic 13.11
A "Design" made by a second-generation Chinese-American girl from San Francisco

2004a: 94–6). From the point of view of Ames and Ilg, however, Mosaic 13.11 might very well be described as a design, a symmetrical pattern filling the whole tray that is made up of two separate compact designs, centrally placed and divided by an imaginary line down the centre of the tray.

Amongst my collection of English children's Mosaics, all mainly taken from London, I have a Mosaic of a collective of abstract patterns made by a twelve-year-old girl, which Lowenfeld would have classified as a collective design.

Mosaic 13.12
A collective design of abstract patterns made by a 12-year-old English girl from London

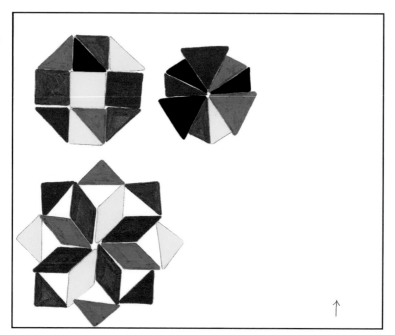

In my paper (Woodcock 1986a: 25–31), I had a possible explanation for the phenomenon of the large number of representational Mosaics, that is, of objects, scenes and collectives, made by the Chinese at the point where I refer to the structure of Chinese Mosaics collected by Thornton in Malaysia. I was struck by the resonance between the structure of those Mosaics and the ideographic written Chinese language, which is the language form that is understood by all literate Chinese and the communication form that unites them. Written Chinese has a long history. It is a perceptual language, in contrast to Western languages, which are phonetic. The form in which a written Chinese word is structured, I had hypothesized, says something about the origins of its meaning. Unlike Western languages, which are rooted in a highly inflected grammar, the Chinese written language is based on pictorial representations, and the words have only one grammatical form. Since the language lacks conjugation or declension and only has very minor uses of inflection, a Chinese character does not specify whether it is a noun, verb or adjective, whether it is singular or plural, or whether it is referring to the past, present or future. The meaning has to be inferred from the context. Thus all thought in Chinese has, when couched in written language, built-in images of their meanings which can only be understood in context.

Furthermore, an ancient Chinese belief underlies that meaning: a belief that meaning can be found in the pattern of events, the natural arrangement of things, as opposed to the causal mentality which underlies Western thought. The principle of causality is linear, whereas the Chinese mind seems to be orientated laterally, based on a synchronistic principle. Jung wrote in a foreword to the Richard Wilhelm translation of the I Ching that, to the Chinese mind when contemplating life's reality, "the matter of interest seems to be the configuration formed by chance events in the moment of observation, and not at all the hypothetical reasons that seemingly account for the coincidence" (I Ching 1951: iii).

Perhaps the Mosaics from these three collections could shed further light on whether the representational nature of Chinese language has deeper roots than we may suppose. Pan reminds us: "The possession of the ancestral language is the supreme mark of being Chinese, imparting as it does a sense of unbroken continuity with the earliest years of Chinese history" (1990: 248). Perhaps the Mosaics can be a language expressive of the cultural identity as well as the individuality of the personality and can reach beyond the building blocks of verbal language.

These three collections of Mosaics from subjects with a common Chinese ancestry, but living in three very different cultural backgrounds, have given further confirmation, in my view, to this explanation, even unto three or four generations away from the original style of thought. It is particularly impressive that the largest number of conceptual Mosaics represented entirely by objects or scenes was in Guangzhou. The children there were of course the only ones educated through the Chinese language, even though the written Chinese characters have now been so simplified that their original objective representations cannot always be easily discerned, as the educators whom I met admitted at the time.

In this context, and even without any knowledge of the Chinese language, there seems to be a residual cultural remembrance of their ancient heritage in the sample of Chinese-American children.[29] Is it possible then that this cultural heritage can continue to play an active role in our lives even though we are unaware of such influences? Quite clearly more research needs to be done, to tease out and identify these cultural characteristics and their effect upon present lives, if any or at all, before any coherent theory of culture, cultural differences and their impact can be formulated.

Colour and shape are not neutral qualities. To take colour first, there is now greater awareness of the fact that the cultural traits associated with particular colours are not universally the same throughout all cultures in the world. Different cultures can and do ascribe different meanings to a specific or even shade of colour. Black is obviously such a colour. This colour is well known to be associated with racial prejudice, but even this trait operates more subtly than this stark description leads us to believe. All over the world, skin colour has always had other significances besides that of the race one belongs to. Both in Asia and Europe, dark-coloured skin, especially amongst women has always been associated with the labouring classes, with

---

29 See the tables in Appendix 5c for comparative percentages of representational Mosaics among the research samples, and that for the preference for shape and colour that will be discussed next.

the corollary that the paler the skin, the more likely it is that one would be a member of the rich leisured classes. In recent decades, it is quite the opposite, especially amongst "white" people. Having a tan has become a desirable "look", and for the same reason, which is that only the leisured can afford to take holidays in the sun. So skin colour has always also been an indicator of social status.

The preference and use of colour in the Mosaics amongst the Guangzhou and San Francisco samples only will be considered next. My data on colour had been collected on a different basis from Ames and Ilg. Whilst they counted the frequency of use in actual Mosaics, I had asked for a preference to be selected and circled (along with other choices, such as gender, urban or rural) on the form completed by each subject, after they had had some personal experience of using the Mosaics. The data collection and analysis provided by Thornton formed the basis for the design of the form for the Guangzhou sample, and Ames and Ilg's findings will be used as the basis for comparison with the San Francisco sample.[30]

It must be acknowledged at the outset that whilst all 301 Mosaics were individual both in process and in product, they also shared a commonality, which was that all the children demonstrated a keen interest in creating bright and vivid Mosaic products. However, it was not surprising that they showed distinct differences as a group among the three samples. The London sample of 31 Mosaics followed Lowenfeld's analysis of Mosaic structure, but differed greatly from Lowenfeld's findings with regard to English children in the percentage of representational Mosaics as against abstract patterns. This fact had not been noted by Thornton in her sample of the Chinese children in Malaysia, and I suspect this was because her research was not looking at cultural differences per se. Turning now to the samples from Guangzhou and San Francisco and looking at the preference for and the use of colour, I will begin with the Guangzhou sample.

In Guangzhou, both boys and girls were united in preferring yellow best by a wide margin from the next colour, and liking the colour black least. In between those two colours, the boys and girls' order of preference for the remaining colours (red, blue, green and white) were totally unlike each other. Interestingly, white was the second choice amongst the city girls. In the West, it is quite well known that white is the colour of mourning for the Chinese, but it is perhaps less well known that white traditionally also embodies the virtue of moral purity and the concrete essence of the female principle. Therefore there is no emotional contradiction in a Chinese bride wearing the traditional Western white wedding dress for the civil or church ceremony often seen in Hongkong (at least at the time this research was being undertaken) and changing into a traditional red (for the Chinese, the colour for joy as well as a symbol of the twin virtues of truth and sincerity) and gold Chinese wedding gown for the festivities afterwards.

In China, yellow is the 'national' colour, traditionally associated with the emperor, and black symbolized personal guilt and depravity. This accorded well with the preferences given to these colours by the children from Guangzhou. It is

---

30 A more detailed study of the Guangzhou and San Francisco samples will be presented in Chapter 14.

thus quite possibly why I was merely baffled and not in the least offended when an obviously angry person shouted at me the words "yellow bastard". I was secure in my knowledge that I was not a bastard, and I had no negative feelings about having the adjective "yellow" applied to me. I did not understand that the word "yellow" was meant to be part of the insult. I did not know then that in English usage, "yellow" was the colour of cowardice. It is not that I was thick-skinned, so my mild astonishment was misunderstood.

It may be of interest to note that the children from Guangzhou also preferred the combination of red and yellow, as being the two colours which go together best, perhaps because traditionally red is symbolic of the Yang principle, whilst yellow is symbolic of the Yin principle. Is this finding an accidental outcome, or does it have a real significance?

When it came to the San Francisco sample, both boys and girls preferred the colour blue. This was also true for the twelve-year-old children in Ames and Ilg's sample. They used more blue tiles than any other. Unlike the Guangzhou children who liked black the least, the Chinese-American children's second colour choice was black. In the case of the Chinese-American boys, the preference for black and blue made up over 76 per cent of the sample of boys. In Ames and Ilg's study, after the blue, both the girls and boys used more white, and for the boys, black shared second place with white. In the San Francisco sample, the girls prefered yellow and green the least, and the majority of boys white and green the least. According to Ames and Ilg, their table (p. 66, table 22) showed a spread of colour usage for the full range of the six colours was between 22 per cent and 5 per cent. This was in contrast to the Guangzhou children's figures for colour preference of between 44 per cent and 2 per cent.

The latest book on psychotherapy using the Lowenfeld Mosaics is by two Americans, Perticone and Tembeckjian (1987), where they devote an entire chapter on the use of colour (pp. 57–65). I would like to refer the present findings (use most or best preference for blue and black as against using or liking yellow and white least) in San Francisco to their findings on the meaning of colour. They say that "blue is considered a cool color and is often used to convey a mood of quietness and calm" and "black is almost always associated with depression". They found that the use of yellow "is perhaps the most difficult to interpret accurately" and the use of white "may simultaneously represent compliance and opposition". It cannot be certain whether this has any resonance with the children from San Francisco; but it is perhaps important to note that they were referring to a specific psychological method, using interpretation as the treatment of choice.

Here too clearly more research needs to be done, for it is clear that the preference and use of colour have a complex and subtle relation with the cultural background of the individual personality. As John Gage has pointed out, "Colour-salience as revealed by language must be related to the wider experience of colour in a given culture" (1999: 79).

Shape, like colour, is a basic way of presenting ourselves: unlike the colour of one's skin, shape, apart from our bone structure, is something that is generally much more within personal control, and has become a particular issue for our present generation. People, when asked about their health, are often heard to reply, "I'm not in good shape," meaning they are not in good health physically and/or psychologically. And the subsequent conversation is likely to continue on the same topic for a while. However, if the reply to "How are you?" was "I'm well/good", the topic of conversation usually shifts onto something else. The two answers are obviously not as straightforward as they sound. And at the present time in the West, being the right shape has become a chief concern amongst young and old alike. Like colour, it also has a social dimension: for both Western men and women, being a "good" shape is not the same as being healthy; being the "right" shape has much more to do with what it says about the personality and presentation of that personality. This is a cultural issue too. Amongst Asian peoples, where poverty and deprivation are common experiences, being plump is often considered a sign of wealth as well as health. In Africa, where starvation is common, being plump would be beyond the ambition of most of the ordinary folk. Survival is more likely to be their main concern.

From the point of view of shape preference and use, all the Guangzhou and San Francisco children gave the diamond shape as their first preference by a big margin. In the Ames and Ilg sample, their twelve-year-olds also used the diamond shape the most, but not by as big a margin. The isosceles triangle was the shape preferred by the smallest number of children in both the Guangzhou and the San Francisco samples. This echoes Ames and Ilg's findings of the use of isosceles triangles for their twelve-year-olds. These findings are thought provoking for many reasons, and highlight another area that might be interesting for further exploration. Both colour and shape probably have cultural meanings about which very little is known at the moment. All that is evident is that they can generate a huge amount of feeling amongst peoples.

***Mosaic 13.13**
A symmetrical
pattern made
by a 10 1/2-year-
old Chinese
boy from
London*

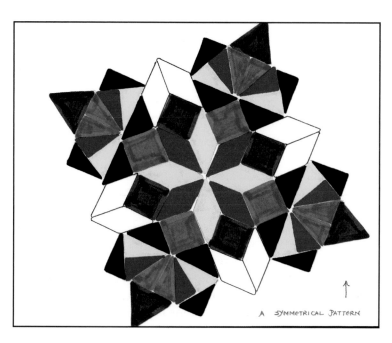

I would now like to present three Mosaics which for me typify the culture from which each came. The first Mosaic was made by a $10\frac{1}{2}$-year-old Chinese boy from London. It was said to be "a symmetrical pattern", a Mosaic that would be described as typically English and age appropriate from Lowenfeld's perspective. In fact, abstract patterns made by the Chinese children conform to those made by the English. This Mosaic (13.13) summarised for me both the cultures within which this boy resided. His internal nature was consonant with his external environment. He was born in London and wholly educated through the medium of the English language, but was likely to be able to converse at least with his parents in Cantonese Chinese.

The next Mosaic (13.14) was made by a twelve-year-old Chinese girl from Guangzhou. This was the translation of her description of her Mosaic: "The road to the happy world." To the Western eye, it may suggest that this road is not a single route, but that one can approach "the happy world" from the four sides of the tray. When I was at university in Hongkong, it was often said that if heaven was like the bull's eye on a dartboard, then one could see that there are many ways to reach the target. Clearly, "the happy world" is not necessarily the same as "heaven", but "happiness" is what people often desire; and for the Chinese, white is also the colour of moral purity.

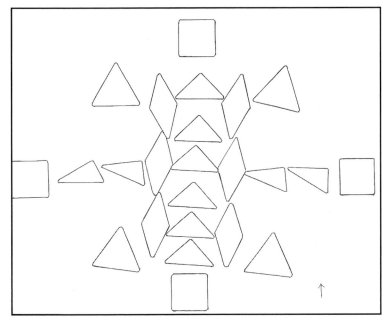

Mosaic 13.14
A conceptual representational Mosaic made by a 12-year-old Chinese girl from Guangzhou

The first appearance of an all-white pattern is recorded in Lowenfeld's Table 2 (2004a: 126–7) and was made by a fourteen-year-old, but irrespective of this age difference, the fact that it was noted by Lowenfeld suggested that others followed. In Ames and Ilg's sample, four twelve-year-old girls used a single colour for their Mosaic: two girls used only blue pieces, and two used all black pieces, while two boys used all blue pieces. Blue and black were also the most common colours used in the Ames and Ilg sample. In Guangzhou, it was not uncommon to see a single colour used to make a Mosaic. These largely occur in conceptual representational Mosaics, which are unknown either for children in England or America. This is the Mosaic I recall when thinking about my Mosaic collection in China.

Finally, an abstract pattern, made by a second-generation Chinese-American boy. On the form, he gave the following description of his Mosaic (13.15): "I just stuck the pieces trying to make them fit and look nice." This Mosaic is likely to be regarded by Ames and Ilg as a successful abstract pattern. It is a single figure "centred horizontally on the paper . . . [where the] pieces on either side of an imaginary dividing line balance each other" (1962: 82). It was his description of his Mosaic which showed the quality which has caused the Chinese-Americans to be placed with the Americans of European ancestry, and distinguished them from the other two samples of Chinese children. He lived very much in the present moment; he wanted simply to see how he could make the pieces "fit" and "look nice". That was an approach identified in American Mosaics by Lowenfeld, to which she had applied the term "Am-type".

Mosaic 13.15
A successful abstract pattern made by a 12-year-old second-generation Chinese-American boy from San Francisco

There were undoubted differences among the three samples, but equally there are distinct similarities. Further analysis in the next chapter will highlight some distinct nuances and the intricate nature of culture. The impact of culture and cultural differences between the family culture of a child and the wider culture of its community inevitably has implications in therapeutic work with children. So, to conclude the next chapter, I shall present a clinical case with an Asian child.

14 Mosaics, culture and the implications for interpersonal understanding

Before my arrival in England, I genuinely had not considered skin colour as a defining trait of personality. I had no opinions on the matter of skin colour as a characteristic determinant of anything as particular as racial difference. After I came to London, I eventually came to realise that it was to be the most distinctive aspect of the physical self, the one that is seen and noticed first. For instance, in my very first job in England, one exasperated colleague finally informed me that by my very presence, she was being forced to think daily about the Chinese and China. She assured me, and I believed her, that it was nothing personal. More generally, simultaneously with skin colour, it is one's shape that strikes another's eye. As noted in the previous chapter, historically physical shape and size have always played a role in how a person is viewed. Throughout the world and down the ages, the use of costume and personal decoration and the changing fashions surely attest to this.

I began to look round me to see if I could identify some other but more general features of cultural differences between the Chinese and British ways of life. Some years later I began to focus on specific issues of living which all cultures face. How had individual cultures formalised certain essential features of living? Can the way a family meal is structured tell us something about an attitude to nurture and the wider issue of socialization? My experience of English hospitality nearly forty years ago had fortunately given me glimpses of a variety of mealtime rituals. Apart from some fine distinctions in the different kinds of meals, as between tea, high tea, breakfast, lunch, dinner and supper, there were ways that meals should be served. It was impressed upon me that the Sunday roast dinner was the best exemplar of English eating, both in the way guests and hosts should behave and in the course the meal should take.

It seemed clear that in post-Second World War England the mother remained the provider of nourishment from the family's earliest beginnings, when the first infant arrived. The way a meal proceeded seemed to have been directly taken from the feeding situation of the infant at the mother's breast. The mother provided the milk and the baby received her gift. In England, this model held throughout one's lifetime. Amongst couples without children, it is still more usual for the woman to prepare the meal, although men are increasingly heard to say that they actually like cooking and women confess to hating it. However, this baby-feeding model is what all cultures start with. What happens next? How do differences emerge?

During the early years of my life in England, it seemed customary for the woman to prepare and cook the meal, and not only did the hostess or host serve the individual portions in turn, but everyone at table waited to be asked whether they wanted further helpings. Meals were also served in courses, singly in succession. The full meal traditionally consisted of a starter, which was anything that could be considered as an appetizer to the "main course", which normally comprised a meat of some description (sometimes fish was served as a precursor to the meat and sometimes instead of) with vegetables and some form of carbohydrates, usually boiled, roasted, sautéed or mashed potatoes. The meal concluded with a dessert and/or a savoury, in fact, anything that would stimulate the digestion. The meal would be taken linearly, in a series of distinctive courses, with all the ingredients cooked and served separately. Once, whilst staying in a modest hotel in France, we were served each ingredient of the meal separately, thus prolonging our enjoyment of it. At mealtimes, the figure of mother continues to play the dominant role as the provider of nourishment. Until recently, the portions continued to be controlled by whoever (usually an adult) served the meal, making everyone else dependent upon their judgement, in terms of which food, what amount, and the timing of the serving. It was a serially ordered experience, with a greater emphasis on power and dependency.

I was, however, brought up to understand that a family meal was a shared experience, both in the cooking and in the eating. Depending on the circumstances, either or both the parents could be involved in the cooking. It was not obvious that one of the mother's chief caring roles was that of actually producing the meal for the family. This was confirmed for me in 1986 in Guangdong, when I was invited to dine with the family of one of the high-ranking officials who was in charge of myself, my son, who assisted me in the project, and my research project. Her daughter had come to help and our offer of assistance was accepted without any of the usual polite protests I had experienced amongst our friends in England. It is however true that we were only given very light work to do. In a while we were joined by her husband, an army general, who immediately joined the working party, and we produced the meal together amidst much merriment and lively conversation. In some Chinese homes, if a cook had been employed to cater for the family, it was not unknown for the cook to eat with the family. It is, however, in the order and manner with which a meal is served and eaten together which most distinguishes the two cultures.

For the Chinese, this clarity in order is missing. It was quite usual to start and end with soup, and often people would continue savouring the soup during the meal. The main part of the meal usually consists of several dishes served together. The chief ingredients consist of meat, fish and vegetables, in any combination. It is well known that the Chinese eat with chopsticks, and one of the reasons for this, tradition says, is to avoid having a knife at the dining table. Whether this was consciously intended or not from the beginning, the absence of knives has the effect of emphasising the amiability of the eating experience. A round table on which the food is placed also implies a sense of equality in the shared experience.

In discussion with the officials from the Education Department in China, this pattern was still very much the case in Guangdong Province. Wherever I went, both formal and informal banquets were arranged for us, always attended by a large number of Chinese people. Anybody who was even remotely connected with officialdom or the project was invited, or so it seemed. Like wedding feasts, speeches were obligatory. These occasions were indeed more like formal wedding receptions and were rather overwhelming for my son and myself, but for such a visit as ours, it was apparently very much the norm for the Chinese. Such banquets, however, have some similar features to the English Sunday roast dinner. They do often have many courses, each course consisting of a main ingredient, all served separately. So it is not that the Chinese cannot conceive of different ways of serving food. Just as in the West, buffet meals where many and various dishes are served simultaneously are also quite common. There is no lack of mental flexibility in either culture. What I am basically referring to is the serving style that has been chosen by each culture as the style within which children are socially embedded.

From an early age in a Chinese family, a child is encouraged to take his place as an equal member of the family, at least at mealtimes. All the members of the family, and according to ability, serve themselves from the dishes on the table (young children are shown and then helped until they can help themselves). The unspoken rule is that one must be mindful of the fact that one is sharing the food, so it would be frowned upon if one was to pick all the choice pieces (the meaty pieces instead of the bony ones, for instance) for oneself (it is permissible to pick out pieces for a young child or one's spouse or the chief guest), or to eat more than one's "fair" share of any dish. It also encourages the young to begin to learn about their likes and dislikes and the size of their appetites. People make visual assessments of the ongoing situation throughout the meal, so an awareness of others is being built into the occasion, which also assists with socialization. Until the one child policy in China, this subtle form of socialisation had served the Chinese well. When I was in China in 1986, it was one of the concerns that the policy might make children selfish and lack personal experience of sharing.

When I was in San Francisco, however, a very different picture emerged from my personal experiences of staying with American families, including a Chinese-American family for the period of my research, as well as on other occasions.[31] There was much more a sense of independence and individuality that was acceptable, and in some cases encouraged. Very few families seemed to eat together or formally. The whole lifestyle did not seem to be conducive to such regularity.[32] Nor

---

31 My grateful thanks to Sai-Ling Chan Sew and her family for welcoming me into their home during the period of my research.

32 This situation has now become much more common in London at the beginning of the 21st century. It is also more common for fathers to take on the role of cooking for the family. And the role of financial provision is now less the sole responsibility of the father. Even at the time of conducting my research in London, this change had already started and the trend has since accelerated.

did parents often cook for the family; "take-aways" or "take-outs" had replaced home cooking. Of course, this made it easier for individual tastes, as well as the fancy of the moment, to be easily catered for. During my various stays in and around San Francisco, I always ate out with my hosts. I was told that guests for meals at home were atypical. People of all ages routinely went out to eat. Thus eating as a family at home seemed to be a rarity, and every such occasion became special.

Reflecting upon the Mosaic findings through the three research groups, it occurred to me that the way a cultural group manages the social aspect of the dining experience might reflect their social identity within the cultural group. Here I am painting with a broad brush, ignoring other social dimensions like class or economic differences. Comparing the Chinese children from Guangzhou with the Chinese-American children from San Francisco, there seemed to be a vast gulf between their respective sense of belonging, their sense of self-worth or self-doubt, their consciousness of being part of a culture or that of self, their independence and individuality. Can such signs be identified in their Mosaics?

Back in 1986, in Guangdong, the sample of urban children came from the two best-equipped schools in the provincial capital city of Guangzhou, with the broadest curriculum, embracing Western scientific discoveries and technological expertise, where attempts were made to combine the latest Western technology and scientific thinking with traditional Chinese art (as in the inclusion of both Chinese calligraphy and painting) in the curriculum of the school. Yet it was unthinkable to the officials that a family would not eat together. The air of expected conformity was palpable. The children were all subject to the same pressure for academic achievement. This was the general attitude, there was no alternative in sight, all children were subject to it. In this realm of life, they were certainly equal.

In San Francisco in 1991, it would be the norm for members of a family to take their meals separately and at different times. At the school where the San Francisco sample was taken, I was told that the school was really not allowed to have on their roll more than 40 per cent of children of Chinese descent. Since the school had a high scholastic reputation, and was in an area where the very sound of the school's name had the added attraction of an auspicious meaning in Chinese, the vice-principal reckoned that actually 65 per cent were really of Chinese descent. Nevertheless, it was very much an all-American school. The emphasis was clearly individualistic. Very few, if any, spoke Chinese, let alone wrote it. I was told that the only noticeable difference between these children and those from another ethnic group within the school was the extra parental pressure towards academic achievement placed on them. This raised the anxiety of the group of Chinese-Americans, since they all knew that this pressure was not an inevitability. There was an alternative for their European or Afro-American peers, which was unavailable to them, purely because of their ethnic or cultural background, which has a strong tradition of pressurising a child to achieve academically.

It was only after I began to write up my findings when I discovered that this phenomena of Chinese expectations of conformity whilst thinking within a broadly world context, had been reported in an article by Ekblad (1984: 578–90), and more particularly in the *Scandinavian Journal of Psychology* by the same author (Ekblad 1986: 220–30). In China, both Ekblad's and my own conclusions from the children's Mosaics show that "Chinese expectations of patriotism and altruism in children are extremely stable and uniform . . . [but that] the price of this adaptation seems compensated [for] by protection up to school age, and by group support in a social network [such as the Young Pioneers] which makes the children appreciated and loved" (1984: 588).

On further reflection, I began to see that the features which most distinguished the group of Chinese-American children from the Chinese children from Guangzhou could also be applied to what Ames and Ilg had found in the large sample of American children whose forebears had come mainly from Europe, chiefly Britain. They too showed that they were "often dissatisfied with themselves . . . doubtful of their design's worth" (1962: x). Modifying Ames and Ilg's categories only slightly, 17 per cent of the San Francisco sample offered a statement about their Mosaic which amounted to not knowing what they had made. They often merely stated what colours or shapes they had used, or just described what they did, without putting a name to their product. When a Mosaic had been named, the subject, usually a representational Mosaic, had features of doubt and uncertainty that had no parallel in Guangzhou.

Examples from both girls and boys might serve to give a flavour of the characteristics I am talking about. The first one was made by a third-generation[33]

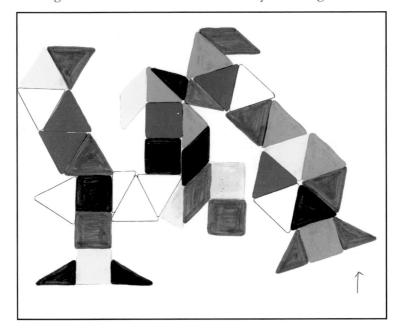

Mosaic 14.1
Mosaic from a third-generation Chinese-American girl from San Francisco

---

33 The form on which children declared their generation was self-determined. This was the school's contribution to the research project in response to the request to supply a research sample of Chinese-American children. A lesson on ancestry had been given by the school staff to the classes from which the research sample were to be drawn. The form was designed so that the children could fill in the research forms themselves at the end of the lesson.

Chinese girl from San Francisco. She wrote afterwards, "My Mosaic started out as a snake but I decided to add more [pieces] so it wasn't a picture of anything when I was done. I tried to use as many colors as possible."

The next Mosaic of a similar vein is from a third-generation boy. Here I have copied exactly what he wrote down, including the punctuation: "My Mosaic is nothing really, its just a bunch of shapes put together ? on either side is color that match." It will be noticed that in fact it is a good abstract pattern, symmetrical along the vertical axis in both shape and colour. This would be classed by Ames and Ilg as an entirely successful symmetrical pattern, and in that sense it is an American Mosaic, although the successful American designs are classified by their placement on the tray rather than on the centrality of the design symmetry. Also in Ames and Ilg (1962), these designs are often along the horizontal axis. Here the whole tone of the statement is one of questioning the worth of the design and showing a lack of self-confidence in his ability to make anything at all.

Mosaic 14.2
Mosaic from a third-generation Chinese-American boy from San Francisco

The nearest to a sense of self-awareness in the Guangzhou sample is a Mosaic made by a girl. In her statement about her Mosaic (14.3), she wrote, "Pattern. I think what I have done is peculiar. I like doing peculiar things." From the point of view of classification by visual means alone, it is clearly an abstract pattern, symmetrical (in the use of shape only, whilst the colours have been used with originality) along the vertical axis, not unlike the previous Mosaic made by the Chinese-American boy. It is a successful abstract pattern, which is rare enough amongst any of the three Chinese samples, it is only symmetrical along the vertical axis, which is considerably rarer still. Perhaps she was semi-aware that it was these features in her Mosaic that had made what she had done "peculiar".

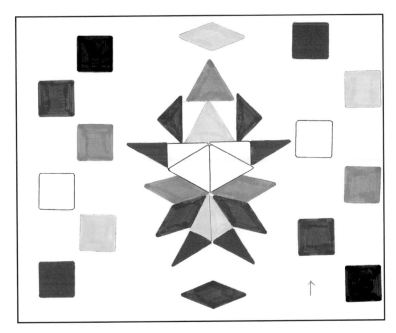

Mosaic 14.3
An abstract pattern made by a girl from Guangzhou

My next choice is from a third-generation Chinese-American girl. Remembering the Mosaic as a Personality in Action, I have chosen this Mosaic particularly to demonstrate how a Mosaic can speak volumes. On her form she stated: "My Mosaic is a question mark." Apart from the question it surely begs, let us examine the product in greater detail. The question mark is made so that it

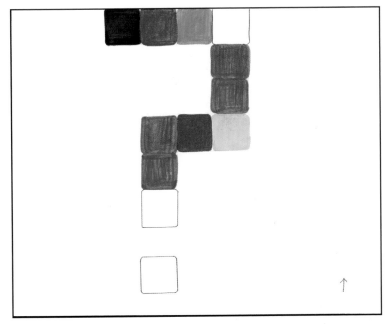

Mosaic 14.4
A "question mark" made by a third-generation Chinese-American girl from San Francisco

appears to be dangling from the top edge of the tray frame, with the defining feature of the question mark at the base of the figure, made with two white squares, thus almost merging this part of the Mosaic with the background. "Does she harbour any doubts about herself?" may be a legitimate question to pose in this case. But it could equally be said that the question referred to was a philosophical one. She may have simply been wondering what the whole project with the Mosaics was about.

The next Mosaic was made by a second-generation Chinese-American boy. He described his Mosaic as a "deformed tree" in small capital letters. It is a totally recognisable representation of a tree. It shares a feature with the previous Mosaic, in that it has a white base from which the tree has developed, and the trunk itself is short and small. The tree consists of one green, one blue and one red square; two yellow squares and four black squares. White was used most often and in a greater variety of shapes: apart from the four squares, there are two isosceles triangles, two scalene triangles (both shapes were used for the sides of the tree) and an equilateral triangle for the top of the tree. The tree is thus framed by a white outline. It is a perfectly symmetrically shaped tree, if slightly lacking in stability due to the short, small white trunk raised from the bottom edge of the tray frame, which did not suggest any idea of roots. This Mosaic begs a similar question to the previous example. In what way is this tree deformed? Does he feel himself to be "deformed" in some way?

Mosaic 14.5
A "deformed tree" made by a second-generation Chinese-American boy from San Francisco

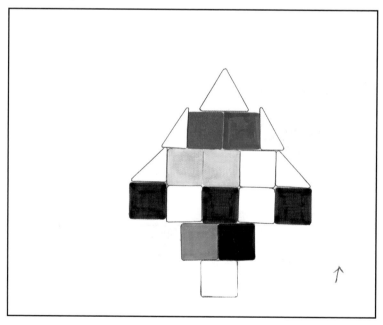

Almost identical to this "deformed tree" is a Mosaic (14.6) made by a third-generation Chinese-American girl. She stated: "My Mosaic is a retarded or deformed flower in the sun and has red petals and yellow inside and has a green stem and leaves."

The closest to this "retarded or deformed flower" that I can find in the Guangzhou collection is one made by a girl (Mosaic 14.7). According to the trans-

Mosaic 14.6
A "retarded or deformed flower" made by a third-generation Chinese-American girl from San Francisco

lation given by the Chinese interpreter provided for the project, it is a representation of "cut flowers for a vase". The representation, however, is full of colour and displayed a variety of flowers. The visual impact of the Mosaic itself suggests more than just the notion of flowers which have been cut (depicting the shortened life of the flowers). To my mind's eye, this Mosaic showed its maker to be a girl with a sunny and lively attitude, not at all lacking in self-confidence.

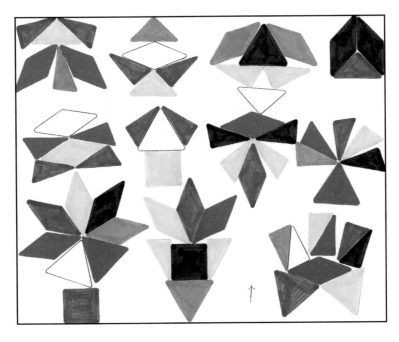

Mosaic 14.7
"Cut flowers for a vase" by a girl from Guangzhou

All these Mosaics suggest a reading that perhaps requires a cultural dimension that is beyond the individual personality of the Mosaic-maker. This dimension may be rooted in the historical context of Chinese migration to the San Francisco area in the late nineteenth century. Pan (1990: 106) writes that "at a time when immigrants [in general] were commonly expected to discard their old ethnic identities and surrender themselves wholeheartedly to the embrace of America, the Chinese immigrants' unwillingness to sink deeper roots was held against him; he was seen as sitting on the fence, not committing himself". This non-participation in the host society was apparently not exhibited by later generations. The earthquake of 1906 destroyed the immigration records, making it impossible to ascertain the legality of people's immigrant status. Citizen status was then granted to the earthquake survivors, which provoked a backlash against them. Local hostility increased and ended in the creation of an immigration processing system that is commemorated evermore in the Chinese psyche by the simple words "Angel Island", which is where the practices of this system were enacted. It may be wondered perhaps whether the feeling of unworthiness, as expressed in many of their Mosaics, underlies the psychic reality of the present generation of Chinese-Americans in San Francisco, however else they may have integrated into American society.

I will now consider the children in Connecticut (where Ames and Ilg 1962 collected their sample of Mosaics), who were also descendants from immigrants, but had a different history. The people of Connecticut became the dominant group in America soon after they cast off the yoke of colonial rule. Their immigration from Europe was spurred on not only by the attraction of wealth and power, but by religious persecution in their mother countries. The East Coast of America was their first port of call, where they became the longest-established group. Yet, as perhaps we can infer from what was noted by Lowenfeld in their descendants' Mosaic responses, despite this positive history their attitude to the Mosaic process itself betrayed a dissatisfaction with themselves and an uncertainty about their Mosaic work that was much like that of the Chinese-American children (Ames and Ilg 1962: ix–xi) in my San Francisco sample. Perhaps this is not a coincidence?

I would now like to turn to another matter. Are there any Mosaics from the San Francisco sample that are not found in the Ames and Ilg collection? The answer is "yes". Does this collection of Chinese-American Mosaics show any examples that have also been found in the Guangzhou sample? The answer is again "yes", and I show a few examples from each sample below. Since the Connecticut children in Ames and Ilg's study did not seem to have made any conceptual Mosaics, I will simply confine myself to examples of these in the Guangzhou and San Francisco samples. There are two types of conceptual Mosaics, as defined by Lowenfeld.

My first example comes from a Chinese-American boy and is entitled "Black Death". The capitalizing of the title suggests it to be a conceptual design.[34] On the other hand, this boy's "Black Death" was probably inspired by the literary genre of

---

34 Lowenfeld has described this type of conceptual design as "designs in which abstract lines and masses are used to convey an abstract idea" (2004a: 64).

Mosaic 14.8
A conceptual design entitled "Black Death" made by a second-generation Chinese-American boy from San Francisco

horror stories and board games at the time these Mosaics were made and not the events in mediaeval Europe. At the time, I was unable to confirm with the Mosaic-maker what his intentions were.

The next Mosaic (14.9 overleaf) example comes from a Chinese-American girl. She had deliberately turned the tray round to the portrait position and made the Mosaic which she went on to describe as "My Mosaic is about a cross and God."[35] It is singularly devoid of colour except for the use of a single red square representing the letter "o" in the word "God". The remaining shapes are all made with white pieces, including the square. She had chosen a square as the shape she liked best; circled white as her favourite colour, but put blue and white as the two colours she thought would go together best. This makes her use of red in her Mosaic intriguing to say the least.

Like the girl in Guangzhou who had made the Mosaic described as "The road to the happy world" (Mosaic 13.14), she used white, the colour she liked best, to represent a higher realm of human psychic reality. Are they referring to a similar sphere of human life? Happiness in life is an aspiration; the cross, when linked with God, contains the essence of the Christian idea of salvation and forgiveness, pointing towards the way to heaven, where supreme happiness resides. In this Mosaic (14.9 overleaf), the cross was divided from God by a line of Mosaics. It can be speculated that this line could be referring to the two realms of earth and Heaven; or, the line could suggest that it was human sin which separated man from God.

---

35 Lowenfeld has described this type of conceptual design as one "in which representations of objects are used to convey an abstract which may be either an emotional or a mental concept" (2004a: 65).

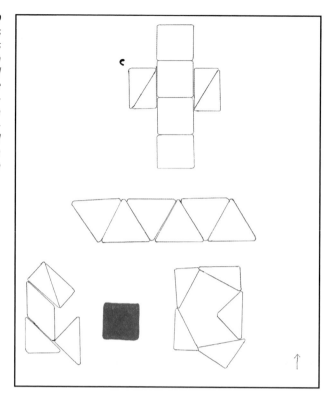

In any case, both of these Chinese-American Mosaics could ultimately be classified as conceptual Mosaics, a sub-group of representational designs.

I will now give examples of conceptual Mosaics from the Guangzhou sample. Considering the fact that neither Lowenfeld nor Ames and Ilg mention this category of Mosaics for children, the Guangzhou sample has, proportionately speaking, a surprisingly large number of them. The first conceptual Mosaic from China I have chosen is one made by a boy (Mosaic 14.10). It is typical of the conceptual Mosaics seen in the Guangzhou sample. He stated on his form: "A house, to symbolize the vigorous development and reconstruction of Chinese society." A straightforward representation of his idea, simply and succinctly stated in a single image. The image is obvious, but the idea is less easily discernible.

The next conceptual Mosaic (Mosaic 14.11) from Guangzhou was made by a girl and gives a subtler picture. Although she stated the representation equally firmly and as briefly as the boy cited in the previous example, she described her idea in greater detail: "An oblong. Made with my beloved white colour and the scalene shape to express a wish that people all over the world would co-operate so that we all can live and enjoy a full life." She used only one shape and all the colours are linked by her favourite, white. Black was not used; in her form she highlighted the fact that it was not a colour she had considered by ignoring it altogether. The idea of different peoples being represented by the different colours but in the same shape (the scalene triangle) and linked by her "beloved white" also conveyed the impression that the idea of universal co-operation amongst equals was central to her wish.

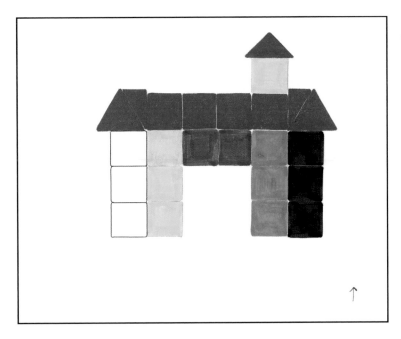

It seems clear that the children from Guangzhou could conceptualise thoughts in the form of representational objects, with a broad contemporary view of the world, whereas the Chinese-American children from San Francisco referred more to a personal interest in their Mosaics. The Chinese-American boy had certainly portrayed "Black Death" very much in an abstract pattern, whilst the Chinese-American girl had used the symbols of Christianity to express a faith based on personal conviction and a direct relationship to God. Nevertheless, conceptual

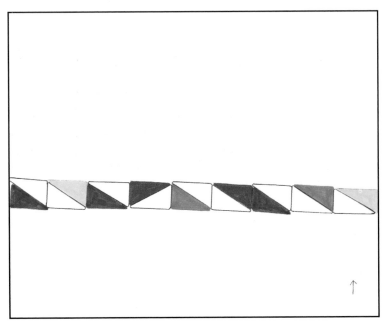

designs were not noted by Ames and Ilg (1962). To that extent then these Mosaics from San Francisco do have a perhaps tenuous Chinese reference. Thus, several dimensions of personality may have become intertwined here to give a subtler and more complex picture than my original research intentions had allowed.

I hope that this brief description of cultural differences, using Mosaics to tease out the finer details, will have been sufficient to demonstrate that the Lowenfeld Mosaics can be used as both a psychological projective instrument and a tool for cross-cultural research, and that culture, cultural background and the educational process within any cultural background may also have a tangible effect on the Personality in Action, which can be visually expressed through the medium of the Mosaics.

Pondering on the visual expression of cultural differences led me to wonder if there was any other objective evidence of such phenomena. Some years ago I came across Shigehisa Kuriyama's remarkably perceptive work *The Expressiveness of the Body and the Divergence of Greek and Chinese Medicine* where he compared two diagrams of the human body (1999: 10–11), the one from Hua Shou's *Shisijing fahui* (1341) and the other from Vesalius's *Fabrica* (1543). He was impressed by the differences: "In Hua Shou, we miss the muscular detail of the Vesalian man; and in fact Chinese doctors lacked even a specific word for 'muscle'. Muscularity seemed to have been a peculiarly Western preoccupation. On the other hand, the tracts and points of acupuncture entirely escaped the West's anatomical vision of reality" (p. 8). I was reminded of the lectures on anatomy and physiology that we were given during my child psychotherapy training. We were taught how the body was structured through descriptions of the skeleton and the musculature. It was particularly interesting for me, since at that time I was more naturally attuned to the Chinese model of the body displaying acupuncture points. But now, seeing these two conceptions of the body side by side in diagrammatic form, the idea of cultural differences as a genuine phenomenon came alive in me again. Perhaps this was evidence of a kind. It is possible that to the Chinese mind, thoughts and pattern are concretely constructed, whereas for cultures with phonetic languages, the idea of pattern is construed in the abstract. "[C]onceptions of the body – not just in the meanings that each ascribes to bodily signs, but more fundamentally in the changes and features that each recognises *as* signs" (p. 272).

To return to thinking about the individual, I will now present a clinical case to show the effect on one family of the complex dynamics of living in a multicultural society. During the summer term of a school year, an eleven-year-old Asian girl was referred to me for school phobia accompanied by retching and vomiting in the mornings. I shall call her Teresa. She was born in London and had only ever attended a convent school. Her convent school enjoyed a high academic reputation, and until that summer term all had seemed well with her attendance. Both the staff and parents were now puzzled by this turn of events. Apparently she had been a keen and studious pupil up until the beginning of that summer term. When Teresa arrived at my consulting room, she appeared to be a shy and quiet girl, which soon wore off as the session progressed. I began the first session as usual by inviting her to do a Mosaic.

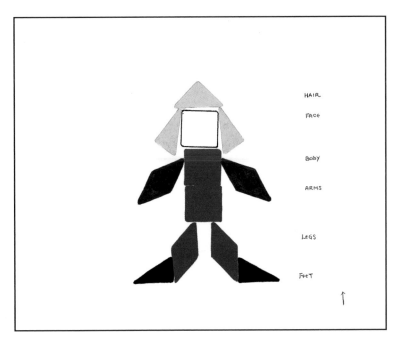

HAIR

FACE

BODY

ARMS

LEGS

FEET

Mosaic 14.12
Teresa's self-portrait

Teresa worked quietly, confidently and quickly. She told me that her Mosaic was that of a person. I was immediately struck by the picture of blonde hair framing a white face. Was I to be challenged on the idea that the Mosaic was a portrait of a Personality in Action? She continued to describe the features depicted by the Mosaic, beginning with the yellow "hair", white "face", red "body", blue "arms", red "legs" and black "feet". She was happy with her Mosaic, satisfied that she had managed to convey the essentials. I asked her which of the Mosaic colours did she like best. Unhesitatingly, she said "red". Is it a picture of anyone, I next asked? She looked up at me sharply and replied with some surprise in her voice, that it was a picture of her.

The question in my mind acquired greater urgency. How had a girl with black hair acquired blonde hair in her own mind? I then asked her to tell me why she thought she had come to see me. She sat in silence for some minutes and then said that she had become unhappy at school towards the end of the last term. I asked her to say what it was that had troubled her about the school, and if she had been happy there before that? This time the pause was shorter. She looked me straight in the eye before replying with a question, "Have you heard about Easter?" I tried to choose my words cautiously and said that I knew it was an important Christian festival. Teresa continued her questioning: "Did you know that they drink the blood of their God and eat His body?" I told her that I had thought it was only a symbolic act in memory of Christ's sacrifice. Teresa insisted that all the Catholics drink the blood of Christ and eat His body.

Realising that she might not have fully understood the Christian symbolism of the act of eating bread and drinking wine, I changed tack and asked her about her own religion. This was a genuine enquiry from me, as I had not been provided with much background information. Instead of talking about her religion, she told me emphatically that they were *very* strict vegetarians, and that she was equally convinced that vegetarianism was an essential part of the religious ethos of her family's religion. I began to see some light; it was the eating and drinking of the body and blood of Christ that had troubled her. And indeed, she was disquieted by the revelation that for a Catholic, this ritual had an equal importance to her own belief in the religious necessity for not eating any meat, which in her mind came also to mean no drinking of blood either. It was this that had put her off going to school after the Easter holidays. It was the school's policy to provide an extensive educational programme on the importance of all the Christian festivals in the Catholic faith for final year students before they moved onto secondary school.

After two sessions, Teresa returned to school and continued to progress well with her education. Nevertheless, the blonde hair and white face continued to concern me. It was fortunate for my curiosity that by her choice, we were to return to her Mosaic again and again during subsequent appointments. She enabled us to discover together the underlying meaning of this self-portrait. It was a picture of the contradictory nature of her daily existence, and how she dealt with this by adopting at least the appearance of assimilation at school.

At home, Teresa lived the life of an obedient Asian girl. She dressed in traditional clothes, and all her friends of the family were invariably from within her own culture. She had a younger brother and was the elder of a family of two. All her classmates talked about their brothers quite differently from her experience of life at home with a brother. They certainly did not have to cater for them in the same way she had to do at home, where she was expected to be mother's little helper, not just in terms of household duties, but also to supply her brother's every need so he could concentrate on his studies. She patiently explained that this was normal for a daughter, any daughter, within her culture.

Her attempts to fit in at school were nothing as sophisticated as integration with the host community. From the picture she obtained of her classmates' lives at home, Teresa simply longed to have a life more like theirs, to have even a fraction of the freedom that she imagined they enjoyed, without any of the responsibilities she felt burdened with. But she was also fearful of the loss of her family's affections, particularly her mother's.

Teresa had recently been acquainted with her father's hope for her future, which was to marry an Asian of the same faith. This man would be chosen for her by her parents. A subsequent meeting with her parents confirmed that these plans were already far advanced. Teresa would not be told about their choice until they decided it was the appropriate moment. Teresa did not look forward to this future.

She was also intrigued by the changes in her body, but was denied any objective knowledge of the developmental process. The parents had forbidden any instruction on the subject to be given to her. And since the convent school's attitude to sex instruction was nearly as illiberal as her parents', there had been very little opportunity for her to access such information. Teresa, however, was keen to have this information. Conflict and unhappiness seemed inevitable not only for Teresa, but for the entire family.

And yet the father was enthusiastic about Teresa going to university and taking up a profession. Implicit and explicit in the conversation with him was also the expectation that she would combine a career with the task of being an Asian homemaker. This, her parents felt was the best, or maybe the only way for Teresa to integrate into English society.

Unfortunately for her, Teresa did not want a professional life in the future; she was convinced she could become successful in business, just like her father, and very early on demonstrated to me an excellent business acumen. However, he would not countenance his daughter taking up business as a career, and only saw a high-ranking position in one of the professions as an aspiration for her. She was not interested in an academic education, certainly not in studying for the kind of examinations that would enable her to take up a professional career. Teresa knew what she was good at, what she enjoyed doing, and she was determined to pursue her own goals.

At school recently, she had begun to embark on a campaign to cultivate a Western attitude in order to at least give an appearance of having the same kind of outlook as her classmates; hence the yellow hair and white face. Thus her self-portrait reflected not what she saw in the mirror, but how she felt about herself, what she aspired for herself. But she was handicapped by the lack of confirmation at home, as well as lack of information; thus the blank face. Every part of her that had contact with the outside world in her Mosaic, her arms and feet had a different colour from that of her body and legs. Somewhere perhaps she realised that these latter parts would be the territory where her battle would have to be fought; hence red, her colour, the colour she liked best, was used exclusively to represent *her true self* in her Mosaic. She would relish the fight, but when would she be allowed even to begin?

Of course this situation is not unique to Teresa. Most of the second-generation immigrant children would share this dilemma with her, whether they be Greek, Turkish, Chinese, Vietnamese, Japanese, Indian, Pakistani or any of the others who regularly migrate across cultural and national borders. Teresa found herself working against all the odds and returned for treatment time and again, using the same symptoms she first displayed as a way to return to talk to someone whom she had perhaps found was at least uncritical as well as sympathetic. The parents finally persuaded themselves that I was either useless or worse, sabotaging their wishes. They had wanted me, the therapist, to persuade Teresa of the error of her ways. I, as the therapist, did not feel that that was my role. We finally agreed that Teresa would stop coming to see me, and to save everyone's face, the parents would consider alternative treatment. The cultural context and the times, together with the character of the individual personalities involved, made this a case filled with individual pain for all concerned, an impasse and a veritable tragedy.

If Teresa and her family's case could be mapped onto an entire community with all its multicultural complexities, the tension thus created might be unimaginably problematic. Even so, perhaps such dilemmas can only be tackled on a personal basis? As we are individuals, so will each of our personalities and circumstances be individual. Having studied the three research samples in some detail and found a few general similarities as well as differences amongst them, I continue to believe that it will only be through individual work that such personal dilemmas can be worked at and life be lived.

15 Our bodies, ourselves and Lowenfeld's theory of E

One of the major preoccupations of my life has been the idea of Life and its beginnings, but it did not acquire any means of expression until I began training at Lowenfeld's Institute of Child Psychology and came across her theory of E. Many years later I also began to grapple with her theory of Protosystem Thinking. As the former underpins all human life, I shall begin my latest thoughts on the theory of E in this chapter and discuss my understanding of Protosystem Thinking in the next.

A broad way of envisaging the nature of Life is perhaps to view it through the kinaesthetic sense of movement. As to what sustains Life, there are many theories, for which such terms as "life force" and "libido" are but examples. My own understanding of what sustains Life derives from the idea of movement, which is perhaps inherent in the Chinese notion of Qi or Chi (Yang 1997: xx). Whether this predisposed me to accept or reject Lowenfeld's theory of E in its entirety, I am unable to decide, but what I accept is that, as a metaphor, it is a plausible and easily imaginable idea. What is being imagined is the active and action potential of Life itself.

Lowenfeld postulated that when the sperm penetrates the ovum, that is, at the moment of conception, there arises a basic charge of undifferentiated energy which she has called E. This E varies in quantity from individual to individual. If it did not and every person had the same charge of E, then in order to account for the extreme as well as variety of difference in any given population within the same culture and in the same period of history, it follows that there would have to be an "enormous silting up of interior friction and tension on the one side and a great hollow as it were, absence of friction and tension on the other side" (Lowenfeld 1952).[36] Her hypothesis was that first we are not all born with the same amount of E, but are each endowed with an individual amount of E, possibly through genetic inheritance. Like the colour of our eyes, our bone structure and our temperament, some people are naturally more energetic than others.

---

36 This series of lectures were given to the students at the Institute of Child Psychology (ICP). The audio tapes are incomplete, and are now housed in the Lowenfeld archives at the Wellcome Library for the History and Understanding of Medicine.

Lowenfeld further postulated that human nature in relation to E functions through the homeostatic principle. A dictionary definition states that homeostasis is "the tendency of an animal or organism to maintain a constant internal environment regardless of varying external conditions". She believed that this principle governs all forms; governs the relationship between size and structure, which gives stability to the final shape of our bodies. Thus the body or mind will show signs of fatigue or stress when physically, psychologically or mentally over-exerted. It is not only part of our physical nature, it is embedded in one of our senses, our vestibular sense, which allows us to perceive our body's movement, our position in space and our degree of balance. According to Lowenfeld the homeostatic principle applies to our psychological selves and is perhaps what is involved when there is mental disturbance. There is a parallel here with the Chinese notion of Qi, which also describes mental distress as a disturbance of this energy, and sees any discomfort in the body as an imbalance of it.

It is astonishing how often this homeostatic principle is invoked in a Mosaic response. From the cases cited in previous chapters, the preconceived idea of symmetry, or an underlying notion of imbalance can be found in a number of the Mosaic-makers. Adam, with whom this book opens, is a case in point. His first statement about his Mosaic was, "It's a pattern – a symmetrical pattern" (Mosaic 1.1). It was not until we had contemplated his Mosaic for some time that a picture that powerfully described his feelings about his inner and outer world began to emerge. Having articulated that "the space in the middle is important", he went on to say, "This" – indicating this space – "feels like a contracting coffin. I am in the middle – squeezed so hard that I've become invisible."

In their Mosaics both Janet in Chapter 9 and Teresa in Chapter 14 show the disharmony within themselves in their depiction of their physical selves. Janet (Mosaic 9.1) used a regular rectangle to represent the trunk, the body of her person, but it is how this shape was made up that was telling. The two sides were composed of isosceles triangles, but the colours of each were entirely different from one another. The left side was red and green, and the right side entirely blue. Furthermore, the use of the isosceles triangles suggested an oblique rather than straightforward split, as though the colours associated with the right also had a place on the left side and vice versa. This matched the way Janet described her feelings about her parents' separation and eventual divorce, showing how this has effectively emotionally unbalanced her. It also became clear that she had never given up the hope that they might be reunited, when home would again feel like home.

Teresa's Mosaic portrait of herself (Mosaic 14.12) made a similar impression to Janet's. Except for the yellow hair and the addition of feet, the shape of the person's torso was identical to Janet's, but was composed entirely in red squares. Her inner feelings about her total situation had been expressed idiosyncratically but clearly. And again like Janet, Teresa's problem was not something that could be addressed directly by Teresa herself on her own; it had to be faced by her family. So the first point about E in any individual is that it is subject to the homeostatic principle and forms part of the economy of individual bodies, so that the total charge of E in each of us is unique to ourselves and requires to be balanced physically and psychologically within us.

The second point regarding E has to do with the physical body in which this charge of E is lodged. Through long professional experience Lowenfeld came to the conclusion that not all bodies are well suited to house the E they are endowed with. "Bodies are either well or badly equipped for the expression of E" was how Lowenfeld (1952) expressed it. Thus there can be a discrepancy between the charge and the suitability of the structures to discharge it. Lowenfeld argued that if this charge is too large for the body to manage, it will cause unendurable tension in the body, which in certain individuals may result in neurosis. It can also be argued that too little charge of E might be expressed in the condition described as endogenous depression. Clearly this idea is also related to both the physical and the psychological aspect of our vestibular system.

From the outset of human life, the notion of splitting creating difference is built into our genetic make-up. With the union of ovum and sperm at the moment of conception, the cell begins the process of growth in a continuous process of division, multiplying at an astonishing speed. Already all the parameters that govern life are in place. To begin with, these cells are generic in nature and as yet have no specific function assigned to them. The first critical moment during the pregnancy comes when gender is determined. We are all said to begin life in the womb with two "X" chromosomes. At one critical point, one of the Xs loses a "leg" so to speak, and becomes a "Y". This "Y" has seemed to define maleness. However, recent researches on the X chromosome reported in a series of articles in *Nature* (17 March 2005) suggests that even at the level of the genome, male and female are already clearly defined and expressed as separate genomes. What I understand from this in relation to E is that men and women have distinct ways of expressing E, because E is moving through two markedly different genetic structures, that of male and female. It is in the realm of our psychological selves that this distinction becomes paramount. I will enlarge upon this thought later in this chapter.

From the beginning of human life, the physical and the psychological in human nature are indivisible. And the survival of the individual E, once begun at conception, compels a being's physical and psychological continuance. Some examples of the way E manifests itself in the realities of human development follow.

Physical survival is an obvious first goal although how this is achieved will vary from individual to individual by genetic makeup and constitution, from culture to culture and according to our external physical and social conditions. Traumas in the womb before birth are not unknown, as in abortion or drug poisoning of the mother; there can be traumas directed from outside the mother, as in the case of rape. Once the child is born, the E is chiefly concerned with the necessities of growth and the maintenance of health, by such means as cries, smiles and other actions for obtaining adequate provision of food, warmth and shelter. Thus the struggle for survival begins from the start of life and continues till life's end. And despite its vicissitudes, people seem to want to continue their life for as long as possible.

Our psychological survival seems to include a wish for immortality, the desire to make one's own mark beyond one's lifetime. This is where the E in each gender plays its part. This is where Woman has a distinct advantage over Man. The most obvious moment to observe this difference in the function of E in men and women is during the time of maturing sexuality. Puberty ushers in adolescence, but it is experienced differently by the sexes. For both boys and girls, distinct feminine or masculine signs appear and generally develop through a period of years. The unmistakable sign for a girl that she has physically matured into womanhood is the onset of menstruation. There is no such defining moment for boys.

Moreover, from the beginning of their lives, women are normally endowed with the physical capacity to carry the next generation, so can have proof of the physical continuance through their offspring. This potentiality is their birthright, and it is this potentiality that gives them the added psychological certainty. Men, however, have no such clear sign to give them this certainty. They can never be sure that the child carried by "their" woman is also a child from their own loins. For a man, perhaps the supreme demonstration of their creativity is in the artistic realm. It is perhaps why the public recognition of an author's artistic endeavours is especially acclaimed and treasured. It is perhaps why women's artistic contribution has been, with notable exceptions, so long sidelined.

In the present age, where greater choice for women, especially in the realm of procreation, has meant greater personal responsibility, men and women have become more equal in their public lives. Thus, for the general populace at large, for example in the political and economic fields, there is an all-encompassing demand for productivity and profit, and for power to be given to those who are wealthy as opposed to those who are knowledgeable or wise. To make goods and to make money seem to have become the chief goals of a lifetime. This is presently the value put on our psychological E, how we express the meaning placed upon both our efforts and our aims.

As the embryo grows and develops, the embryonic cells begin to differentiate by function and placement. Depending on where they are within the body map, and their specific functions in the development of the embryo into a foetus, the cells thus positioned will develop into eyes, ears, lower or upper limbs and so on, and eventually the human form become distinctly recognisable. Thus, from the very beginning, function and pattern are fundamental to life, and go hand in hand with the E that powers them. In the reality of a life, this functioning and patterning is also likely to be reflected in a corresponding psychological need for status and relationship.

In her imagined model of E and its function, Lowenfeld subdivides the flow of this neutral force E into channels, the physical and the psychological, which is further divided into the intellectual and emotional channels. These channels are only images of E in movement, actively passing through an individual person throughout a lifetime. The E in itself has no goal; the direction of its movement is generally shaped by our individual desires for personal survival and continuity. It is E which takes us forward through our lives, supporting us in the search to fulfil our goals and desires. E diminishes with age, following the natural parabola of a life's span. So when someone dies in an accident, we lament the event because we deem the death to be premature; the parabola has in this case been cut short and seen to be incomplete. On the other hand there are occasions when we decide to give up our lives for a cause.

This idea or image of E flowing through channels has perhaps another parallel with the Chinese idea of Qi, which is often explained by the Chinese in metaphoric language. It may not even be true to describe these channels as interrelating in any particular way. Perhaps we can use another metaphor. Let us imagine our personality as a tapestry of colour: we can see threads of many colours, but these threads of colour, of E in its physical or psychological channels, do not represent the whole picture. We may even be able to see how the picture has been created, to identify which is physical and which is psychological, but what we must ultimately know is that we can never arrive at the meaning of its contents without any reference to the source and history of its subject.

Indeed that is how Lowenfeld has chosen to describe E, by the use of analogy. At the time of her lecture in 1952, she likened the force of E to the force of electricity, in that the way E manifests itself is determined by the nature of the form through which it flows, and in itself, apart from the function it infuses, has no goal. So these are not special channels, like our blood vessels in our physical selves. We have to imagine the E that expresses our urge towards physical development, growth and repair as that which moves through the physical channel, and the E that expresses the strivings of the human intellect as that which moves through the intellectual channel. And the E that moves through the emotional channel expresses the feelings of pleasure, of pain, and all the shades in between. Like the acupuncture map of Qi (Kuriyama 1999: 10), it was an imagined map of the function of E that Lowenfeld was charting, in order that she could make her next point.

It appeared to Lowenfeld that all these channels branch off from a common stem, and that any blocking of one channel will tend to increase the discharge of E in other channels. If the E in any of these channels is not flowing smoothly, E will be dammed up in that channel and imbalances will occur. If two of the channels have been blocked for whatever reason, then the accumulated E will eventually be expressed exclusively through the remaining channel. It is well known, for example, that in an accident the brain produces a substance called endorphin to suppress the feeling of pain in order that the accident victim can think clearly about the quickest way to effect treatment for the physical injuries. Equally, the numbness felt on hearing shocking news in an emotional crisis is the natural response to dampen the emotional pain in order that the crisis can be better coped with.

The case of Oliver (Chapter 11) is perhaps a good example that these channels are not strictly defined. At his referral I was given to understand that he was emotionally disturbed and intellectually performing below his ability. He was also accused of anti-social behaviour, disrupting family harmony, stealing within the family and disrupting class learning at school. There was no reference either to his increased physical activity or a noticeably greater lethargy. What was clear was that the E in his intellectual and emotional channels was being diverted to unproductive activities that were unsatisfying for Oliver and unsatisfactory for others.

This is how Oliver expressed it in his Mosaic responses. To begin with, he showed us the problem in his role as Jesus, the bearer of all our sins. Later, through his exploration of the meaning to him of each of the Mosaic colours, Oliver found out he was unable to use yellow in any shape or form. E as expressed in the colour yellow was blocked, and this was why he could not use it. This blockage was reflected in his life at the time of the making of this Mosaic. The moment he found himself unable to use yellow was also the moment he acknowledged he needed to work upon himself psychologically. He had found out why his previous Mosaics had been emotionally unsatisfactory. And when he finally decided he could end his treatment, he showed that he could now use the yellow in a meaningful way that satisfied him. In fact, his Mosaic (11.6) at that point showed that he had realised how central yellow, whatever yellow represented to him, was to his life. He placed it at the heart of his final Mosaic, and the Mosaic developed in a flowing movement outwards to all corners of the tray. Centred firmly and balanced on this yellow, his life was to take off brightly in all areas of his life. At least that was his hope. He was able finally to demonstrate to himself that his E had achieved a good balance and was flowing smoothly.

Lowenfeld hypothesised that if no appropriate channel exists for discharge, E may be experienced by the individual in a number of adverse ways, as anxiety, epileptic fits, hyperactivity, explosive headaches and inability to think rationally, or as outbursts of anti-social behaviour which may or may not have an aggressive content. Lowenfeld accepted that such blocking may arise from unconscious conflict but as a number of the above examples show, is not necessarily the origin of it. For instance, we now know that our diet can affect our behaviour. If children grow up on a diet of junk food, they are known to become argumentative, easily distracted and cannot concentrate on their schoolwork. They also become hyperactive and generally unmanageable.

Here is an example of what can happen if there is no appropriate channel for the discharge of E. Consider the plight of the child who has begun to be mobile and to take his first steps towards independence, yet who suddenly finds himself strapped into a pushchair or stroller! His E has begun to take its first step towards self-directed purposeful movement, yet he finds himself abruptly prevented from exercising it. What picture of the world does this check to the flow of his E give him? Does it have any connection with what I have often come across in a supermarket: a difficult eight- or nine-year-old riding in the shopping trolley, which is being rapidly filled up with goods by an adult. Is he in the trolley because he was being unhelpful or simply tired? Is the adult being especially indulgent, or do they simply want to get round the shop quickly? Or is it also to do with a habit that was formed when the child was first strapped into a pushchair or stroller?

Generally, however, blocking is one of the normal ways a person deals with particular kinds of experience. Furthermore, I would add, the eventual emergence of its expression may even rest with the specific style of response of an individual personality. Presumably there is rarely a universal rule of survival. For example, we all need oxygen, but breathing it in through one's nostrils is but the most common way to do so. In an emergency, people take in air via other means, such as directly into the trachea and by mouth-to-mouth resuscitation.

Lowenfeld also postulated that there is a special area of the brain that is solely concerned with directing or governing E. We now know from researches in modern neuroscience that the entire brain is involved, that there is no specific centre for what she called the Primary Noticing Centre. Our brain functions in an entirely co-operative way, moment by moment, and often involves the entire human organism.

This theory is not unlike the Chinese idea of Qi or Chi, an ancient philosophy that has been refined into the Taoist religion and is exemplified in the Book of Changes or I Ching, and the Chinese medical practice of acupuncture. Lowenfeld formulated her theory through images of the movement of E. Like the Chinese in their ancient symbol of the opposing archetypal poles of the Yin and Yang in cyclic movement, it is a way of describing the dynamic nature of the rhythm of Life. This convergence of Western and Eastern thought began at the beginning of the twentieth century with Einstein's exposition of his Theory of Relativity, when the linearity of the world of classical physics was forever altered to a view where movement was central to it and the world became multidimensional. Not only was it central, but it brought into consideration the idea of relativity and relationship. It became clear that truth was better served if we viewed objects relative to their place in space and time in history. From then on, and during the remainder of the twentieth century, physics moved beyond the Newtonian world and delineated a relational, multidimensional world. In the nineteenth century, the most original thinkers in the Western world had sought to describe their world in linear terms: Darwin (with Wallace) in their theory of evolution by natural selection; Marx in his account of a new theory of political, social and economic history of our world, which gave us the communist ideology; and Freud, who gave us his psychoanalytic theory of our inner life and its intimate connection with our sexuality. These were mainly linear theories based upon an a priori acceptance that the principle of cause and effect underlay all cognitive explanations. All these ideas were expounded prior to the age when Einstein brought into being the new physics after which relativity and multidimensionality became accepted notions. This set Lowenfeld's own theories nicely in their own historical context. She saw her own ideas as no more than working hypotheses within a continuum of the history of thought, but from my point of view, they have provided me with a good basis for developing my own thinking. In this and the subsequent chapter, I have given my interpretation of Lowenfeld's theories, and in places given my own extensions to or angle on her ideas.

16 Our thoughts, our feelings, ourselves and Lowenfeld's theory of Protosystem Thinking

During my last year at school, I was a volunteer teacher for a small class of children. Their families were unable to send them to school, and these classes were run by a religious charity. I was interested in finding out whether I had a vocation for such work. What I came away with was a profound sense of curiosity about how the human mind worked, having noticed that even in this small class of fewer than fifteen children, none of their minds worked in the same way; each child saw the subject from a different angle. To be sure, only a few children could not actually understand my presentation of the subject, and it would have been very easy to assume they lacked the intelligence to grasp the point. However, I decided to ask each of the children to explain their point of view to me, and I was utterly spellbound by the impeccable reasoning they all displayed.

The most striking example has remained in my memory since that time. Throughout the arithmetic lesson a nine-year-old boy had sat at his desk, clearly bemused by what he had been asked to do. This was already his third arithmetic lesson, yet he was still unable to add up a few single numbers, and I was intrigued. I sat by him and asked him if he could tell me what it was about the work that was puzzling him. With his eyes still fixed on the paper in front of him, he said that because these numbers were not attached to specific objects, he was unable to assume they all referred to the same thing and so add them together. He was saying that if each number referred to a different thing, say this two to chairs, and that five to apples or the seven to stars in the sky, he did not feel or think he was entitled to consider them as belonging to the same category and that he could add them together. "How could things be simply represented by a number unless the number was attached to an object?" he had asked. It was for him a genuine difficulty. I suggested that if he could imagine that these objects were all of the same kind but simply unnamed or unknown, perhaps he could then add them up? He thought for a while and said that he could not imagine unknown objects. We were now up against what he could or could not imagine, and I had no adequate response. This incident was what fired me to train as a teacher. Thus, very early on in my own experience of others, I learnt that it is not necessary that we all think alike, once we move into the realm of what we believe it is possible to imagine. There, answers clearly depend on the mind that is facing the facts or questions. It was my first glimpse that different ways of thinking and feeling could be both possible and legitimate.

Before we come to consider Lowenfeld's concept of Protosystem Thinking it may be useful to consider the nature of human thought and thinking in general. What do we mean when we say "That's a clever thought," "That's an amusing thought," "That's not a thought, it's a feeling," or when we talk about "musical ideas" or "artistic thought"? Are we referring to the same kind of process or are there different kinds? Do we have a unified view about thought and thinking in general?

To begin to answer these questions, I propose to start from a fundamental point, which could perhaps be phrased as two questions: What is the task facing the foetus as it rapidly develops into a baby? To do this work, what are the tools with which nature has equipped the infant?

It seems to me that the answer to the first question, the question of the task, can only be "survival"; and the answer to the question of the tools for the task has to be "the entire bodily structure, that which is bounded by our skin". Here I should emphasise the importance of not separating the mind or the brain from the body, as of course personal experience is an indivisible whole and not really divisible into the physical and psychological.

Let us begin with survival first, survival in the womb, then survival in the world outside it. To survive in the womb E must enter the organism. With the entry of E, movement begins. The delight of the moment when the mother-to-be can feel the thrusts of limbs within the womb is a moment to be relished. At birth we lack knowledge of life experience and are at our most vulnerable. To survive we need first and foremost to make sense of the world around and in us, to be able to judge what is "good" or "bad" for us, what advances or diverts us from the goal of survival. Curiosity, a feeling, is the principal expression of this need. From the start therefore, feeling accompanies thought.

We now come to the tools that we need to survive and sustain our survival, certain of which begin to develop whilst we are in the womb, and these are our senses. The earliest to develop is that of touch. It is now known that the foetus can respond to gentle prods on its cheeks as early as eight weeks into gestation, and by twelve weeks, as we can now see from pictures, it is sucking its thumb. Hearing is another early tool. Towards the end of gestation the foetus can hear and respond to sounds. Our entry into the world outside the womb is marked by our first breath, and the emergence of our voice which immediately brings the possibility of expression into use. Like curiosity, voice is an indication of the presence of feeling in our psyche, as the cry can carry many meanings. It is chiefly an instrument for expressing need, used when we feel neglected or when our needs are unfilled, abandoned when unattended and out of touch with a caring environment, and when injured or ill. Our first response is to make our needs known and register a negative response to the world at large. It is what we might call a 'crying need'. The smile of approval and satisfaction registers this as a positive response and emerges somewhat later. Is this why it comes more easily for a parent to chastise their child, and less readily to the adult to praise that same child?

A newborn is thus well on the way to become fully equipped to respond to its environment in ways which allow it to survive. The next questions are: how does an infant make sense of the multidimensionality of its experiences? How does an infant organise its experiences? How does an infant communicate thoughts and feelings? How does it distinguish between its own personal preferences and learn to value its own judgement in matters vital to its interest? According to Lowenfeld, the answer to these questions is that the infant needs a form of thinking that incorporates feeling.

Lowenfeld, after years of watching children play, came to the conclusion that babies think and feel, using what she called Protosystem Thinking. She used various other terms as well, such as Non-verbal Thinking, Pre-verbal Thinking and even Pre-logical Thinking as well as Primary System Thinking, but they were all found to have disadvantages: "Non-verbal Thinking" focuses our minds on what it is not rather than what it is; the term "Pre-verbal Thinking" gives the impression that it is a process which predates verbal thinking but is replaced by verbal thinking in later life; and "Pre-logical Thinking" suggests that it is simply not logical rather than that it has a logic of its own. The term Primary System Thinking was eventually rejected for a different reason: she did not wish to have the notion confused with Freud's Primary Process. This idea of babies being able to think, in the 1920s and 1930s, was quite a bold concept, given the state of contemporary neuro-scientific knowledge, when verbal language was regarded as the pre-eminent, if not the only medium of thought and communication. At the same time, Lowenfeld came to understand that play and playing were the means by which children expressed and communicated with themselves, ordered their experiences, and made sense of their experience of themselves and their environments. The Mosaics is one of the tools that Lowenfeld designed for the expression and understanding of Protosystem Thinking.

Protosystem Thinking is notably different from verbal thinking. (You will recall the exercise that I had suggested in Chapter 3.) First it is impossible to put into words, because it is not possible to convey the totality of an experience in words without serious distortion; Protosystem Thinking *makes sense of the totality of experience and has a logic of its own.* Lowenfeld postulated that this kind of thinking is active in us throughout the course of human life from the last stages of intrauterine life to the end of our life.

Considering the child in its first few years of life, the most obvious feature of the child at this time is that it is unmediated by any previous experience of its internal and external environment, apart from that of being in its mother's womb. In other words, *all its knowledge of itself and its world comes through its senses.* That is, all its experience is essentially sensorial. Protosystem Thinking is thus its key to the knowledge derived from this personal experience, and essential for acquiring the knowledge it needs to survive.

We are born with the tools to ensure our survival, and these are what we call the five senses: touch, taste, smell, hearing and sight. We experience our world through them, and it is through their simultaneous interplay that our picture of the world is formed. This picture is imaged, not cast in words. To these five senses I should like to add the proprioceptive sense (the sense of the body's movement or muscular effort) for motor development (Eliot 2001: 261–89), which enables a person to experience how their body is disposed in space. This sense enables us to locate ourselves physically, to know the positions of our bodies or our limbs: whether it is right way up or upside down, whether the arms are raised and whether the body or any part is at rest or in action. This, combined with the sense of balance given by our ears, gives us our sense of ourselves in relationship to our surroundings in space, using gravity[37] to centre ourselves. These provide us with a sense of context and a sense of continuity in time. The proprioceptive sense also dynamically joins the other five senses to give expression to our E (the subject of Chapter 15) through our behaviour and our emotions. Thus the personality forms a dynamic whole. Together, working simultaneously, these six senses provide us with the basic data for our Protosystem Thinking.

It is perhaps useful to see how each of our senses operate within and contribute to the Protosystem thought process. Of the five senses noted, I shall concentrate mainly on the three senses used in the Mosaic process: touch, vision and hearing or voice. Touch is the most pervasive as well as fundamental. It is indeed the touchstone of our experience. It is the sense that brings us closest to our environment, the sense of intimacy par excellence, as well as the sense that enables us to differentiate between ourselves and the other, that separates our external from our inner world. Skin stimulation of premature babies has been shown to have a positive effect on their survival. On a functional map of the brain, the hands occupy a disproportionately large space, second only to vision (Damasio 2000: 300–2; Eliot 2001: 123–56). Touch is the sense that binds all our senses together. Touch provides information about the world external to ourselves and allows our inner world to communicate and interact with the outer world.

Our sense of taste is closely allied to our sense of touch. Eliot (2001: 172–95) states that taste buds are developed very early in the foetus, and that the ability to taste begins in utero. The neuroscientist John McCrone tells us: "The experience of taste is partly tactile" (1999: 85). The sight of babies stuffing something, anything and everything into their mouths is a very common one, and it is one of the ways they use to explore their worlds. Our tongue is also capable of magnifying the feel of things inside our mouth, so that we have a detailed and multidimensional image of an object.

Taste provides one of the essential features of the feeding experience, the knowledge of what is "good". As food is basic to life, it is useful that what tastes good should also be good for our health and ultimately our survival. We now know that the nutrients coming through the umbilical cord carry with them the tastes in the food that the mother has eaten, and the same mix of tastes is present in her milk. Perhaps this already gives the newborn a set of criteria for what is "good".

---

37 Elizabeth Burford, a graduate of Lowenfeld's Institute, has explored self-representation using spatial concepts and her work appears in the Further Reading list.

Whilst touch and taste bring us closest to the external world, our sense of smell prescribes a small area around us that has a direct though often transient effect on our knowledge of our immediate surroundings. "Scents are laid out along an axis from pungent to flowery, or fresh to rotten, rather than having the more obvious spatial co-ordinates for sight, hearing and touch" (McCrone 1999: 85–6). In later life, we seem to believe that our sense of smell has a strong influence on our relationships with other people. The perfume industry relies on and is a good example of our underlying belief. In nineteenth-century England there was certainly the conviction that foul smells indicated the presence of disease. At that time this miasmatic theory informed one of the major planks of public health policy.

Touch, taste and smell together are important for the first period of infancy. And in this period of life, the cry of the baby dominates its response to the outer world. Already, feeling is integral to its expressive repertoire. It is the way of expressing its judgement and making this judgement known to another.

Hearing has a different but significant role to play in our Protosystem Thinking. It is now known that foetuses can distinguish the mother's voice from other voices. The timbre of our voice tells the listener at the other end of the telephone line who they are talking to. Our voice is our personal signature. Hearing also has a particular importance to our knowledge of our world: it extends the field of our senses. For instance, it goes where the eyes cannot follow: that is, we can hear a shout when we cannot see the person doing the shouting. What is more, it is the only sense that allows us to share as well as to communicate our experiences. When we make sounds directed at a listener, we both hear the same sounds, thus enhancing the experience of sharing. It is certainly a fact that an infant can be soothed from a distance by hearing its mother's voice. Eliot also points out that "music is both a source of pleasure and a particularly effective way of promoting children's cognitive development" (2001: 259). The timbre of our voice is both distinctive and expresses our feelings. It is the sense that finally enables us to communicate fully, to be recognised as having fully established a relationship with our external world. And hearing is also the last of our senses to leave us at death.

Our sight develops last. This is understandable, as the environment within the womb cannot be apprehended by sight. Once we are born, however, it gives us the furthest and broadest view of our surroundings. From the point of Protosystem Thinking, its singular importance lies in its ability to include motion within its frame, even when we cannot hear the movements. It enables us to discern the dynamics of action and, possibly more importantly, the dynamics of the reaction to us, thus allowing us a chance to detect warning signs of danger from a distance and time to organise a thoughtful response. In the context of our relationship to other people, how others see us remains the most potent influence. We use others as a mirror to reflect ourselves from moment to moment. We have come to feel that our very reputation, our sense of self-worth is reflected through our presentation to the world. We now know that vision occupies a major part of our brainscape and is located next to that for the hand. This arrangement helps us to link the information from this sense with that coming through our other senses, particularly that of touch, thus giving us a rounded picture of our external world. Eliot has given a detailed description of the complexity of the brain's visual system (2001: 196–227) and she states that "*experience* [my italics] actually seems to play a more important role in acuity development *after* [her italics] the first few months of life" (p. 214).

Thus sight gives us a much larger area of awareness and hearing gives us a bigger range of expression. They also have other, separate and different functions. Hearing can bridge distance without objects being in view of us, and without seeing them we can locate the source and direction of the sound, whereas sight can show us objects even when we cannot hear them. Above all, sight can show us objects in movement, it can show us an event in space-time.

Having examined the working of our senses, our tools of survival, let us consider how they contribute to the Protosystem thought process. Our senses work co-operatively to reflect the global nature, the multidimensionality and simultaneity of personal experience which ultimately leads us to an idiosyncratic understanding of our world. This idiosyncrasy derives from the fact that when our understanding is formed we are unable to compare our Protosystem thoughts with others. At the time of our experience, we are unable to know that our image of the world is or may not be an accurate reflection of how the world is perceived by others. So the nature of our senses, the personal perceptions and the idiosyncratic understanding of subjective experience are our primary consideration in thinking about Protosystem Thinking.

The picture formed by our senses is dynamic and comprehensive, and it is Lowenfeld's contention that they are perceived together as a pattern. It is the pattern formed and informed by our senses that determines our total view of our world, joining together our inner and outer worlds. Patterning, according to Lowenfeld, is an important capability for us to make sense of the world around us. I am reminded of the piece of research that showed that babies respond with interest to an unknown meaningful language, but not to meaningless gibberish. Perhaps they are responding to the pattern of the language. Recent research studies have shown "that networks obtained by linking words exhibit seemingly *universal patterns of organization* [my italics], provided the words are syntactically related" (*Nature*, 17 March 2005, p. 289).

This *patterning* is a primary function of Protosystem Thinking and develops during the last stages of intrauterine life. Furthermore, this patterning is across the senses. In a study in the 1970s, it was shown that a baby, within twenty-four hours of its birth, will react with more interest to the sight of its mother's face accompanied by the mother's voice than to that of a stranger's face and voice. What is of particular interest is that this infant will show discomfort when presented with its mother's face accompanied by a stranger's voice (or the other way round). In a literature review by Trevarthen and Aitken it seems as though the infant has recognised the incongruity of the presentation, which suggests that the accepted pattern is multi-sensory, across sense modalities (*ACPP Journal*, January 2001). There is also evidence that the brains of children diagnosed with Autistic Spectrum Disorder (ASD) are not integrated – ASD children tend to see details without seeing the context or the whole picture, and how the details relate. It would be my contention that this would have significant effects on their Protosystem Thinking.[38]

Whilst we make sense of our world through the pattern made by our senses, we also express ourselves through our senses. We communicate visually when we write, draw or paint; we invoke another's (or sometimes our own) hearing when we speak or when we make music; and we do both when we dance in a ballet, or perform in a Peking opera, where we make use of the whole of our bodies, expressing both the story and the emotion through gestures and movement, using the proprioceptive sense as well as our other five senses.

Touch, however, is involved in all our activities: we wield a pen or brush or tap the keys on the keyboard; we stir the ingredients in a pan; cut up food on our plate; taste the food and drink; and we handle the Mosaic pieces. Above all, our intimate relations with objects as well as other people, our shallowest, most fleeting and deepest feelings all are expressed through our sense of touch – from love to hate in all its fine gradations, from a passionate embrace through an introductory handshake to a punch in the nose; from caressing a favourite bowl to crumpling an unwelcome letter. When we come to the expression of feelings, we also need to consider the role of Culture. The same gesture, the same touch may not have the same meaning for the giver and the recipient. Touch is involved at some point and at some level in all human intercourse.

Touch represents the cornerstone of personal experience; it touches us at all points of life. Remembering Quentin's experience of making a Mosaic (p. 111), I am now more than ever convinced that touch is the bedrock round which we judge any experience. We say, "He is touched" meaning he is not himself, but "I'm touched" to refer to an act of sympathy or generosity from one whom we feel "touched" by. It is of interest that the first is always applied to someone else, while the second is mostly applied to oneself. Nevertheless both refer to a feeling. Two further examples might make this clearer. We say that we are going to "keep in touch", but we do not mean actually touching, more usually we mean contact by telephone, letter or email. Meeting would be only one of the options. Equally telling is the remark about people that they are "losing touch with reality" or that they are "out of touch". This comment invokes touch in conveying an abstract idea that is the opposite of "being in touch" and is based on assumptions made through observation of an individual's behaviour. These are all judgements summarising our feelings. Touch not only makes survival possible, it makes life meaningful.

Mosaic-making utilises all our major senses: sight, hearing and above all touch. Harry is a good example (pp. 55–9). He had used the Mosaics without any preconception of how it might help him out of his difficult relations at home and at school. As he was doing his first Mosaic, he declared that his aim was towards "symmetry". After three Mosaics (8.1–8.3) in two sessions he found that the Mosaic process alone, using mainly touch and sight and occasionally augmented by words, served to clarify for him both his predicament and the solution. It was the

---

38 See also Grandin and Johnson (2005), where Grandin's understanding of animal behaviour was derived from her observations of their non-verbal behaviour.

feeling of certainty with which he ended his therapy that determined and revealed his knowledge that he no longer needed any further treatment. Touch and action are what distinguishes the Lowenfeld approach to therapy. Of all the therapeutic approaches that presently abound, play therapy as practised in its varied forms bears the closest resemblance to Lowenfeld's original use of objects, miniature toys and action in her therapeutic work.

As the infant grows, it begins to get a picture of what kind of world it inhabits. Always included in this picture-making is the internal status of the infant. This picture is influenced by the ongoing moment-by-moment information formed simultaneously through our multidimensional sensorial experiences, and enlarged or developed depending on its present and previous experiences as well as what it has already made of its previous experiences. This picture can also be dramatically changed, and this too will be interpreted accordingly. All this is based on the infant's subjective and therefore idiosyncratic view of the meaning of its experiences, because of course the infant has not been able to share this view and check whether this view is also that of the other people around it. It is why children who have been sexually abused from a very early age often consider abuse to be the normal way to show affection.

There are other factors in infancy that Lowenfeld noted which need to be taken into account: for instance, that infants lack a sense of time and the elapse of time, which means that although babies are aware of movement, they do not recognise the direction of movement. They are also unable to grasp the notions of here and there: something is either present or it is not. This is developmentally quite logical. You will remember that the three senses, touch (as in the grasp reflex), sight and hearing, are fully developed only after birth, and these are mainly to do with the spatial dimensions of sensorial experience. So it is not surprising that modern research has confirmed another observation of Lowenfeld's: very young infants have no sense of whether a sensorial event is happening inside or outside their bodies. For example, a pain is experienced as a sensation, but not as something located inside or outside the body. Thus, for an infant every experience is global in nature and timeless. These ideas develop as the infant grows. It takes time and personal experience of space/time for a sense of continuity to develop, and ideas formulated in early life can usually only be modified by later personal experience. A sensitive imagination, an ability to imagine another's situation, to be able to put oneself in another's shoes, can be another route to being able to modify one's ideas (Harris 1989: 51–77).

Lowenfeld goes on to say that when an infant has a sensory experience, this experience simultaneously arouses in it a feeling. As the infant is not able to make a distinction between itself and the external stimulus for that experience, nor the feeling the stimulus has aroused, the infant's mind registers all this as one totality. It follows that the baby cannot detach the qualities of an object or aspects of its experience from the object or the experience: the infant only knows a series of total experiences. The sensorial qualities are not separated out; the experience is perceived as an indivisible whole: ". . . therefore that quality which arouse [*sic*] in him the most powerful, or the clearest affect are to him the quality of the object arousing the affect . . . There is no means for the external observer to know *which* quality of the perceived object has thus reached pre-eminence and has become joined to [the] affect in the child's mind" (Lowenfeld 2004b: 257–8). The feeling and the object become identified, they merge into a single whole. Children thus *organise experiences by the feeling that the experience invokes*, and they do this by classifying experiences through the *similarity of feeling*. So for the child an experience of "this hurts me" becomes "that is a hurting me thing or person" and would go together with similarly hurting experiences. So it is quite possible that, having once experienced a cat scratching him whilst he was cradling the cat in his arms, the child might shrink from the arms of his mother when she is wearing her fur coat. To these groupings Lowenfeld has given the term *clusters*. For the child a feeling has the ring of truth about it. These feelings are absolute to the child: because he feels them, they bear the stamp of universal truths. This is the basis for our development of a sense of discrimination at one end of the spectrum and a belief system at the other. Harris has argued that "young children grasp that people's emotional reactions differ depending on the beliefs and desires they have about a situation" (1989: 2).

Lowenfeld recounts an anecdote that nicely illustrates the primacy of feeling in the working of Protosystem Thinking and the cluster:

> A little boy of three and a half with a pretty, social mother had a green, smooth, shining toy duck to which he was much attached. He used to put it under his cheek when sleeping. This duck quacked. His mother used to go out a great deal in the evening, and so came up to his nursery, usually wearing a green silk evening dress, to read to him a good night story. She then sat in a low chair, and being rather tall, her knees came just to the height of his cheek. It was their custom that when he had had his bath he came in from the bathroom to his nursery with his duck under one arm, paused at the door, looked at his mother, then ran forward, stroked his cheek on his mother's knee, said "Pretty Mummy", climbed on her knee and cuddled down, and she read him his story. Every night this little ritual was carried out. But one night his mother came up wearing a red dress. The little boy paused at the door and looked at her very hard before he came forward rather slowly, did not stroke her knee with his cheek, and climbed up rather soberly on to her lap. This happened two nights, and at the third he stood at the door and burst into tears and said, "Oh, Mummy why do you not put on your *quacking dress* [my italics]?"
>
> (Lowenfeld 1964: 13–14)

Lowenfeld's observation was that "the whole combination of *affection* [my italics], greenness, smoothness, cheek-stroking, etc., and *quacking* had come together into a whole, and it was a matter of chance which of this composite group of qualities he might hit upon to characterise this whole" (1964: 14). Feelings tell us the significance of what we are experiencing. It is feeling that ultimately drives the decision process. Feeling is that which tells us when to take a decision, that which determines the timing of any action. Without feeling we will have no means of knowing the judgements our Protosystem Thinking has led us into formulating. Without feeling we will not know what value we have placed on a thought. Without feeling we will not know when to put thoughts into action. Without feeling we are seriously disabled. The role of feeling within our Protosystem Thinking is integral to our survival strategies.[39]

So the language of Protosystem Thinking is chiefly expressed multidimensionally, using all our senses, which for people is by definition through action. Is that why the punch or the hug are the most basic forms of human expression of feeling? Furthermore, it is in the quality of the physically felt punch or hug that the meaning of the action becomes clear. What we presently call civilised behaviour removes the physical element from the action. It is why we deem talking to be more civilised than fighting.

However, the Mosaic language has permitted the inclusion of one physical element, the sense of touch, without violating the client's own sense of space. In my own clinical work I have found this element of touch an essential factor in the therapeutic communication process. The case of Adam offers a clear demonstration of the importance of this process. What the Mosaic allows is time for the Protosystem thought to *emerge*. Adam (Mosaic 1.1) worked on his Mosaic silently. It was not until he had completed it that I invited him to tell me about it. He began by telling me it was "a pattern", but after a brief pause he added "a symmetrical pattern". Protosystem thought is indeed patterned, and Adam further described his pattern as an attempt "to balance the colours and shapes symmetrically" (p. 1). After I had reflected back to him his Mosaic process, he saw something momentous, that "the space in the middle is important" (p. 2). When I repeated the word "important", Adam seemed finally enabled to articulate his *feelings* in words. After pondering a short while, and with a quiet, firm and steady voice, he was able to articulate his feelings in a multidimensional image. Pointing to his Mosaic, he said: "This *feels* [my italics] like a *contracting* coffin. I am in the middle *squeezed* so hard that I've *become* invisible" (p. 2). Not only was Adam able to put himself at the heart of his communication – he was in the middle – and recognise his own worth by saying that the space in the middle was important, he was also able to describe his feelings about himself within his present situation: he was "*in a contracting coffin*" which had been "*squeezed*" so hard, he had "*become invisible*". It was using the Mosaics within the Mosaic process that made it possible for Adam to express something that had been inexpressible in words before, and finally articulate it with words of great eloquence.

---

39 See Antonio Damasio's seminal work *The Feeling of What Happens* (2000), specifically Chapter 6, on a neurological account of how patterning in brain activity and feeling are linked to our consciousness of self.

17 Ending and postscript: my personal experience of the Mosaic process

It was at Lowenfeld's Institute of Child Psychology that I personally experienced the Mosaic process for myself for the first time. I had come to the Institute seeking to understand children, child development and how to bring up my children within British culture. It is now clear in retrospect that it was not simply that I had wished to benefit my children from my better knowledge, but that I also wanted to increase my understanding of myself.

Mosaic 17.1
My first Mosaic [40]

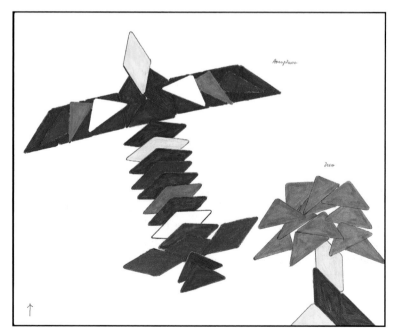

---

40 This Mosaic was first referred to in Chapter 2, p. 10.

The feeling engendered by this first experience of doing a Mosaic has carried me through the intervening years: the enthusiasm remains undimmed; the knowledge has deepened and broadened. Learning is one of the things that the Chinese are reputed to revere, and I seem not to be an exception. In the early years after completing my training, I continued to make my own Mosaics, but always as an isolated event, almost as an exercise to keep up my Mosaic muscle tone. I tried hard to put aside my own professional experience, to let myself be free to explore. I did not at the time examine the possible reasons why I might have wanted to make a Mosaic just at that juncture of my life. And it never once occurred to me to look at my own Mosaics as part of a series. Looking through them now, just before beginning this chapter, was a revelation. My memory was that I had mostly made trees, and indeed, that is generally true. But the truth of the detail was the more telling. Each Mosaic told of a unique moment in time and personal history. As with everyone else recounted in this work, I fit neatly into a mould, however singular.

Even so, it was a long time since I had last done a Mosaic. Moreover, there was now a defined purpose to this present project: it was to conclude my book with an account of my own Mosaic process. I wanted very much to know how far my inner life had travelled with me and whether the faith shown to me by others was reflected in a corresponding faith in myself. I am however convinced that all beginnings have at their heart their own endings, and so with this work. Thus somewhere I was certain that my first Mosaic already held the key to what would be in all my subsequent Mosaics, including my latest, the one I had decided would conclude my book on my Mosaic work. I had therefore spoken to my colleague and friend Shona about how I should like to end my book, adding that I would do the Mosaic when a publisher accepted it for publication and that I would like her to observe and write up the process, which was to be included along with my own thoughts and feelings about it. It was a "nice" idea, with all the simple rounded flavour of the word. We did not think at the time that we would have to honour our word.

I now give an account of the Mosaic-making in Shona's own words, with permission:

> It was some time ago, during a conversation with Thérèse about her Mosaic book, that she explained that her plan was to close the book with a Mosaic made by herself. I was very enthusiastic about the idea, until she mentioned that she would like me to observe her making the Mosaic and write up the process afterwards. My enthusiasm waned somewhat at that suggestion and I took several weeks to think about what was being asked and whether or not I felt able to take part.

Clearly, Shona had taken the proposal sufficiently seriously to consider it in earnest. It was fortunate that she did, for it turned out that we had to do it after all. When the signed contract landed on my desk, Shona and I duly arranged a time to meet. We decided that after the Mosaic-making, we would have a convivial evening together. We both looked forward to the evening, I thought. The time came. Here is Shona's account of it.

This was a Mosaic observation I approached with more than usual interest and apprehension. The prospect of observing the process of a Mosaic being made by someone who has been an admired and respected colleague and tutor for many years was both exciting and a little daunting. However, Thérèse pointed out that this Mosaic was about her experience, not mine, and with this thought firmly in mind I began to feel more confident about the process. I was aware that the process was likely to be harder for Thérèse than for any observer, because the satisfaction of using the Mosaics to express inner and perhaps unacknowledged thoughts and ideas can be affected by the comments of the observer. The maker can also experience powerful emotions, which need to be acknowledged and considered. I remembered my own first Mosaic-making experience when a thoughtless fellow trainee responded with "Finished? Good I'm off to the pub then." It taught me the importance of valuing what is produced and allowing the maker time to explore both the process and the finished product!

My recollection of the occasion is one of keen interest. I had assumed that the calm of knowledge would replace the enthusiasm of my first experience. Up to the point I began, the day had been totally preoccupying, but when the moment to start came, I had a strong sense of being given specific materials to accomplish an undefined task, and it was as Lowenfeld had written, "whatever response he makes must come from himself alone" (2004a: 153). I prepared myself by emptying my mind of Mosaic ideas, and simply focusing on the blank tray space in front of me. There was a strong sense of having been here before and vaguely remembering the way, but also one that this moment was entirely unknown. It was all new, but I did not feel lost.

When Thérèse and I sat down to begin the process, I was pleased to discover that we seemed to be sharing an attitude of relaxed interest in what was going to be made. . . . We chose to work at a low table. Thérèse sat in the centre and I sat to her left. There was no need for me to do the usual introduction to the Mosaics and I sat quietly, waiting, observing and hoping I would be able to remember the whole process by the end. Thérèse asked me if I would like to take notes and I declined, preferring to work as I usually do with clients and simply give my full attention to what is being made. There were moments in the following ten minutes when I regretted that decision!

I knew instinctively that I would begin at the centre of the bottom edge of the boundaried space. And as soon as I began, I also knew I was likely to make a tree. What kind of tree, how it would grow, those might have been the questions, but I was too involved with the shapes and colours by then.

Thérèse began with a black diamond, placed on its point near the bottom edge of the tray. To the left, she placed a green isosceles triangle, which was quickly replaced with two green equilaterals, one either side of the diamond.

Thérèse commented that she always got it wrong at the start. She then placed a blue diamond to the right of the black diamond and a green diamond to the left. Two further green diamonds were added, one to each side so that the shape began to branch outwards.

Another upright green diamond was placed above the first one and again two more diamonds were added to either side. The one to the left was blue and the one to the right was black. I noticed that the second black diamond was placed on the inside face of the one below it, whereas the second blue one was placed on the outside. Thérèse continued to be engrossed in her construction and murmuring "Sorry about this",[41] she began to place three green equilateral triangles over the top of what had been made so far. The Mosaic-making continued in this fashion, with the central core being built up using diamond shapes and then covered with equilateral triangles placed on top.

At times these pieces were almost woven into the existing structure, and I became aware that this Mosaic wasn't just a two-dimensional construction, but a structure with depth, subtlety and an overall sense of vibrancy. All the colours except white were used in the process. When placing the green diamonds on the outer edge of the structure, Thérèse made a remark about the ageing process and its effects on her. I agreed that we had both reached the stage where we might become more aware of the ageing process, but I was thinking as I looked at the Mosaic that there was little evidence here of any loss of strength or vigour. Thérèse finished her Mosaic by overlapping a black equilateral, then a blue, on top of the red equilateral which was in the centre of the top row of the design. She indicated that it was finished and began to reflect on how she had made the Mosaic. It was clear to me that Thérèse had intended to construct a tree and we spoke about how she had made other trees over the years.

Whenever I make a Mosaic, apart from my first, I always seem to make a false start. What was novel, however, was my recognition of this during the process, and with some surprise. Recollecting the story of my birth, as told to me by my mother, now made sense of the inevitability of this faltering start. I was a premature baby, by the "wrong" number of weeks. I was too young to nurse at the breast before the advent of intensive care, so I fell between many stools and nothing much could be done for me. I spent the first few months with little food and much crying. It was three months before the right formula could be found and I could begin to grow and develop properly. I had indeed made a faltering start to life. All this had remained somewhere in my psyche throughout my life, and it was only now that I was able to make the connection. The point is not that I had only now seen the connection, the point is that it was I who found the truth in it.

---

41 I realised that Shona would have to draw round the shapes and then colour them, in order to reproduce the final Mosaic product. The intricate overlapping of the Mosaic pieces would make this a much more complicated task, hence my apology.

Throughout the making of the Mosaic, I became increasingly aware that with this tree I was drawing the strands of my life into a cord of meaning. During our subsequent conversation this became ever more apparent, and I found Shona a sympathetic listener.

Beginning at the bottom, Thérèse explained that she had wanted to give her tree more support at the base than she had done in the past. She acknowledged that she was now aware that things which had happened in the past had contributed to her strengths and had helped her to have greater insight into the needs of her clients. I thought of Margaret Lowenfeld's writing about experiences having the power to open doors in the mind, which leads to greater awareness and understanding of others. Thérèse also said that it had been important to retain spaces within the structure to give it depth, and I thought she had succeeded in this aim.

Giving feedback on the process was something I had felt particularly anxious about, but Thérèse needed little help to begin exploring what she had created, and I was fascinated to hear about her experiences and her reflections on them. I asked about the cultural aspects of her Mosaic, because something about the three equilateral triangles at the top and the green points of the diamonds projecting below made me think of dragons. I was careful to own this as my thought and rightly so, because it had no resonance for Thérèse. She told me, however, that red and yellow together were common in Chinese culture and although her favourite colours were blue and green, she had wanted to include some red and yellow pieces.

Looking at the Mosaic now, as I write about it, I am aware that I would really like to sit down with Thérèse again and discuss it further. It may be that I felt inhibited at the time, but on reflection, I think this is part of the power of Mosaics, that there always seems to be something new to discover in them.

Shona drew round the Mosaic pieces and went on to colour them. The plan was to make a digital image of this drawn and coloured image which Shona could have available in front of her to assist her in writing up the Mosaic process, leaving me the coloured Mosaic drawing to write my part in the process. That was the plan.

However, "Of mice and men, the best laid plans . . ." I was in the room whilst Shona drew and coloured away, hovering between friendly but distracting inconsequential talk and non-intrusive silence accompanied by a loud presence. We had both gone out of our comfort zones into unknown social territory. Shona failed to shoo me out of the room, thinking it still to be my room; I stayed, feeling it unsociable to leave her to do all the work whilst I went off to relax before dinner. We were undone by our individual social manners. There was a small squeak; Shona had used a wrong colour and was trying to fix it. The mark stubbornly refused to be removed. The error glared at her. I had steadfastly averted my gaze and was not to see the result until the end of the evening when Shona had left for home.

I was quite unprepared for the howl of grief that issued from me when I saw it. It was utterly bewildering. How could something as trivial as a smudge of colour in the wrong place have such a devastating effect? Out of this I began to realise that of the entire Mosaic, there must be something particularly significant about this piece which had been glossed over in the original discussion.

I tried to eradicate the wrong colour from Shona's colouring before making the real discovery that it was a piece of work on myself that clearly I had to do. The meaning of that grief could not be ignored; I felt I needed urgently to understand its meaning. This need became a subscript to my life for some time, for days to stretch into weeks, whilst I went on with chores requiring more immediate attention. I had tried to comfort Shona with what another friend and colleague had said to me about the incident, that it showed powerfully the importance of the total commitment of the therapist to the client's Total Response. But this was no comfort to someone who felt she had clearly failed to protect this total commitment. Shona was inconsolable. I was appalled at the depth of feeling in each of us, unleashed by something so seemingly minor.

And the beginning of understanding came at last, the meaning emerged one dawning day through the mists of sleep, startling me into wakefulness. In our conversation I had been recounting to Shona my childhood adventures as a refugee in China, after the fall of Hongkong during the Second World War. In retrospect, I had always felt it was my experience of this broad slice of life in those extraordinary times (which seemed to me at the time entirely ordinary), that had helped me to communicate with the children and young people who came to me for help. I did not at that point make any connection between this insight and the part of my Mosaic process that the final placement of the red isosceles triangle represented.

My thoughts returned to my Mosaic, and I remembered how I had been moving pieces up and down my Mosaic tree. And although I had made a sweeping acknowledgement of my use of personal experience to deepen my understanding in my professional work to Shona at the time, I had not truly understood the significance to myself of this movement of pieces up and down the tree as represented by my own Mosaic process. This red piece was only one of several I had relocated. As I lay awake that morning, I could see it coming back down from near the top to near the beginning of the tree, and being carefully centred on the tree trunk. I remember feeling pleased with its final resting place. The significance of this single movement now flooded me with indescribable contentment. I realised then that, having served the children in my work, I could now place my wartime experiences again where they belonged. These experiences had first served me in my life; they needed now to be recognised, not as something that had spoilt my life, but as something which gave meaning to my life. I had failed to recognise the true nature of its significance and, more importantly, failed to give my own response to life's travails due honour. So if Shona had not unintentionally made an error, I might never have found the jewel in my latest Mosaic. The best-laid plans indeed.

Appendix 1   Guidelines for using Lowenfeld Mosaics with individuals

The Mosaic set

The set consists of a box which has been divided into two identical sections, and a tray with specific dimensions. The Mosaic pieces and the space of the tray form the vocabulary of the communication.

Each section holds the same type and number (228) of pieces. Each section is further subdivided into 5 compartments in which the pieces are stored.

The pieces are made up of 5 mathematically interrelated shapes. The basic shape is the square, from which is derived the diamond, the isosceles triangle (= half-square), the equilateral triangle and the scalene triangle (= bisected equilateral triangle), each arranged in one compartment of the half box so that the shapes are more easily recognised.

All the shapes are available in 6 colours. The colours should always be arranged in the same order within the compartment, the traditional order being red, blue, yellow, black, green and white.

In either section, *for each colour*, there should be 4 squares, 8 diamonds, 8 isosceles triangles, 6 equilateral triangles and 12 scalene triangles.

The pieces are designed to be used on the tray fitted with a white piece of paper. The edges of the tray thus form the symbolic boundary of the task.

These simple and clear properties of the Mosaics allow the therapist to focus on the way in which the child/adolescent/adult creates meaning from minimally directive or culturally biased material.

How to introduce the Lowenfeld Mosaics

1. Present the opened box above the tray, traditionally in the landscape position and fitted with white paper to allow for a traced record to be made. Always present both the box and tray in the same way, so that it would be immediately clear what if any changes have been made by the Mosaic-maker.

2. Present the 5 shapes following the colour order in the compartment, that is a red square, a blue diamond, a yellow isosceles, a black equilateral and a green scalene, demonstrating with each piece how the shape is mathematically related to the previous[42] shape shown, laying down each shape on the tray in such a way so as to show this relationship (Figure 3.2).

3. Present the colours by saying/showing that all these shapes are available in all these colours, naming them in the order you have shown them, as you return them to the box (thus also showing again where each is housed in the box) adding that they are also available in white.

4. Ask the child/adolescent/adult to *"choose some shapes, as few or as many as you like, to make something, anything you like, on the tray"*.

5. Should you be questioned about the above instruction, do not be tempted to elaborate, simply *repeat the instructions*, so as not to limit the choices that can be made. Suggestions or examples tend to focus and therefore narrow the choice. Thus it is of the utmost importance that any instructions should be as clear as possible in the first place. Give simple and direct answers to questions.

6. Should the subject be doubtful or reluctant, encourage her/him by pointing out that there is no right or wrong way of doing things with the Mosaics, that we all do something different, unique to us, capturing that unique moment. We all have *our own signature*.

7. End the instruction with the request "Tell me when you have finished".

How to use the Mosaics in personality assessment and therapy

1. The need for keen observation of the Process as well as the Product equals the Total Response. The need to attend to the process includes any activity or conversation which may precede, accompany or follow the making of the Mosaic. It is essential to learn the subject's Mosaic language; it follows that the presenter should always use the *vocabulary or name* supplied by the child/adolescent/adult in referring to any Mosaic tile when discussing their Mosaic with them.

2. It is often useful to *go through the Process with the child/adolescent/adult* and in the recapitulation or "reflecting back" it may be possible to demonstrate to the child/adolescent/adult her/his normal response (something we are usually unaware of) to new situations – that is, the Total Response can reveal our personal style of approach to living situations, it can show *the Personality in Action*. If appropriate, "*link*" any feature in the Mosaic which reflects directly or metaphorically to his personal background, *but* the therapist must own this linking, this thought as her own idea, in case the "link" is untimely for the subject or the therapist is off the mark.

---

42 The order of showing the diamond and isosceles triangle can be changed so that the relationsip between the isosceles triangle and the square could be more immediately shown; but this could be done after the isosceles triangle has been shown to be first related to the diamond then to the square as the present order allows.

3. The need to begin with an *awareness of one's own Mosaic Response*, that is, before any session, acknowledge and put aside one's own preconceptions about shape and colour, about the right way to represent a subject or what constitutes an unpleasant or pleasing pattern and what might be a normal or pathological Mosaic.

   It is of the utmost importance for a therapist to be familiar with their own pattern of response, which means doing a Mosaic with a therapist who is already experienced in using them. This leads to an accepting attitude and an awareness of the cultural as well as the personal dimension of the Mosaic Response.

4. The processes of "reflecting back" and "linking" apply to all work using the Lowenfeld approach.

Appendix 2 Guidelines for recording a Mosaic session

Basic file data

The following brief details should be on the front or top page of the file:

1. Plan of therapy room used.
2. Summary of therapy room rules if room is used mainly with children.
3. Reason/s for treatment referral.
4. Personal history (including updates of information).

The therapist's own thoughts and feelings during the entire process should accompany (if only in your own mind) every sessional write-up.

Information on file

Update this information as more comes to hand. This includes the following facts:

1. *Name/identification* with personal details of subject, including gender, age, ethnicity.
2. *Family background if the subject is a young person*: parents: age, ethnicity, occupation and relationship to each other; siblings; referred person's place within the immediate family and in the wider family, if known.
3. *Reason/s for referral*: should include information of when, by whom and what action was taken. It should also conclude with information on the outcome.

Write-up of sessions

The Mosaic may or may not occupy the entire session. The Lowenfeld approach makes no distinction between the subject's use of Mosaics or any other activity, such as use of Lowenfeld World material (sandtrays with miniature toys), drawing, painting, puppet or doll house play. The write-up should be under the following headings:

1. Names of the child/adolescent/adult and that of the therapist.
2. Date of session: include here any further update of background information and current circumstances.
3. Subject's appearance: physical and emotional appearance.
4. Subject's manner: how the child approached the session, including any changes during the session.
5. Process: work in the session in narrative form, that is, describe in sequence and in detail where, how and with what the person started, how they proceeded, what they said and how you responded to both the proceedings and the conversation.
6. Any thoughts and feelings of the therapist not articulated during the session and later, for example, during the write-up, should be included as a matter of self-audit and part of an evidence-based practice.

Work session summary

Think about the movement of the session and what has been communicated. Note what might need to be taken up at the next session or at an appropriate time later. If the Mosaic-maker was a child, note what practical steps need to be taken on their behalf, and if possible diary in for action.

Children, adolescents and adults may not only do Mosaics within a session. Thus, any other activity should be recorded in similar detail in narrative form. All the above notes apply to a Lowenfeld Projective Play Therapy clinical session.

Recording Mosaic session

1. Show the position of the Mosaic-maker in relation to their Mosaic and the position of the therapist in relation to the Mosaic-maker.
2. Note whether and at what point the Mosaic-maker changes the orientation of the Mosaic or tray, for example, from landscape to portrait position.
3. Note how and when each Mosaic tile was chosen, placed and moved or removed, including any accompanying dialogue and or actions. Weave into the narrative the therapist's own responses.
   a. To record the Mosaic Process, draw and number the pieces as the process happens, i.e. draw and number the pieces as they are put down in the tray space, including the colour of the tile used. Note the particularities of the Mosaic tiles, e.g. the need to identify the different triangles (equilateral = largest of the triangles; scalene = half the equilateral; isosceles = half the square). An example for indicating a black scalene triangle would be to draw a rough shape of the scalene triangle and write "K" to indicate black, so as not to confuse it with blue, and "Sc" for scalene triangles so as not to confuse it with a square.

b. To recreate the Mosaic, draw round each tile of the subject's Mosaic design, removing the drawn tiles whilst preserving the design. Colour in the shapes afterwards. The process of colouring in a Mosaic by hand may be time-consuming, but is the best way for the therapist to understand the Total Response. It is the ideal time for the therapist to contemplate the Mosaic session.

4. The therapist's unspoken thoughts and feelings, either during or after the session, should be separated from the above. Preferably they should be within brackets in the text of the narrative to show when these thoughts and feelings occurred or at the end of the sessional notes when they occur later.

5. Be aware of the Total Response in your recording and describe
    a. the individual style of approach to the Mosaic task and
    b. how the self portrait has been realised. The more detail that is recalled and recorded, the more easily will this task be achieved.

Appendix 3 Lowenfeld Mosaic guidelines for use with deaf people

These guidelines were developed for the purposes of using the Mosaic material to meet the needs of deaf people who have additional physical and mental health difficulties resulting in acute problems of independence and social integration within the community.

This adaptation in use of the Lowenfeld Mosaics was pioneered as a supervised research project and evolved over a period of more than ten years, allowing the teachers, social workers, carers and users alike to recognise that the Lowenfeld Mosaics could indeed contribute towards giving those deaf people who used it a non-verbal tool to access their thoughts and feelings. Communication between teacher, social worker, carer and the deaf Mosaic user was often given enhanced relevance through acknowledgement of the completed Mosaic and discussion about it. Lowenfeld Mosaics were used as part of a comprehensive assessment process, either at the beginning and end of a placement, or as part of a case review, and important information on the emotional concerns of the deaf person were often clarified or identified through this medium.

It became clear to the research team that the Lowenfeld Mosaics encapsulated many complex facets of conscious and unconscious thought processes as well as an integral emotional element. However its entirely non-verbal essence made it invaluable in work with people experiencing communication difficulties. Therefore, the presentation of the Mosaic material had to be carefully considered, and guidelines were developed for reference when presenting the Lowenfeld Mosaics to a deaf person for the first time.

At the beginning of any Mosaic work, the material is introduced in the same way it would be presented to hearing users of the medium. At its simplest and most basic, the demonstration of the Mosaic tiles (pieces) can be understood through sight alone. During the developmental stages of these guidelines, it was discovered that carefully selected key signs, often personal or idiosyncratic to the user, were needed to supplement the information. Sign language was selected carefully and specifically to make the explanation simple, clear and appropriate to the communication level of the user.

Over the years, it became clear that the demonstration procedure had to be sufficiently flexible to allow it to be sensitively adapted to reflect the breadth of variety in communication levels of the deaf person, whilst remaining within agreed and accepted parameters of information, vocabulary and style.

The demonstration devised is detailed as follows and should be read in conjunction with the general guidelines in this Appendix. There are no additional terms to the Lowenfeld Mosaic terminology being used which are devised specifically for use with deaf people.

The Mosaic tray should be placed prominently on the table in a landscape orientation, with the long edge of the tray fitted with white paper in an accessible position to both the Mosaic user and the person demonstrating.

Place the Mosaic box on the table above the tray, with the box half open. This is to convey the fact that the Mosaic box contains two identical sets of Mosaic pieces and to make it clear that all the variety of colour and shape is contained in one half of the box. Putting the box above the tray serves the same purpose as for hearing users: it emphasises the visual nature of the tool from the beginning of the presentation. Placing the box centrally does not bias the left or right-hander, especially if the presenter later indicates that the Mosaic box could be moved to a more convenient spot. The Mosaic user can then choose to place the box in a different position after the demonstration.

- Show the box and explain that this is a box with different coloured pieces by:
- Signing: "Box, different colour pieces (in there)."
- Explain that you are going to show some different shapes by:
- Signing: "Show you, pieces (and pointing) in there."

The 5 shapes are then selected one at a time and held up for the Mosaic user to see. The pieces are then laid centrally on the tray, side by side along the corresponding edge of the previous piece, to demonstrate visually how the Mosaic pieces relate to each other.

The colour order takes the Mosaic user through each colour in the sequence it appears in the box: red, blue, yellow, black, green and white; however, the colours should not be named during the demonstration. Any references should be conveyed to the Mosaic user by visual means and not through the use of words or signs if at all possible.

The shapes are shown on the tray as follows: (1) square (red), (2) diamond (blue), (3) isosceles triangle (yellow), (4) equilateral triangle (black), (5) scalene triangle (green). A second scalene triangle (white) is used to complete the visual demonstration of the Mosaic colours as well as the half relationship (see below).

Within this one demonstration, the process takes the Mosaic user through both the shapes and the colours visually and succinctly, beginning with the most basic piece (the square) and proceeding to the most complex (the scalene triangle), and shows each of the mathematical relationships between the pieces. As with the colours, the shapes are not named and are simply shown.

The relationships of the shapes' edges are also shown visually, augmented by signs for "same"/"different"/"half". These signs are used for emphasis as the sides of the pieces are being visibly compared.

- To demonstrate the same lengths of two different shapes, for example, place any side of the diamond against that of the square, and sign "Same".
- To demonstrate the difference in lengths between two shapes, for example, place the hypotenuse of the isosceles triangle against any side of the square or diamond, and sign "Different".

The "half" relationship between two shapes, for example between that of the isosceles triangle and the square, or the preferred option, between that of the equilateral triangle and the scalene triangle (see above) may also be shown thus:

- Whilst demonstrating the sides of the green scalene triangle against that of the black equilateral triangle already placed, finish by placing the green scalene triangle on top of the black equilateral. Then, place the white scalene triangle alongside the green scalene on top of the black equilateral triangle, thus showing that two of the scalene triangles together make up one equilateral triangle. Sign "Half". This process can also be used with the isosceles triangle and the square. By demonstrating in this way the "Half" relationship between the equilateral and the scalene triangles, the demonstration of colours including white, is neatly completed.

The mathematical relationships are thus revealed by visual means and independent of language ability. Thus the presenter of the Mosaics uses a visual language comprising actions performed by hand using two different shapes, the scalene triangle paired with the equilateral triangle and the isosceles triangle paired with the square.

- When all the pieces and colours have been shown, lift the pieces from the tray one at a time, replacing first the scalene triangles and working backwards through the demonstration procedure to the square. Hold up each piece for the Mosaic user to see again before replacing it in the correct compartment of the box as a reminder of which pieces are located in which part of the box.
- Make a display of replacing them in their space in the box. Draw a finger along all the pieces of the same shape in this uncovered section, signing: "All same (here)."
- When all the pieces have been replaced, remove the lid from the other half of the box, explaining that this is another set, the same as the first. Sign/gesture: "Here, other/more piece(s), same, these pieces."
- After the demonstration, make a point of showing whose turn it is: deliberately move the tray and box over to the Mosaic user. At this point, ask which side the user prefers the box to be placed by signing: "Which?" and indicate either side of the actual tray.

- The Mosaic user should then be encouraged to express him or herself. Signing: "Now, yours, different (to) mine. Yours (with emphasis)."

If the Mosaic user interrupts the demonstration process, the presenter should stop the demonstration and discuss the subject raised to the Mosaic user's satisfaction before resuming.

If the user places pieces on the tray during the demonstration, accept this and allow the Mosaic-making to continue.

If the user adds to any part of the demonstration, accept this also and allow the user to take over if that is their clear desire.

Accept and acknowledge all that the Mosaic user does, because any and every response from the Mosaic user is part of the Total Response.

Be relaxed and reassuring. Concentrate on eye contact and body language. Remember this Mosaic is theirs. The presenter should be there to act as a mirror in the first instance. Acceptance and acknowledgement are essential.

The Mosaics have been used in many ways among this deaf and multiply-disadvantaged research group, not least as a calming device and as an alternative way to the usual physical means to express feelings. It allows the projection of emotion into a material that distances the individual sufficiently from the heat of the emotion and allows them to refocus on making something still closely and directly connected to them, positive and attributable to them, but in a visual form which they may then be able to discuss. Thus their emotion is acknowledged and often offered relief. Mostly, the deaf user finds the Mosaic a beneficial and therapeutic experience.

The Lowenfeld Mosaics never fail to present a picture of how the Mosaic user sees him or herself, and is therefore uniquely informative to the presenter. However, the experience of sharing something that is valued and visually retained boosts the Mosaic user's self-esteem and enhances rapport between the user and the presenter.

Appendix 4 Brief guidelines for using Lowenfeld Mosaics in cross-cultural research

Lowenfeld's original advice for using the Mosaics for cultural research with non-Western peoples was to utilise a half-set, which was then supplied separately in its own box. In recent times, it has become uneconomic to produce sets of two sizes and only the fuller set is now available. In my own research work, it has proved to be quite easy and inexpensive to make two sets out of the set used for therapeutic treatment. My own research was conducted solely with such half-sets, and the time taken to collect the sample was shortened by such usage.

There were good reasons for Lowenfeld to give the advice.[43] She was aware that without a Mosaic developmental profile of the people from whom Mosaics were to be collected, it would be impossible to "distinguish that part of the response which arises from immaturity in itself and that which is caused by unfamiliarity with the material" (2004a: 343). Another of her concerns was the need to give maximum priority to the spontaneity of the subject's response. And she feared that the larger set would be too overwhelming. With the Chinese subjects from China and San Francisco, I decided that allowing twenty minutes for each subject to respond to the Mosaics seemed to be ample time to allow for familiarity and spontaneity to work together to produce a unique portrait of a Personality in Action within a particular cultural context.

Bearing in mind the wide variations in the cultural contexts for which any anthropologist may wish to use the Mosaics, possibly as only one of a battery of tests, it is obvious that there can be no hard and fast rules about which sized set of Mosaics would be more appropriate. It must surely be ultimately down to the judgement of the individual investigator. The clinching argument for me was the time factor, which also would have an impact on the total cost of the project.

---

43 Lowenfeld's suggested modifications in technique of administration are to be found in Appendix D of her work (2004a: 343–4).

Having experienced the time it took me to collect 31 Mosaics in London, one at a time, I decided to use a group method. I had six half-set boxes made by woodwork trainees, which allowed me to collect six Mosaics at a single session. This cut down both the time I had to stay in China and in San Francisco, and made it easier for me to arrange for assistance locally. It is certain that collecting, drawing and colouring 301 Mosaics using the bigger set would have been a much more time consuming process, making it likely to be unattractive to any funder of such a project.

Clearly, each project has to be designed with the conditions of the target sample in mind. It may be useful if I relate some of the problems inherent in my own cross-cultural research work. In China it was my intention to use people who would be familiar to the pupils to read out the instructions. I was grateful that the pupils' teachers offered to do this for me. Designing the instructions was however more problematic than I had envisaged. For both the instructions and the questionnaire I was fortunate to have the services of a fluent bilingual speaker[44] to translate the English text into written Chinese and with time to discuss and revise the resultant document. This reminded me of the problem of the linearity of language. As Chinese is also a concretely based pictorial language, it was difficult to convey the vagueness of the usual request "to do something, anything you like, with the Mosaic pieces, with as few or as many pieces as you like, on the tray". To avoid the inevitable bias towards making either the representational design or the abstract pattern more prominent by putting the words of one or the other first in the sentence, I had two versions made and used these in alternate sessions. Experienced anthropologists are unlikely to need any advice from me.

---

44 I owe my brother, Dr Ronald Lo Joy-Pak, an enormous debt of gratitude for undertaking the task of translating the instructions and the questionnaire for me. He was quick to see my difficulties and understood that it would be easier for him to take on the translation with me in attendance for any clarification if necessary.

Appendix 5a Research protocol, Guangdong, China, 1986

RESEARCH INTO PERSISTENCE AMONG CHINESE CHILDREN OF CHARACTERISTIC RESPONSES TO THE LOWENFELD MOSAIC TEST

Summary statement

This research is concerned to establish whether Chinese upbringing and education creates a common perception of the world. Moreover, it is concerned to discover whether there is a link between the common perception of the world and the language used in children's education.[45]

Background to the proposed research

Some thirty years ago Lowenfeld Mosaics (see section "Research instrument" below) were collected from a group of 109 Chinese males, aged between 10 and 26 years from a rural and an urban district of Malaya.[46] A statistically highly significant proportion of the subjects from this sample demonstrated two common characteristics in their responses to the Lowenfeld Mosaic Test not observed in other collections. This is the only extant collection of Mosaic Responses from Chinese subjects.

Research aims

This research project is a descriptive study with two main objectives in mind:

1. To see if the results of the earlier study could be replicated in mainland China, and more specifically:

---

45 This protocol was submitted nearly 20 years ago. I have reproduced it here unedited.
46 This collection was made by Peggy K. Thornton in the early 1950s – see References.

a. to see if there are any differences between the Mosaic responses of the boys and the girls;

b. to see if there are any significant differences between the urban and rural groups;

c. to refine the category differences.

2. To see if and how far Chinese children educated in an entirely different educational medium (i.e. in a language other than Chinese) and environment retain the characteristic Mosaic Response. This part of the research is in progress and being conducted in the UK.

Research methods

For Objective 1 the total sample in China would be taken from Guangdong, with half the sample from urban Guangzhou and the remaining half from the rural area of Panyu in Guangdong.

In the Malayan study, the ancestry of the subjects came from a wide-ranging area of China. As the sample for Objective 2 will be mainly Cantonese in origin, it was decided that the matching sample should be obtained from Guangdong.

The minimum sample to yield statistically significant findings would be 200 subjects *if* the age range is narrow. There should be 50 girls and 50 boys in the urban sample and similar numbers of boys and girls in the rural sample.

The age was chosen because it is the age of transition from primary to secondary education in England, when the educational foundations have been laid.

Research instrument and administration

Research instrument

The Lowenfeld Mosaic Test is to be administered to each child individually or in groups of no more than four. It is a non-verbal projective test that has been widely used by anthropologists, psychologists and educationalists in many parts of the world. It is particularly suitable for the study of large numbers of people (subjects) from different parts of the world because it is unaffected by language differences. It does not impose preconceived interpretations on the results, and yet the test material is sufficiently strictly defined to allow general observations and comparisons to be made.

Administrative procedure

The material used in the Lowenfeld Mosaic Test consists of 228 geometric pieces in 5 different but mathematically interrelated shapes. Each shape is available in the same 6 colours. These Mosaic pieces are laid out ready for use in a box, grouped by shape and displaying all the colours in each shape.

This box is presented to the child alongside a tray fitted with plain white paper. The child is shown the variety of pieces available and then asked to do something with the pieces on the tray, using as few or as many as they choose. When the child has finished, they will be asked about what has been done.

Statement of requirements

Sample of subject
I would appreciate it if you would provide 200 children all of whom were born in either 1974 or 1975: 100 from urban Guangzhou (50 girls and 50 boys); the remaining 100 (50 girls and 50 boys) from rural areas in Guangdong, preferably near Guangzhou.

Setting
I would need a private room with 5 chairs and 5 level-topped tables (approximate size 1×0.5 metres) so that 4 children can do the Lowenfeld Mosaic Test simultaneously without being able to overlook each other.

The requirement
Although each child will only need from 15 to 20 minutes to do the Test, I shall require sessions of no less than one and a half hours for 4 children to be tested simultaneously.

At most I can manage 5 such sessions per day, with appropriate breaks.

I am able to stay in China up to a maximum of 5 weeks. However, I would prefer to complete the research work in less than the 5 weeks if at all possible.

Explanatory note to Chinese colleagues

There is a UK-based project concerned with the effects of education on children from different cultural backgrounds. This includes the study of Chinese children who are being educated in China and Chinese children who are being entirely educated abroad, e.g. England.

The Test that is being used for this project has been chosen because it does not need words in the response and thus largely surmounts the problem of different languages.

The data obtained from Guangzhou will form the standard for the Chinese children of the age group which is being studied. Therefore, it is essential that the children respond spontaneously.

Form

The form for the children from Guangdong was in essence identical to the one used for the children in San Francisco, except that it had a Chinese translation underneath the English text. The form was designed to be filled in by each child, but had the approval of the authorities. The interpreter provided by the authorities for the project translated all the replies. All quotations are verbatim transcriptions of her verbal translation.

LMT 嵌鑲構圖答案表 九八六

廣州
GUANGZHOU   LMT MOSAIC FORM   1986

Date Mosaic taken   日　期　：

(1) Student No.   學生編號

(2) Date of Birth   出生日期   年 _____ 月 _____ 日

* (3) Sex : F/M   性別：女／男

* (4) Urban/Rural : U/R   出生地   城市／農村

(5) What the child says about his/her Mosaic.   (Preferrably exact wording)
這孩子怎樣説及他／她做的嵌鑲構圖
（請記録小孩自己的字句爲要）

* (6) Shape preference 形狀的寧擇

Square   Diamond   Isosceles   Equilateral   Scalene
正方形   菱　形   二等邊三角形   三等邊三角形   不等邊三角形

* (7) Colour preference   顔色的寧擇

Red   Blue   Yellow   Black   Green   White
紅   藍   黄   黑   緑   白

* (8) Pair of colours 顔色配合

Red   Blue   Yellow   Black   Green   White
紅   藍   黄   黑   緑   白

* = Circle whichever is applicable
在適用的答案劃上圈綫。例如(8)(紅) 藍 (黄) 黑 緑 白

Appendix 5b Research protocol, San Francisco, USA, 1990

RESEARCH INTO PERSISTENCE AMONG CHINESE CHILDREN OF CHARACTERISTIC RESPONSES TO THE LOWENFELD MOSAICS

Summary statement

This research is concerned to establish whether there is a common perception of the world among people of Chinese descent but living in different social/cultural backgrounds and being educated under different schooling systems. Moreover, it is concerned to discover whether there is a link between the common perception of the world and the language used in the children's education.

Background to the proposed research

Over 30 years ago Lowenfeld Mosaics (for explanation, see Research instrument below) were collected from a group of 109 Chinese males, aged between 10 and 26 years from a rural and an urban district of Malaya. A statistically highly significant proportion of the subjects from this sample demonstrated two common characteristics in their responses to the Lowenfeld Mosaic Test not observed in other collections.

In 1985–6, Mosaics were collected from 12-year-old children in Guangzhou and Panyu, a rural district of Guangdong, China; and from Chinese children in London, UK, who have been wholly educated in English schools, but who also attended extra-curricula Chinese language classes. The two characteristics identified in the Malayan collection were common to these two collections as well, although there were differences in other respects between the three collections.

Research aims

This part of the research project is a descriptive study with four main objectives in mind:

1. To see if the same results are obtained from children of Chinese descent whose families have been established overseas for several generations. More specifically, to see if there are any differences between the Mosaic responses of the girls and boys who live in a society where equality of treatment is a conscious and established aim of that society.
2. To see if and how far third- and/or fourth-generation Chinese children educated entirely in a language other than Chinese and whose parents are also likely to communicate in American English, demonstrate the characteristic Mosaic response.
3. To see if there are any differences in the Mosaic responses between Chinese children who attend schools where the Chinese language is taught and those who attend schools where it is not.
4. To compare the responses of third- and/or fourth-generation American children of Chinese descent with those of American children of European descent.

Research methods

In the previous two studies, the ancestors of the subjects were mainly Cantonese speakers from Guangdong Province, China; hence the importance of finding a matching sample from San Francisco.

For the findings to yield significant results, a minimum of 100 subjects in each group is required, provided that the age range is narrow.

The age (i.e. 12 years) was chosen because it is the age just after transition from primary to secondary education in England (in China, it was the final year of their primary schooling), when it is judged that the educational foundations have been laid.

Research instrument and administration

Research instrument
The Lowenfeld Mosaic Test is a non-verbal projective test that has been widely used by anthropologists and psychologists in many parts of the world. It is particularly suitable for the study of large numbers of people (subjects) from different parts of the world because the response is unaffected by language differences; it does not impose preconceived interpretations on the result, and yet the test material is sufficiently strictly defined to allow general observations to be made.

Administrative procedure
The Lowenfeld Mosaic Test is to be administered to each child individually in groups of four.

The material used for field research in the Lowenfeld Mosaic Test consists of 228 geometric pieces in 5 different but mathematically interrelated shapes. Each shape is available in the same 6 colours. These Mosaic pieces are laid out ready for use in a box and are grouped by shape and display all the colours in each shape.

This box is presented to the child, alongside a tray fitted with plain paper. The child is shown the variety of pieces and asked to use a few or as many as they choose to make something on the tray. For the purposes of this research, the child is allowed a maximum of 20 minutes to do the Mosaic. When the child has finished, they are asked to complete a short questionnaire by writing about the Mosaic they have made and on such matters as colour preference, shape preference and so on.

Statement of requirements

Sample of subjects
I need 200 third-generation Chinese American children, preferably those whose families originally spoke Cantonese, the number made up of 100 whose education does not include Chinese language in their curriculum and 100 whose education includes learning the Chinese language. Of each group of 100 children, 50 should be boys and 50 girls. All the children should be aged 12 or born in the same year so that the majority would be aged 12, whichever is easier to obtain.

If this sample is not easily obtainable, the sample could be reduced to 100 third- and/or fourth-generation Chinese-American children whose families originally spoke Cantonese, the number of boys and girls should be as nearly equal as possible.

Setting
Assuming that the work be done in one stretch of time, I would need a private room with 5 chairs and 5 level-topped tables (approximate size 28 × 36 inches) so that 4 children can do the Lowenfeld Mosaic Test simultaneously without being able to overlook each other.

Although each child will only need approximately 30 minutes to do the Test and answer a brief questionnaire, I shall require sessions of no less than 2 hours for 4 children to be tested simultaneously. At most I can manage 4 such sessions per day, with appropriate breaks.

A volunteer assistant will be necessary. Perhaps an undergraduate student from the Chinese community might be interested in participating in the project.

Forms

THE LMT MOSAIC FORM

* = Circle where appropriate

Date Mosaic taken: _____ Year _____ Month _____Day

1. Student No: _____

2. Date of birth: _____ Year _____ Month _____Day

3.* Sex: Female / Male

4.* Residence: City / Suburb

5.* Do you consider yourself second, third or fourth-generation Chinese
    American?   second / third / fourth

6. Briefly describe your Mosaic.

7. Circle the Mosaic shape you like best:
       Square / Diamond / Isosceles Triangle /
       Equilateral triangle / Scalene Triangle

8. Circle the Mosaic color you like best:
       Red / Blue / Yellow / Black / Green / White

9. Circle the two colors that you think go best together:
       Red   Blue   Yellow   Black   Green   White

SCHOOL NAME_____

ANCESTRY FORM

Provided by the school to be completed by participating pupils

1. Name _____

2. Age _____

3. Date of birth _____

4. Birthplace _____

5. Please name the places that the following relatives from your family
   were born:

   Mother _____

   Father _____

   Maternal grandmother _____

   Maternal grandfather _____

   Paternal grandmother _____

   Paternal grandfather _____

   Maternal great grandmother _____

   Maternal great grandfather _____

   Paternal great grandmother _____

   Paternal great grandfather _____

Appendix 5c Comparative data

TABLE ONE

Comparative data for colour preferences or usage amongst the Mosaic collections for Connecticut, Guangzhou and San Francisco.

GIRLS

Connecticut			Guangzhou			San Francisco		
T	C↓	*U%	T	C↓	P%	T	C↓	**P%
	B	21	22	Y	44	16	B	44.0
	K	17	11	W	22	8	K	22.0
	R	17	9	R	18	6	R	18.0
	G	17	4	G	8	4	W	11.0
	W	16	2	B	4	1	G	2.5
	Y	12	2	K	4	1	Y	2.5
50		100%	50		100%	36		100%

BOYS

Connecticut			Guangzhou			San Francisco		
T	C↓	*U%	T	C↓	P%	T	C↓	**P%
	B	22	16	Y	32	14	B	41.0
	K	19	14	G	28	12	K	35.4
	W	15	7	B	14	4	R	11.8
	G	15	7	R	14	2	Y	6.0
	R	14	5	W	10	1	G	3.0
	Y	5	1	K	2	1	W	3.0
50		100%	50		100%	34		** +100%

Key to abbreviations: C↓ = Order of preference or use of colour is graded from the most preferred or used to the least preferred or used; P = Preferred; T = Total number; U = Usage.

Key to letter symbols for the Mosaic colours: B = blue; G = green; K = black; R = red; W = white; Y = yellow.

* "To determine which colours are used most at different ages, we have figured for each age, and for girls and boys separately, what percentage of all pieces used are blue, red, white, etc. These numbers are determined by figuring each child's product separately and then averaging." The figures referred to are taken for all the children at twelve years old, from Ames and Ilg 1962: 66, Table 20.

** The percentage figures for the San Francisco children have been slightly adjusted without affecting the order of their preference.

TABLE TWO

Comparative data for shape preference or usage amongst the Mosaic collections for Connecticut, Guangzhou and San Francisco.

GIRLS

Connecticut			Guangzhou			San Francisco		
T	S↓	*U%	T	S↓	P%	T	S↓	**P%
	D	29.5	31	D	62	19	D	53.0
	Sc	24.5	7	E	14	10	S	28.0
	S	16.5	6	Sc	12	3	E	8.0
	E	16.0	3	S	6	2	Sc	5.5
	I	13.5	3	I	6	2	I	5.5
50		100%	50		100%	36		100%

BOYS

Connecticut			Guangzhou			San Francisco		
T	S↓	*U%	T	S↓	P%	T	S↓	**P%
	D	23	23	D	46	16	D	47.0
	S	23	10	Sc	20	8	S	23.5
	Sc	20	7	S	14	5	Sc	14.7
	E	19	7	E	14	4	E	11.8
	I	15	3	I	6	1	I	3.0
50		100%	50		100%	34		100%

Key to abbreviations: S↓ = Order of preference or use of shape is graded from the most preferred or used to the least preferred or used; P = Preferred; T = Total number; U = Usage.

Key to symbols for the Mosaic shapes: D = diamonds; E = equilateral triangles; I = isosceles triangles; S = square; Sc = scalene triangles.

* "The percentage figures for Connecticut are taken from Ames and Ilg 1962: p. 61, Tables 16 and 17. These figures refer to average percentage of use of the different Mosaic shapes according to age which were calculated for the girls and boys separately.

** The percentage figures for the San Francisco children have been slightly adjusted without affecting the order of their preference.

TABLE THREE

Comparative data for the class of Mosaics produced by the children from London, Guangzhou and San Francisco.

Classification of Mosaic products — The percentage for the London and San Francisco children's Mosaics have been slightly adjusted without affecting the overall proportion of class total of the Mosaics	#	GIRLS London N	%	Guangzhou N	%	San Francisco N	%	BOYS London N	%	Guangzhou N	%	San Francisco N	%
		17	100.0	50	100	36	100.0	14	100.0	50	100	34	100.0
Positive naming of Mosaic product	1	17	100.0	50	100	29	80.6	14	100.0	50	100	28	82.3
Uncertain or non-naming of Mosaic product	2	0	0	0	0	7	19.4	0	0	0	0	6	17.7
Representation of objects	3	11	64.7	15	30	11	30.5	9	64.0	24	48	13	38.3
Representation of scenes	4	4	23.3	15	30	12	33.5	4	28.5	14	28	10	29.4
Representation of a collection of objects	5	1	6.0	14	28	0	0	0	0	11	22	0	0
Mixed collection of objects and non-representational design	6	*1	6.0	2*	4	2†	5.5	0	0	1*	2	0	0
Non-representational designs with pattern	7	0	0	4	8	10	27.5	1	7.5	0	0	6	17.6
Non-representational designs without pattern	8	0	0	0	0	1	3.0	0	0	0	0	5	14.7
All representational designs, 3–6*	9	17	100.0	46	92	23	64.0	13	92.5	50	100	23	67.7
All non-representational designs, 6†–8	10	0	0	4	8	13	36.0	1	7.5	0	0	11	32.3
TOTAL	11	17	100.0	50	100	36	100.0	14	100.0	50	100	34	100.0

* Mosaics consisting of a mixed collection of objects and designs specified as "shapes" have been classified with the representational Mosaics.

† These Mosaics lacked clarity and have been classified with non-representational designs.

Further reading

Simon Baron-Cohen, 1995. *Mindblindness: an essay on autism and theory of mind.* MIT Press.

Paul Broks, 2003. *Into the silent land: travels in neuropsychology.* London, Atlantic Books.

Elizabeth Burford, 1998. *Gravity and the creation of self: an exploration of self-representations using spatial concepts.* London, Jessica Kingsley Publishers.

Brian Butterworth, 1999. *The mathematical brain.* Basingstoke, Macmillan.

Guy Claxton, 1998. *Hare brain, tortoise mind: why intelligence increases when you think less.* London, Fourth Estate.

Robin Dunbar, 1997. *Grooming, gossip and the evolution of language.* London, Faber and Faber.

Kate Fox, 2004. *Watching the English: the hidden rules of English behaviour.* London, Hodder and Stoughton.

Daniel Goleman, 1996. *Emotional intelligence: why it can matter more than IQ.* London, Bloomsbury.

Temple Grandin, 1996. *Thinking in pictures and other reports from my life with autism.* New York, Vintage.

Temple Grandin and Catherine Johnson, 2005. *Animals in translation: using the mysteries of autism to decode animal behaviour.* London, Bloomsbury.

Ivan Guzman de Rojas, 1985. *Logical and linguistic problems of social communication with the Aymara people.* Ottawa, International Development Research Centre Manuscript Reports: IDRC-MR66e.

Steve Jones, 2002. *Y: the descent of men.* London, Little, Brown.

Jean Liedloff, 1986 [1975]. *The continuum concept.* London, Penguin Books, Arkana.

Karen Machover, 1980 [1949]. *Personality projection in the drawing of the human figure; a method of personality investigation.* Springfield, Illinois, Charles C. Thomas Publishers.

Maryrose Margaretten, 1956. The Lowenfeld Mosaic Test: a study of the responses of young children. 2 vols. Submitted, as part of the MA requirement, to the University of Chicago.

Rhoda Metraux, 1977. Typescript of seminar on Iatmul Mosaics given at the ICP on 21 January 1977.

Desmond Morris, Peter Collett, Peter Marsh and Marie O'Shaughnessy, 1979. *Gestures: their origins and distribution.* London, Jonathan Cape.

Steven Pinker, 1994. *The language instinct: the new science of language and mind.* London, Penguin Books.

V. S. Ramachandran and Sandra Blakeslee, 1998. *Phantoms in the brain: human nature and the architecture of the mind.* London, Fourth Estate.

Jonathan Rèe, 1999. *I see a voice: a philosophical history of language, deafness and the senses.* London, HarperCollins.

Martin Richards, 1980. *Infancy: world of the newborn.* London, Harper and Row.

Ian H. Robertson, 1999. *Mind sculpture: your brain's untapped potential.* London, Bantam Press.

Steven Rose, 1993. *The making of memory.* London, Bantam Books.

Ian Stewart, 1998. *Life's other secret: the new mathematics of the living world.* London, Penguin Books.

Peggy Kathleen Thornton, 1968 [1956]. Visual perception among the peoples of Malaya. 2 vols. PhD thesis, University of Reading, Department of Psychology.

Richard N. Walker, 1957. Children's Mosaic designs; a normative and validating study of the Lowenfeld Mosaic Test. (Incomplete copy seen.) Doctoral dissertation, University of Minnesota, University Microfilma, Ann Arbor, Michigan.

Duncan J. Watts, 2004. *Six degrees: the science of a connected age.* London, Vintage Books.

Robert Winder, 2004. *Bloody foreigners: the story of immigration to Britain.* London, Little, Brown.

Thérèse Woodcock and J. Hood-Williams, undated typescript. Analysis of Iatmul Mosaics. London, Lowenfeld Archives, housed at the Wellcome Foundation Library.

References

All publications and unpublished papers by Margaret Lowenfeld and Thérèse Woodcock are housed with the Lowenfeld Archives, at the Wellcome Library for the History and Understanding of Medicine.

Louise Ames and Frances Ilg, 1962. *Mosaic patterns of American children.* New York, Harper and Brothers.

Ville Anderson and John Hood-Williams, undated. *Handbook for use with the Lowenfeld Mosaic Test.* London, Dr Margaret Lowenfeld Trust.

Fritjof Capra, 1991 [1976]. *The Tao of physics: an exploration of the parallels between modern physics and Eastern mysticism.* London, Flamingo.

Antonio Damasio, 2000. *The feeling of what happens: body and emotion in the making of consciousness.* London, William Heinemann.

Solvig Ekblad, 1984. Children's thoughts and attitudes in China and Sweden: impacts of a restrictive versus a permissive environment. *Acta psychiatr. scand.,* 70, 578–90.

Solvig Ekblad, 1986. Relationships between child-rearing practices and primary school children's functional adjustment in the People's Republic of China. *Scandinavian Journal of Psychology,* 27, 220–30.

Lise Eliot, 2001 [1999]. *Early intelligence: how the brain and mind develop in the first five years of life.* London, Penguin Books.

John Gage, 1999 [1995]. *Colour and culture: practice and meaning from antiquity to abstraction.* London, Thames and Hudson.

Alison Gopnik, Andrew Meltzoff and Patricia Kuhl, 1999. *How babies think: the science of childhood.* London, Weidenfeld and Nicolson.

Richard Gregory, 1997. *Mirrors in mind.* London, Penguin.

Paul L. Harris, 1989. *Children and emotion: the development of psychological understanding.* Oxford, Basil Blackwell.

C. G. Jung, 1951. Foreword. *The I Ching or Book of Changes,* trans. Richard Wilhem. Vol. 1. London, Routledge and Kegan Paul.

Shigehisa Kuriyama, 1999. *The expressiveness of the body and the divergence of Greek and Chinese medicine.* New York, Zone Books.

Margaret Lowenfeld, 1964. The non-verbal 'thinking' of children. Paper read at a conference at ICP, 1948. London: Institute of Child Psychology.

Margaret Lowenfeld, 1968. The use of the LMT in the study of personality. Paper read at the 7th International Congress of Rorschach and other Projective

Techniques, London, 5–8 August 1968. In typescript, from the *Rorschach Proceedings*, 838–43.

Margaret Lowenfeld, 1991 [1935] *Play in Childhood*. London, Mac Keith Press.

Margaret Lowenfeld, 2004a [1954]. *The Lowenfeld Mosaic Test*. Brighton and Portland: Sussex Academic Press.

Margaret Lowenfeld, 2004b [1988]. *Selected papers of Margaret Lowenfeld: child psychotherapy, war and the normal child*, ed. C. Urwin and J. Hood-Williams. Brighton and Portland: Sussex Academic Press.

Margaret Lowenfeld 2004c [1979]. *Understanding children's Sandplay: the Lowenfeld World Technique*. Brighton and Portland: Sussex Academic Press.

John McCrone, 1999. *Going inside: a tour round a single moment of consciousness.* Faber and Faber.

Rhoda Metraux, 1975. Eidos and change: continuity in process, discontinuity in product. *Ethos*, 3 (2), 293–308.

Lynn Pan, 1990. *Sons of the Yellow Emperor: the story of the overseas Chinese.* London: Secker and Warburg.

Lynn Pan, ed., 1999. *The encyclopedia of the Chinese overseas*, Richmond, Surrey, Curzon Press.

Eugene X. Perticone and Renée M. Tembeckjian, ©1987. *The Mosaic technique in personality assessment: a practical guide.* Rosemount, New Jersey, Programs for Education Inc.

Oliver Sacks, 1990. *Seeing voices: a journey into the world of the deaf.* London, Picador, Pan Books.

Ursula Stewart and Loraine Leland, 1952. American versus English Mosaics. *Journal of Projective Techniques*, 16, 246–8.

Peggy K. Thornton, 1956. Visual perception among the peoples of Malaya. DPhil thesis, University of Reading.

C. Trevarthen and K. Aitken, 2001. Infant interrsubjectivity: research, theory, and clinical applications. *Journal of Child Psychology and Psychiatry*, 42 (1), 3–48.

C. A. S. Williams, 1976 [1941]. *Outlines of Chinese symbolism and art motives: an alphabetical compendium of antique legends and beliefs, as reflected in the manners and customs of the Chinese.* 3rd edn. New York, Dover Publications Inc.

Thérèse Woodcock, 1972. Lowenfeld's theory of "E" as demonstrated by play in childhood. Thesis for the Postgraduate Diploma of the Institute of Child Psychology.

Thérèse Woodcock, 1984. The use of the Lowenfeld Mosaic Test in child psychotherapy. *Brit. J. Projective Psychology and Personality Study*, 29 (2), 11–18.

Thérèse Woodcock, 1986a. The Lowenfeld Mosaic Test in the study of cultural differences. *Brit J. Projective Psychology*, 31 (1), 25–31.

Thérèse Woodcock, 1986b, A patchwork of Mosaics. Paper presented at the Annual Lowenfeld Day Conference at Cambridge University, 1 November 1986.

Thérèse Woodcock, 1987. Chinese Mosaics and culture: Lowenfeld Mosaics from Chinese subjects from different cultural backgrounds and at different times.

Paper presented to the British Society for Projective Psychology in London, 26 June 1987.

Thérèse Woodcock, 1997. Communicating the uncommunicable: the use of Lowenfeld Mosaics as an expressive tool for the deaf. Paper presented at the European Society for Mental Health and Deafness Congress, Manchester, England, 2–4 October 1997.

Thérèse Woodcock, 1999. The homeostatic and epistemological principles and theory of E. Lecture given to Unit 1 students on the Lowenfeld Child and Adolescent Projective Play Therapy Course.

Thérèse Woodcock, 2001a. Emotions, emotional development and Protosystem Thinking. Lecture given to Module 1 students on the MSc Course on Lowenfeld Projective Play Therapy.

Thérèse Woodcock, 2001b. Expressing the inexpressible: the use of Lowenfeld Mosaics in therapeutic communication. Paper presented at the Association for Child Psychology and Psychiatry Conference, Cambridge, 8 June 2001.

Thérèse Woodcock, 2001c. On culture, cultural differences and therapy. Lecture given to Module 1 students on the MSc Course on Lowenfeld Projective Play Therapy.

Thérèse Woodcock, 2001d. On Protosystem Thinking and Lowenfeld Projective Play Therapy. Lecture given to Module 1 students on the MSc course on Lowenfeld Projective Play Therapy.

Thérèse Woodcock, 2002. The use of Lowenfeld Mosaics with adolescents in relation to their emotional development. Lecture given to Module 2 Students on the MSc Course on Lowenfeld Projective Play Therapy.

Dr Yang Jwing-Ming, 1997. *The root of Chinese QiGong: secrets for health, longevity and enlightenment*. YMAA Publication Centre.

Index

Page numbers in italics refer to illustrations.

How to obtain Lowenfeld Mosaic Sets and books by Dr Margaret Lowenfeld

The Dr Margaret Lowenfeld Trust was established after her death with the aim of ensuring the continued availability of the equipment needed to practise her methods and of the books that she authored.

Mosaic sets may be ordered from the Trust by visiting its website **<http://www.lowenfeld.org.uk>**, which also contains information about where to get her publications, or by writing to:

> The Dr Margaret Lowenfeld Trust
> PO Box 277
> Worksop
> S80 9AU, UK

"Throughout her long and innovative life, Margaret Lowenfeld emphasised the development of new forms of communication with children, especially devoting herself to the diagnosis of troubled children . . . By understanding and using the tools she developed, we can experience, and so partake of, her insights." *From the Introduction by Margaret Mead, world renowned anthropologist and author of* Coming of Age in Samoa, *to Margaret Lowenfeld's* Understanding Children's Sandplay

---

The following books by Margaret Lowenfeld can be ordered by visiting the Press website **<http://www.sussex-academic.co.uk>**, where information on ordering from the UK, the US and the Rest of the World, is provided.

THE LOWENFELD MOSAIC TEST
Including a Full Colour Supplement of 140 Mosaics
ISBN 1 84519 083 1
£35/$50, a two-volume set, 360 pp.; *Colour Supplement*, 140 mosaics

UNDERSTANDING CHILDREN'S SANDPLAY
Lowenfeld's World Technique
ISBN 1 84519 082 3
£17.95/$42.50, 292 pp.

SELECTED PAPERS OF MARGARET LOWENFELD
ISBN 1 84519 084 X
£19.95/$45, 408 pp.